D0058995

PUGETOPOLIS

Knute Berger

PUGETOPOLIS

A MOSSBACK TAKES ON GROWTH ADDICTS, WEATHER WIMPS, AND THE MYTH OF SEATTLE NICE

SASQUATCH BOOKS
SEATTLE

Copyright © 2009 Knute Berger
Electronic edition published 2009

All rights reserved. No portion of this book may be reproduced or utilized in any form, or by any electronic, mechanical, or other means, without the prior written permission of the publisher.

The essays on pages 32, 35, 38, 42, 47, 62, 66, 69, 84, 93, 96, 108, 117, 121, 124, 128, 147, 160, 164, 183, 193, 204, 217, 220, 224, 233, 240, 247, 257, 260, 264, and 271 first appeared in slightly different forms in the *Seattle Weekly*, a Village Voice Media Publication, and are reprinted with permission. The essays on pages 112, 132, 157, 200, 207, 252, and 268 first appeared in slightly different forms in *Eastsideweek*, a Village Voice Media Publication, and are reprinted with permission.

Printed in the United States of America
Published by Sasquatch Books

15 14 13 12   9 8 7 6 5 4 3 2

Cover photograph: Simon Tullstedt / Stock.XCHNG
Cover design: Rosebud Eustace
Interior design and composition: Rosebud Eustace

Library of Congress Cataloging-in-Publication Data

Berger, Knute, 1953-
Pugetopolis : a mossback takes on growth addicts, weather wimps, and the myth of Seattle nice / Knute Berger.
    p. cm.
ISBN-13: 978-1-57061-626-6   ISBN-10: 1-57061-626-4 (e-book)
ISBN-13: 978-1-57061-572-6   ISBN-10: 1-57061-572-1 (paperback)

1. Seattle (Wash.)--Social life and customs. 2. Popular culture--Washington (State)--Seattle. 3. Seattle (Wash.)--Social conditions. 4. Seattle (Wash.)--Politics and government. 5. Seattle (Wash.)--Economic conditions. 6. Natural history--Washington (State)--Seattle. 7. Puget Sound Region (Wash.)--Social life and customs. 8. Popular culture--Washington (State)--Puget Sound Region. 9. Puget Sound Region (Wash.)--Social conditions. 10. Puget Sound Region (Wash.)--Politics and government. I. Title.
F899.S45B47 2009
979.7'772043--dc22
                        2008037593

Sasquatch Books
1904 Third Avenue, Suite 710
Seattle, WA 98101
(206) 467-4300
www.sasquatchbooks.com
custserv@sasquatchbooks.com

For CP, the perfect reader.

CONTENTS

Columnist Laureate

By Timothy Egan

He looks the part, of course. Just as people start to resemble their dogs—or vice versa—Knute "Skip" Berger is our city's image in all its woolly, fleeced, untied-shoes essence. He'll never be identified with one of those awful fads that made people think everyone in Seattle was a grunge guitarist, a twenty-something millionaire, or an accountant with a rock-climbing wall in the second office. He's neither old school nor new school, which is to say he's fad resistant. The most overused, most sought-after word in modern American life? *Authentic!* That's Mossback—the alter ego he's used for his columns of the last half-dozen years.

More important, he sounds the part. Read him and hear the music of the Pacific Northwest: contentious, sometimes out of tune, our soundtrack. He could easily write about anything in the public realm—a failed presidency, the overselling of light rail, the danger of becoming a city without children—for a national readership. He would find a large audience, I'm sure. But he's chosen to write about our backyard, and we are the luckier for it.

It's tempting to call him a crank with a conscience, but that's not quite fair. Mossback is not the raving uncle in Seattle's attic. He's not the cynic in black (see *The Stranger* or any blog). He's certainly not Mr. Sunshine. Mossback is the contrarian, with just enough of an edge, funny when the occasion calls for it.

I love the column, I told him some years ago, even though I disagree with half of what he writes. Why do I love it? The other half. They say if you hit .300 in column-writing you're doing well. Think of Emmett Watson, pounding out one a day, seven days a week, during the time when he was Seattle's voice. Or Mike Royko in Chicago, toiling away at nearly the same pace. They hit their singles, to keep the baseball metaphor rallying, but suffered through long Richie Sexson–like whiff streaks. When Mossback nails it, you can hear the connection. The tone is that true. And for the record, he easily tops the .300 average.

Here is his description of cruise ships, now parked at the city's front door for five months of the year in the space we used to cherish as our own:

> Spring has sprung, and the giant crap-spewing barges have returned to that Capistrano of the Sound, Elliott Bay. Ah, the cruise ships, part of that so-called clean tourism industry that every year seems to flush more and more tourists into our city. Given the economy, we're supposed to be grateful, and indeed we have spent megamillions to make the tourists happy: new piers, a mall-ified downtown, hotels, trolleys, and restaurants no local would be caught dead in. It creates jobs and keeps some hustle in our bustle. But it costs.

Or here's his take on the invertebrates occupying the legislative branch of Seattle government:

> The City Council is chock-full of poster children for Who Wants to Be a Gutless Wonder? Even those on the council who claim to be holding Seattle accountable find a way to cave when it counts.

If you find yourself in Mossback's crossfire—and that means you, Mr. Mayor, or you, sports team owner with hand outstretched—it hurts. It should. And his observations, for the most part, have the added value of being true, as Henry Kissinger once said. Column-writing about the blood sport of politics and the culture wars that rage around our social lives is not a Kumbaya exercise. Seattle may love process, but Mossback loves to poke.

Every region needs a well-informed, ridiculously well-read, common-sensical smart-ass to cry foul before the citizens do something awful. Ideally, this person should be curious—above all else—with a nose for news, and open-minded enough to stay out of the rut. This person should also not be content to simply play the same chords to an audience of nodding heads. The propensity for outrage, for wit, for surprise—all character qualities needed for columnist laureate. He would decline the honor, no doubt. Still, Mossback fills this role.

With Berger you get the bonus of institutional memory, no small thing in a city where most residents are transplants. We hear a lot about Seattle as the most literate, best-educated, well-read city in the nation. It makes us feel good to hear this, though many such surveys are full of nonsense. We win these designations in part because Seattle continues to produce original voices like Skip

Berger. He's actually from here! Quick: On what day did Tex Johnston do the famous barrel roll in a precursor to the 707, pushing Boeing into the Jet Age? Where did Senator Warren Magnuson reside between martini breaks, and sometimes during them? And what was Seattle like before the Kingdome was imploded? Summon Mossback. He's the Wet Side Google.

I once spent an entire lunch hour listening to him describe what happened on Whidbey Island 150 years ago when Indians raided the island and decapitated prominent pioneer Isaac Ebey. I was spellbound. And if you get him going on Norse sagas from the era when Berger's ancestors roamed northern Europe draped in animal hides, the next thing you know he'll have you eating lutefisk for breakfast.

He's a product of Seattle's Scandinavian values, but Berger must have been absent when they gave the lesson in the nice part. Oh sure, he's a big-hearted man and plenty nice when nice is needed. But anyone who calls his experience in the Boy Scouts "a cross between *Animal House* and *Lord of the Flies*" was not stamped with the seal of Beaver Cleaver's Ballard.

He comes by his quirkiness from a résumé of pleasantly off-plumb experiences at several Northwest landmarks. High school at Lakeside, when Bill Gates and Paul Allen were haunting the same halls. Then off to The Evergreen State College, "where the only organized sport was stoner Frisbee," as he writes. He had an early infatuation with world's fairs, as in the event that left Seattle its most prominent landmark, and with time capsules, about which he became so knowledgeable that he calls himself "one of the world's foremost experts on something almost nobody cares about." The Washington State Centennial Commission hired him in 1989 to devise a way to keep the state from losing track of its time capsules. What followed was the perfect solution: capsule children, keepers of the information, who would pass it on to their children.

Skip has had numerous love affairs with regional publications, some of them doomed (*Washington Magazine*), some of them institutions (*Seattle Weekly*). His voice on local public radio every Friday is so sweet you wouldn't know he's the Mighty Mossback. And he blogs—a term that doesn't do justice to the weight of his product—for *Crosscut*, our regional Web newsmagazine. When he started the last job, I wondered how he could possibly come up with original insight on a daily basis. I envisioned sample entries: Tuesday morning, ate honey nut cereal for breakfast. Noted that it tasted better with 2 percent milk. Tuesday afternoon . . .

But surprise: The flow is full, rich, and eventful.

I would guess, from reading him and listening to him rant and dream aloud these many years, that among his Seattle heroes is Ivar Haglund, the clam magnate and sometime folk singer. Ivar gave us fries that tourists toss at seagulls and an annual fireworks show, among other things. When Skip tried to explain the word "Mossback" once in a column, he gave a long historical dissertation that invoked the late clammonger. It seems that Ivar was fond of singing his advertisements, on occasion an old song that included these lines:

No longer a slave to ambition,
I laugh at the world and its shams,
As I think of my present condition
Surrounded by acres of clams.

And now that I'm used to the climate,
I think that if ever man found
A spot to live easy and happy,
That Eden is on Puget Sound.

In those verses, Skip wrote, was the classic mossback experience. "A newcomer gets a foothold here, doing whatever it takes to stay. But by hanging on when the going gets tough, he finds that the magic and beauty of the place are irresistible. Now he can abandon traditional material values—gaining his freedom from the chains of ambition."

It also reminds me of the Western poet Gary Snyder, who has some connection to these parts and once spent a summer as a fire lookout in the North Cascades. The poet offered up a way to live in the transient West, at the edge of the continent. He said, "Find your place. Dig in. Defend it."

A Mossback manifesto, if ever there was one.

Timothy Egan, also a Seattle native, won the National Book Award for nonfiction in 2006 for The Worst Hard Time: The Untold Story of Those Who Survived the Great American Dust Bowl.

Appreciation

This book would not have happened without the support of a whole bunch of remarkable editors. First among them is Lawrence W. Cheek, who pushed me to do this book and then took it upon himself to compile, sift through, and suggest articles from nearly 16 years' worth of output that he thought worthy of inclusion. He then took on the task of editing the entire book. I met Larry when he freelanced articles for *Eastsideweek* and have edited his outstanding stories over the years. I was delighted to learn that he sought no revenge for any red-pen marks I left on his work, and that he edits as well as he writes. I would also like to thank Gary Luke of Sasquatch Books, an old friend and colleague who has been so supportive over the years in encouraging me to write about Seattle and Pugetopolis. I'm grateful to Gary and Sasquatch for making this book happen. Thanks goes also to the Sasquatch editing team of Kurt Stephan and Diane Sepanski.

Many of these columns and commentaries were previously edited and shaped by a host of other excellent editors I've had the pleasure of working with over the years. I've been very lucky to have had free rein to make a fool of myself with my writing, but I would have done so much more often without these people. From *Seattle Weekly* and *Eastsideweek*, I want to thank David Brewster for hiring me and giving me two bully pulpits—one on each side of Lake Washington—during my years there. Gratitude also for David's hiring me onto his online venture, *Crosscut*, which allows me to explore a larger swath of "the Great Nearby." Thanks also to David Schneiderman, formerly of Village Voice Media, for the incredible backing he gave me and the Mossback column during his tenure. I'd also like to thank the current owners of VVM for giving me permission to draw on material I wrote for their newspapers. And big thanks to Chuck Taylor, my managing editor during my last stint at the *Weekly*. He is also my editor at *Crosscut*. Chuck has a very large fan club, but I demand my right to be president for life of it.

I am grateful to Priscilla Turner of *Eastsideweek* and *Seattle Weekly*, who was so inspiring and spirited—an editor who always told me whether a piece worked or not, which can be tough to do with the boss. Others who have helped shape these chapters: Steve Scher and Arvid Hokanson of KUOW-FM, Seattle's public radio station, who signed me up to do commentaries for *Weekday* and coached me in the art of writing for radio; Beth Taylor and Shannon O'Leary for editing my contributions to *Washington Law & Politics* magazine to a standard that passes muster with their audience of lawyers; Rachel Hart and Virginia Smyth for bringing me on to write the "Gray Matters" column for *Seattle* magazine. It's a gift to have such a great platform to write about your hometown for a hometown audience.

I'd also like to thank my friends, family, and colleagues who have been so tolerant over the years hearing me discourse, rant, and rave on various topics. If we have dined or had drinks together, and somewhere along the line you heard me shift from conversation mode into a kind of composing-while-talking speech that signaled I was essentially writing my next column, well, I thank you for your tolerance and true friendship. Lastly, I'd like to thank my partner, Carol Poole, who is a wonderful writer, editor, and reader in her own right. Her feedback on columns and her willingness to drop everything to look at a draft have been invaluable over the years, as has been her endurance and understanding of the weird demands and moods of the creative process. More important, though, is that she is what I describe as the "perfect reader," the person you have in mind as you make your case: interested, skeptical, engaged. I once talked to an editor who said he felt like his work had been merely an exercise in "screaming into a hole in the ground" for all the good it did. Writing doesn't mean much without knowing that someone is listening—and hearing—what you have to say. What I've written may not have changed the world or even our small corner of it, but it has been enough to know that Carol was always there to listen and respond.

—Knute Berger, 2008

SEATTLE MYTHS AND TRUTHS

Pugetopolis Unbound

I.

Pugetopolis is a dirty word.

At least it was in my family. I remember talking about the future with my mother. We were in our summer cabin in the San Juan Islands some time in the 1960s. One day, she predicted, they'll cut down all the trees and pave everything. We'll look just like Los Angeles. People will cease to walk and will travel everywhere in cars or on moveable sidewalks. The human race will become soft and obese. Kids will have to go to museums to see trees. That, she said, is the logical outcome of what we're doing.

To my mother, Pugetopolis was a fighting word. It still is. When I told her it would be the title of this book, her voice flashed anger—as if she'd been betrayed. Now in her nineties, a Bainbridge Island poet whose creative life has been devoted to capturing the essence of this place, she spit the word back at me in disgust: Pugetopolis! I could almost feel her reaching for a bar of soap to wash out my mouth. The concept conjures dystopian visions.

No one I've talked to is exactly sure of the word's origins. The earliest reference I've found is in a May 27, 1966, article in *TIME* magazine about boom times here:

> Throughout the entire Puget Sound area, stretching 140 miles from Tacoma through Seattle, Everett, and Bellingham to the Canadian border, the land where settlers thought

they had found a paradise, with sheltered waterways on the front step and mountains in the backyard, is bursting with new industry. Already, natives are dubbing it Pugetopolis. Said Washington Governor Daniel Evans last week: "In our state's history, the present expansion is second in significance only to that during the gold rush of 1898."

I suspect the term was inspired by Jean Gottman's 1961 landmark book *Megalopolis*, an influential work on the shape of American cities. Gottman focused on the sprawling Boston–New York–Washington, D.C. corridor and explained how it exemplified a new kind of urban form. It was an archipelago of interconnected cities that formed a polycentric supercity. For developers and promoters, it was a new paradigm. Some critics, Gottman later wrote, described it as "pathological."

Today, planners and marketers use various terms to describe the sprawling-cities phenomenon: "urban agglomeration," "metro area," "megapolitan area," "city-region," "metroplex." The Puget Sound area is too small to be a true megalopolis like the Northeast corridor or the Chicagoland region. Gottman insisted on a population of at least 25 million for a real megalopolis; other experts say 10 million will do. Whatever the measure, we're headed in that direction.

Looking at it geologically, the Puget Sound lowlands stretch from British Columbia to the Willamette Valley in Oregon—a habitable, fertile zone carved by glaciers and fed by abundant water. A satellite map of the Pacific coast from Oregon to Alaska reveals just how unusual this region is. Filled with waterways and level land for agriculture and development, it stands in contrast to the foothills, mountains, and plateaus that surround it. It's no wonder some eight million (and counting) residents have spilled into this glacial bowl. Dan Evans's comparison to the Klondike gold rush was apt. Puget Sound has seen multiple rushes of people hurrying here to take advantage of a "paradise" that nature provided.

But when people talk of Pugetopolis, they really mean the heart of the Puget Sound region. Greater Puget Sound runs from Port Angeles on the Strait of Juan de Fuca to the San Juan Islands, then south to Mason and Thurston counties. It's an elaborate cul-de-sac that features more than 2,500 miles of shoreline, deep navigable waterways, peninsulas, long channels, and endless islands all linked to the Pacific.

The metropolitan core is so-called central Puget Sound, mainly King, Pierce, Snohomish, and Kitsap counties. In these four counties now live roughly 3.5 million people, with another 1.7 million expected by 2040. If true, that means these counties will have as many people as the entire state did in 1990—around 5.2 million.

My mother's fears have proved to be well-founded, though things haven't played out exactly as she imagined. Development here is expansive: No other ecological zone in America has undergone as much transformation as these lowlands in the past 35 years, most of it conversion of forest to development. Despite the state's Growth

Management Act, sprawl continues and commutersheds proliferate. People drive daily across the Cascades from places like Cle Elum to work in the Seattle suburbs. Bellingham has become a kind of bedroom city. The Seattle and Bellevue skylines are sprouting new towers like dueling branches of the Medici family. As my mother feared, deforestation has continued. Metro Seattle has half the tree canopy it had in the 1970s, according to satellite images. Meanwhile, the Sound itself suffers from a million little cuts—or little flushes. Studies have shown that Puget Sound's orcas are not only endangered, but full of contaminating PCBs. The local chinook salmon test positive for mercury and flame-retardant chemicals. Prozac is in the food chain, along with hormones from birth control pills and traces of many of the drugs we take every day to keep ourselves going. Just after Thanksgiving in 2007, the Sound even tested for higher-than-normal levels of vanilla and cinnamon, a testament to the fact that everything that goes into our bodies makes its way there. A *Seattle Post-Intelligencer* headline described today's Sound as a "toxic stew."

Every two years, runoff from our roads and driveways alone dumps oil and gas into Puget Sound equal to what the *Exxon Valdez* spilled into Alaska's Prince William Sound. Big oil tankers are banned from the Sound, but our everyday life ensures that the spills keep coming, one drop at a time. Septic systems leak into the depths of Hood Canal, and sewer water, treated and untreated, is dumped into the Sound by the millions of gallons each day.

Trees aren't relegated to museums yet. Well, that's not quite true. At the Seattle Art Museum's Olympic Sculpture Park in downtown Seattle, one of the works is the *Neukom Vivarium* by artist Mark Dion. It is a greenhouse that encloses a 60-foot nurse log from a nearby watershed. In this climate-controlled environment, you can see a tree that fell in the forest and the habitat it provides for other living creatures like moss, ferns, and slugs. The exhibit is a comment on traditional methods of scientific categorization and display, but it can be seen without irony. It suggests we have entered an era when trees are specimens for exhibit, like giant pandas or polar bears. It's a good bet that many of today's Seattle residents have never seen a nurse log in the wild.

The park also exhibits a large stainless steel tree by artist Roxy Paine and a giant abstract eagle painted industrial orange by Alexander Calder. As Pugetopolis gobbles the countryside, we salute what we have displaced with a whimsy that masks a grim reality.

Back in the 1960s, Pugetopolis was shorthand for our future. Boosters saw it as a virtue—a way to promote growth. A 1962 Seattle Area Industrial Council pamphlet bragged that we were "not a solitary city, but a vigorous, integrated commercial and industrial community extending the length of Puget Sound." A drawing showed a modern factory set against a backdrop of pristine, snow-capped mountains. The council promised "natural splendor," "lively, sophisticated, cultured cities," and a "community-wide welcome extended to industry."

Skeptics worried about what later became known as "Californication," which in the emerging ecological consciousness of the late 1960s was more politely called "California Tomorrow." A 1967–68 Puget Sound League of Women Voters report worried about the gap between our technology and our ability to handle the environmental consequences. The problem, they wrote, "is summed up by the caustic prediction that 'Americans will soon be standing in waste up to their knees, launching rockets to the moon.'"

That prediction was too optimistic. We're surrounded by the pollution of Puget Sound, but no one's going to the moon anymore.

2.

I'm not sure when I stopped living in Seattle and became a resident of Pugetopolis. It could have been years ago. It could have been at birth. Seattle might always have been a myth.

If so, it's been a powerful one. Seattle has always seen itself as unique, a "world-class city" with a global role: gateway to the Last Frontier, portal to the Pacific Rim, launch pad for the Space Age. Today, we're synonymous with Starbucks coffee, Microsoft software, Amazon and Costco retailing—when we're not talking about Boeing, Nordstrom, or Eddie Bauer.

Seattle has long been the 900-pound gorilla—or is it the 70-pound chinook salmon?—of Puget Sound, the winner in a long war of attrition against regional rivals for supremacy.

In the beginning, pioneers saw potential in the land and sheltered waters. The first white man to probe the sound, Captain George Vancouver, surveyed the scene in 1792 and imagined that its forested countryside would one day be habitable like the English countryside—a generous prediction, since he found so much of the Northwest coast gloomy and miserable. Later settlers, full of steam from the Industrial Revolution, saw the Sound's commercial potential in grander terms: Settlements received names and slogans bursting with aspiration, like New York Alki (Seattle's original name) and Boston Harbor. Tacoma was dubbed the "City of Destiny," Port Townsend the "New York of the West," and Kirkland was sold as the "new Pittsburgh." (One of my favorite names was selected for a timber community closer to the Pacific coast than Puget Sound: Cosmopolis, near Aberdeen, was named by people who reckoned it might one day be the center of *everything*. Its 2006 population: 1,679.)

People thought big because Puget Sound was a place with enormous natural advantages. Early on, settlers believed there would be one dominant city here. The race was to be that city. Here's how a writer in the *Tacoma Herald* laid it out in 1877:

> Nature has destined that such a metropolis shall be planted as the key-note to remarkable prosperity in the Pacific Northwest. He who dares deny the importance of natural advantages, or who will not be guided by the index

finger of nature, had best set his stake in Oregon, at once, "there to live and die." Every purchaser of real estate in the Northwest wants to locate his property or home near THE GREATEST CITY WHICH IS TO BE.

What drew and held everyone was the waterway. Pugetopolis is a city with a liquid hole at its center. For the soon-to-be-displaced Native Americans who lived on its shores, the Sound was central to their way of life. They traveled across it by canoe, fished its waters, camped and traded on its beaches, and ate when the tide went out, leaving behind mountainous multigenerational middens of discarded seashells.

On the west side of the Sound, busy ports emerged to mill and ship timber destined to build other cities: Port Angeles, Port Townsend, Port Ludlow, Port Gamble, Port Blakely, Port Madison, Port Orchard. Most of these have since mellowed into charming residential communities with marinas.

On the eastern shores, big cities cropped up on bays near the mouths of rivers: Seattle on the Duwamish, Tacoma on the Puyallup, Everett on the Snohomish, Bellingham on the Nooksack. Not everyone flourished, though. In the late nineteenth century, a group of speculators intended to build the premier city of Puget Sound near the mouth of the Nisqually in Thurston County. They called it Puget City. Like scores of other schemes, the plan sputtered and died. And thank goodness. The Nisqually Delta is now a wildlife refuge, something rarer than another burg with ambitions.

The cities on the mainland side had a big advantage over their cross-Sound brothers and sisters: They could link with the transcontinental railroads. Thus they competed for the affection and approval of the robber barons. The railroads, developers, real estate agents, and con men (sometimes they overlapped) played one would-be Manhattan off another.

The legacy of greed set up a dynamic we have to this day, a competitive balkanization. The cities, counties, towns, and suburbs of Puget Sound still compete, still view their futures through the eyes of self-interest and suspicion. You can see that now when you look east to the skyscrapers of Bellevue or hear about yet another "Tacoma Renaissance." No one truly wants to concede Seattle's supremacy.

Regional governance is still viewed with great skepticism. It was a sticking point fifty years ago when the locals bickered over whether to have a central planning entity to help them achieve a regionwide vision. The Puget Sound Regional Council was set up to study and plan, but not govern. Its prime accomplishment has been to pack file cabinets with studies and reports. Actual progress on many issues remains stymied because there are so many local entities—from county and city governments to local sewer districts and private homeowners' associations—often working at cross-purposes. Pugetopolis is a budding supercity without a supergovernment.

Seattle has tried to fill the role of supercity itself. As the winner of the frontier phase of the competition, it has long been the region's powerhouse. But Seattle is the Evil

Empire to many of its competitors and neighbors, the spider at the center of the regional web, hoping to grow and flourish at the expense of everyone else. That was one of the prime factors in the defeat of regional mass transit and water cleanup plans decades ago. The notion of "Greater Seattle" has a hegemonic ring outside the city limits. Seattle has brawled with its neighbors over watersheds and sewers, transportation and spending priorities. It's been seen as unfriendly to rural property owners and suburban cities. Seattle wants bike lanes and mass transit to whisk people in and out of the city; much of the rest of central Puget Sound wants more roads and better bus lines connecting the suburbs. In recent years Seattle has also been viewed as a collection of lefty snobs, a Berkeley with rain. In turn, Seattle sees the suburbs as pointless sprawl.

And yet the region is becoming increasingly like Seattle. After sprawl came Starbucks. In the 1990s, the coffee chain proliferated and created a suburban necklace of cozy-yet-corporate "third places" that matched a growing suburban desire to get out once in awhile. Many of the new suburbanites populating young cities like Newcastle and Sammamish were refugees from Seattle proper; still others came from big cities elsewhere for jobs at Microsoft and Boeing. To cater to their desire for urban amenities, developers built housing tracts that mimicked classic Queen Anne Hill architecture. Influxes of immigrants expanded the ethnic dining options in strip malls and revitalized neighborhoods like Bellevue's Crossroads while adding an Asian flavor to once-white-bread Factoria.

Bothell touted itself as "pedestrian friendly," once-conservative Bellevue was suddenly "gay friendly," and Renton, a one-time blue-collar town known mostly for freeway traffic jams, began to advertise itself on TV as "ahead of the curve." Suddenly, we were all Seattle.

In the meantime, Seattle became more suburban. The downtown retail core took on a generic flavor with national chains proliferating, and developments like Westlake Center, Pacific Place, and the rehabbed University Village competed with Bellevue Square. Bungalows were torn down for new megahouses, neighborhoods became more affluent and upscale, and many lost some of their variety and character. Many of the new condo neighborhoods exhibited the sameness of suburban subdivisions—call it vertical sprawl. The city also began to enforce drinking, noise, loitering, strip club, and other "nanny" laws because while Seattle professed to be a big-time city, it really wasn't comfortable with the mess that comes with that.

The result is a city that no longer feels like itself, and worse, is starting to feel like everyplace else. While Seattle dominates the flavor of Pugetopolis, the character of the whole region is becoming homogenized, its flavor corporate vanilla. We're turning into the civic equivalent of a Starbucks Frappuccino.

History suggests that balkanization won't be entirely wiped away as city and suburbs come together in one cultural stew. I suspect that Pugetopolis will continue to be competitive and dysfunctional for decades to come—

certainly if the past is any guide. Besides, a true megalopolis is a multiheaded hydra.

The problems of parochialism will be aggravated by global warming and the challenge of cleaning up Puget Sound. Both demand that we understand the big picture and intricate interplay of the region's moving parts. To save orcas, you have to have fish for them to eat; to save the salmon, we need new development practices and water rules. To have clean water we need to radically change our ways. All of this will be exacerbated by climate change's uncertainties and costs.

Despite Seattle's own welcoming of density, growth will still disperse throughout Puget Sound in various urban and industrial centers. In spite of the intention to rein in sprawl, the Growth Management Act remains generous in allowing Pugetopolis to grow outward. One of the huge growth areas will be the long-neglected western shore of the Sound. Development will splash up to the foothills of the Olympics just as it has against the Cascades in the east. Seattle will become Pugetopolis's most dense, most expensive neighborhood, but even more people—newcomers and Seattle refugees—will spread out to seek the dream that a denser Seattle can't offer: places with affordable single-family homes, better schools, less crime, more trees.

On top of that, the urban model Seattle is currently selling will not make us happy. Seattle proper is volunteering to take a massive amount of growth in the coming years, but that means changes for which Seattleites are not prepared. Gentrification is already driving out the middle class with unaffordable housing. Long-settled neighborhoods are being squeezed by new demands for higher densities. Preservationists are racing against the clock to save potential landmark structures just one step ahead of swinging wrecking balls that are drastically reshaping the city center. Taxpayers will be even harder pressed to pay for the parks, amenities, and other infrastructure improvements that such densities demand. Already, the egalitarian city that persisted into the 1990s is largely dead.

Seattle's underlying mythology is also being challenged. Many of our old points of pride are gone, or in jeopardy. Our mascot, the wild salmon, is poisoned and threatened, no longer a food staple but a tourist prop for Pike Place fish tossers. We were once a chilly rain-soaked town that prided itself on being hardy; now we may face a warmer future without enough water. The red cedars are struggling, and the people who planted palm trees years ago seem absurdly prescient.

We once considered our semi-isolation an asset: Seattle was a place where you could hear yourself think and take nourishment from the clean air, water, and greenery. Now, thanks to the Microsoft-driven computer revolution, we're experiencing the pressures of outside competition and influence. In addition, globalization, "free" trade, and instant communication are bringing new pressures to conform to global norms. Seattle is losing its sense of place, its unique geographic attachment.

This loosening of connection is a tragedy. When Boeing was founded here, it made sense because the forests provided the right wood for Boeing's planes—we literally helped to grow airplanes. As the company grew, it shaped the city into a kind of company town of engineers and well-paid workers who helped keep Seattle a city without a wide class divide. But in the new economy of this century, Boeing left for Chicago and now outsources its Dreamliner parts overseas. Instead of being the launch pad for a Space Age as envisioned by our 1962 Century 21 world's fair, we've become an assembler, an integrator, a software supplier. Which is nice work, but it also means the creative class that dreams this stuff up could live anywhere.

Many of the city's new downtown urban dwellers are part-time residents, childless couples, or folks whose business is elsewhere (selling software in China, fighting malaria in Africa). Writer Wallace Stegner talked of the West as having "boomers" and "stickers," people who exploited a place and those who nested. Add to these today's new high-rent locust—the "hoppers"—affluent global transients who swarm through on their career paths. The effect of this is a class of people who regard our locality as a temporary roost. Hoppers live a "lifestyle," rather than a life in an actual physical place that makes demands on them. They don't have to adjust to the land and climate, know the local history, or be touched by any of it. They can live in a generic high-rise with concierge service and enjoy a view that might as well be a hologram.

The commercial vision of Pugetopolis is of a place always adapting to the market demands of more and more and more. The Puget Sound Regional Council's plan for the year 2040 addresses a single question: "How can the region accommodate another 1.7 million people and 1.2 million new jobs by 2040 while enhancing the environment and our overall quality of life?"

Call this the have-your-cake-and-eat-it-too goal. It offers the false promise of suggesting that we can experience virtually unlimited growth without real costs; that we can enhance the quality of life without limiting growth and consumption. It shapes a new myth that pleases the Chamber of Commerce while courting environmentalists. It suggests that Puget Sound and its people are infinitely malleable. It also rests on the assumption that American-style prosperity, done thoughtfully, produces only winners.

It is not much different from the mainstream vision we had 150 years ago, when growth and industrialization were seen as inherently good. We've dolled it up with some awareness of environmental consequences, but we're stuck in the same mentality. Here's a breathless passage from the *Seattle Intelligencer* in 1868:

> The snorts of the iron horse shall be heard in the mountain passes; the splash of the factory wheel and the hum of its machinery shall be heard at the waterfall; the fire of the blast of the iron furnace shall be seen on the mountain slope; the eye as it follows the railroad track, shall rest awhile in the valley of prosperous agriculture, and then hasten on to the busy city, where the stately ship shall grow from the shapeless lumber pile; while the Sound shall be

studded with sails innumerable, indicating that
on the deep also is man's prosperity; and the
yawning coal mine, the busy mill yard, and the
seins of the fisheries shall show that the bowels
of the earth, the primeval forest and the depth
of the sea, each adds to man's wealth and to
the prosperity of Puget Sound.

A century later, the Seattle Area Industrial Council
merely updated that vision with its image depicting a factory and pristine mountains side by side. We know they
can coexist, but at a cost. We also know that the "pristine" lakes and snowpacks of the Cascades and Olympics
are polluted with chemicals from that factory. We now
know that the wildlife of those mountains is depleted
because of the press of development. We now know that
driveways and lawn fertilizers and the antidepressants
popped by the factory's employees are helping to con-
taminate our drinking water and spoil the food chain. We
now know that those snowy mountains might be bare in
the future because of the carbon we're pumping into the
atmosphere.

Yes, the "index finger of nature" is pointing at us, but
it appears to be the middle finger of accusation: You came
to "God's Country" and screwed it up.

3.

It's a beautiful, warm summer evening in the early 1990s,
and I'm on a cruise across Puget Sound with a group of

conventioneering journalists. We're returning to Seattle from a salmon feed, the kind visitors will always remember as being so essentially Northwest. I'm standing at the bow looking down as it cleaves the dark waters and I see a swimming ghost. I shake my head and look again. There's a porpoise swimming in the bow wave just below the surface. But the waters are filled with bioluminescent life forms so the porpoise is glowing brightly in the dark. With sleek, fluid motions she escorts our ship, an illuminated apparition of astonishing beauty. Then she's gone.

The golden cetacean seems like a symbol of the dreams that Puget Sound country has evoked in many people. The glow is a reminder of the kind of idealism many of the pioneers brought to this place. Historian Charles LeWarne documented some of this in his book *Utopias on Puget Sound 1885–1915*, which looked at the experimental communities that came and went during formative decades here. Places like the Puget Sound Co-operative in Port Angeles, Freeland on Whidbey Island, Equality in Skagit County. While much of our DNA comes from the boomers and city builders, deep in Pugetopolis's soul is a corner saved for the eccentric, the radical, the outcast, and the misfit. These were people who saw a blank slate on Puget Sound, but instead of re-creating New York or Boston they hoped to create a New Jerusalem or a New Age here, long before the hippie communes of the '60s or the J. Z. Knight-Ramtha Yelm compound of today.

The most fascinating of these experiments is a modest place called Home, originally more ambitiously called Home City. Outsiders referred to it as Home Colony.

Today, it's a collection of modest houses on the Key Peninsula, south of Gig Harbor on Van Geldern Cove. It's a charming, post-utopian, pre-gentrification kind of place—the kind that reminds you that there are still some places apart from McNeil Island where nonmillionaires can have a home with a Puget Sound view. The exurban Pierce County peninsula isn't on the way to anywhere, and while chunks of forest are being cleared for housing sites and a few McMansions are popping up, it still hasn't made the transition from blue-tarp suburb and rural hideaway.

Founded in 1896, Home in its heyday was a community of individualists. Not a commune—Home residents owned their own property—and not devoted to a single ideology like some other Puget Sound colonies that tried to be paragons of socialism or communism. Home resident Jay Fox described it as "a community of free spirits who came out into the woods to escape the poluted [*sic*] atmosphere of priest-ridden, conventional society." Northwest writer and historian Stewart Holbrook described Home in a way that might be very familiar to people who attend places like The Evergreen State College in Olympia, or live in neighborhoods like Fremont, or read the message board at their local food co-op:

> What a yeasting it was, the boiling and bubbling at Home! Spiritualists came. . . . A school for Esperanto was opened. Exponents of various food fads came and went, among them Dr. Hazzard, an eloquent female who spoke to such effect that John Buchi, a Swiss butcher at Home, wished 'a Got damn on all

her wegitarians.' Local enthusiasts started a class in Hatha-Yoga, another in straight theosophy. Russellites came to report the imminent end of things, which was all right with the anarchists. Pantheists, Freethinkers of all shades, Monists, Mormon missionaries—they all came, and Home gave them all a hearing.

LeWarne writes that, unlike the alternative communities of the late twentieth century, Puget Sound's utopian experiments weren't mainly founded by disenchanted, upper-middle-class kids. Their residents were mostly middle-age, working-class people, often tradesmen—mill workers, farmers, loggers, sailors. They were often people making a dramatic midlife change. They usually brought practical skills: Colonies immediately set about clearing the land, milling timber, building houses and wharves, planting crops and orchards. They sought a kind of frontier self-sufficiency that could sustain their efforts to be secessionists from the dominant culture.

They were not necessarily quiet about their efforts. Most of the communities began publishing newspapers and pamphlets. Home had numerous newspapers over the years, including ones called *Discontent: Mother of Progress, Demonstrator, The New Era,* and *Clothed with the Sun.* This active, alternative press served to reach out to the world and like minds. It explored radical topics. The papers often got colony members into trouble by publishing articles that offended outsiders or provided an excuse for official harassment. Home members were jailed for offenses such as writing and distributing "obscene" material (an article about venereal disease) and running a story defending nude bathing (author Jay Fox was prosecuted and jailed for advocating "disrespect for law"). But they also recruited new members and gave voice to radical ideas: the rights of labor, anarchism, socialism, free love, women's rights, free speech. Prominent visitors to Home included anarchist Emma Goldman, union leader Big Bill Haywood, and long-haired proponent of the Arts & Crafts movement and founder of New York's Roycroft community Elbert Hubbard (whose adopted nephew became Scientology's founder, L. Ron Hubbard).

Virtually all the early Puget Sound utopian experiments eventually fell apart. Local officials harassed Home after a self-proclaimed anarchist assassinated President William McKinley in 1901. Eventually, Home lost its post office and was infiltrated by government spies who were convinced it was a hotbed of active revolution and bomb-making. But most utopian communities unraveled because of worldly arguments over things like property and control of community assets. Home was no exception. Outsiders enjoyed exposés of the colony's struggles in the Tacoma newspapers, with headlines like "Inside Workings of Anarchist Colony Are Revealed." Home fell apart, and community members ended up tangled in litigation. The irony of anarchists using the judicial system to settle property disputes was duly noted.

One of the interesting legacies of colonies like Home is how much their countercultural ways still endure as part of Northwest life and image. Puget Sound has spawned thriving alternative scenes that include music, theater, art, newspapers and Web sites, co-housing experiments, consumer and health cooperatives, tree-sitters, vegans, neo-pagans, animal rights activists, protest martyrs, and eco-saboteurs. Seattle neighborhoods from Capitol Hill and Georgetown to the University District, college towns like Bellingham and Olympia all are "yeasting" like Home. The old "Soviet of Washington" still occasionally makes headlines when its radical genes kick in, whether it's the national phenomenon of rebellious grunge rock or the tear-gas-scented protests of the 1999 World Trade Organization "Battle in Seattle."

It percolates into mainstream thinking as well, particularly in regard to the environment. Politicians like Seattle Mayor Greg Nickels and King County Executive Ron Sims have made names for themselves by pursing green agendas. Nickels gained national notoriety (and his picture in *Vanity Fair*) for getting America's cities to embrace the Kyoto accords on global warming, and Sims has instituted tough new development regulations. Farmers' markets proliferate to help people buy locally and seasonally to help break the carbon-dependent corporate food chain. Everyone's visionary plans feature 1,001 things we can do to make Pugetopolis greener, from restoring wetlands and watersheds to mandatory recycling, taxes on grocery bags, and converting Seattle's Crown Victoria taxi fleet to fuel-efficient hybrids.

Perhaps the most influential utopian road map was the one laid out in the mid-1970s by Ernest Callenbach, the Berkeley writer who authored the futurist fantasy *Ecotopia*. That book envisioned a time when the Pacific

Coast, from Northern California to Oregon and Washington, seceded from the United States, walled itself off, and built the perfect, sustainable, ecologically sensible society. Many of Callenbach's ideas—including resurfacing urban streams and expanding alternative energy—are now part of everyday policy discussions.

The concept of the "bioregion" Callenbach popularized has now come to the fore. The British Columbia-to-California corridor that formed the heart of Ecotopia is also awash in green thinking and progressive politics. While the region has not formally seceded from the United States, the early part of the twenty-first century saw local officials determined to go their own way on green policies because the administration of George W. Bush seemed generally hostile to eco-initiatives. Ecotopians found a way to make progress despite the feds—sometimes in defiance of them. Nickels pushed Kyoto, and California passed emission standards that are tougher than the federal ones. Others have advocated that parts of the Northwest form a cohesive economic and trade entity called Cascadia that will help the region become even more globally competitive; while not based in a particularly "alternative" view of the world, it reinforces an underlying sense that the Northwest is better off looking out for itself. Pugetopolis might be the urban vision, but the goal is actually Pugetopia.

Much of the green talk is just well-intentioned talk—still trapped in old assumptions and economic markets that undercut its very goals and ideals. And the powerful forces of commerce and development are always ready to co-opt good intentions. Big dam projects are touted as a needed response to global warming's water challenges despite the wetlands and wildlife areas they would destroy; expensive mass transit projects are pitched as greener than cars, yet overlooked is the fact that when expanded they also tend to drive growth and boost land prices. Suburban megamansions are jammed onto rural lots, displacing habitat and threatening aquifers, yet because they contain some recycled materials and highlight density, they are called "green." Many efforts to make Puget Sound "greener" are simply a greenwashing of old agendas to build and profit regardless of the long-term cost and consequences. Improvements are often small, incremental, and fragmented, if they are improvements at all.

And much environmental thinking still fails to take into account issues of economic justice and fairness: As Seattle becomes a greener city, it is also becoming one that is too expensive for the middle and working classes. As with any alternative community, idealists often become narrowly focused on their own agendas and self-righteously contemptuous of those who don't "get it." Radical cyclists periodically break traffic laws and block the streets to protest the dominance of cars, disrupting minimum wage workers trying to get to their jobs. Some see themselves as front-line warriors in the fight against obesity by promoting walking and biking, yet they seem less interested in the practical struggles of people forced to buy cheap, fattening calories with food stamps. Groups like the Earth Liberation Front commit arson against targets that don't fit into their scheme of things, from suburban homes to university research facilities.

Despite these excesses, we are never better than when we are trying to go our own way and trying to do something new. While I think ELF violence is morally and tactically wrong, the ELFs do act out of a sense many of us have that business as usual will lead to further—and worse—destruction. It may be wrong to burn houses down, but it can also be disastrous to build them in the wrong way in the wrong place. Eco-vandalism should not be allowed to give alternative thinking a bad name. Rethinking is crucial to figuring out how to stabilize, perhaps even reverse, the pathologies of Pugetopolis. There is hope for all of us in the legacy of Home.

4.

Much of what there is to love about Puget Sound is still present in abundance, despite crowding and pollution. There are also threats that aren't man-made. Massive earthquakes, volcanic eruptions, tsunamis: These things are recorded in the land, and scientists tell us one day they are certain to radically change the course of life here. It's hard to believe "paradise" could be so dangerous. As the rock song by the Seattle band The Presidents of the United States of America goes: "You don't believe me / that this scenery / could be a cold-blooded killer / It's gonna blow . . . Volcano!"

For the most part, these worries exist outside of us, well beyond daily life. The geologic clock ticks in centuries and millennia. Sure, there have been reminders of what can happen. I distinctly remember being told as a child that Mount Rainier was sleeping and harmless—a position I reconsidered after Mount St. Helens blew in 1980. And I wasn't in town for the Nisqually quake in 2001, but I remember watching helplessly from a motel in California while CNN broadcast images that gave the impression my hometown had been flattened. Much of Pugetopolis is in the shadow of volcanoes or was built without regard to fault lines.

Most of us see the volcanoes as snow-capped beauty that makes a nice backdrop for photographs. The other hazards are out of sight. It's even easier to forget these hazards because we have lives to live, good lives for many of us. You can still go to a public beach and dig fresh clams for dinner, still watch the bald eagles and ospreys overhead, still enjoy the scent of red cedar, still shop for salmon and fresh mushrooms at Pike Place Market. These seem as eternal, somehow, as the landscape itself. But we now know that they are highly ephemeral—-they can disappear not just in geologic time, but within our own lifetimes and by our own actions.

I sometimes wonder if we would have built on Puget Sound if we could do it all over again. Say we just stumbled upon this place in the early twenty-first century and instead of settling here, we chose to study it first. What would we do with it? How would we plan its development or protect its environment? Would we concentrate so many people in earthquake zones or allow so much sprawl in valleys where lava and lahars once flowed? Would we really place cities on the shores of such an environmentally sensitive area? Would we cut the old growth or dam the rivers or overfish the salmon?

We can't go back, but I wonder what we could learn by running a thought experiment about what we would do if we could start from scratch. An imaginary reboot of Puget Sound country might help us envision a future that isn't just more of the same. A place we can aim for.

I'd like to think that if we could do it over, we would do it better. But then, what would the "market" demand of us? I suspect even with all the right science and research and understanding on our side, we would find it tough to hold back the forces of demand that gather like so many Visigoths on the horizon.

There is something so human about soiling our own nests. Humans hunted out the prehistoric megafauna of North America and used practices like burning forests to make hunting easier. The fur trappers couldn't be satisfied with catching and slaughtering some sea otters or beavers; they had to hunt them nearly to extinction. Even today, you occasionally see logging trucks hauling old-growth giants to the mill, long after we know that they return so little as wood for what they gave us as forest. There is a level of greed and shortsightedness that we can't seem to escape.

On the other hand, there is no better alternative than trying to get it right. We have the advantage in this modern age of drawing on the world's wisdom to help us do better. What we also need is a renewed commitment to raising generations that will want to take on the task of being stewards of the battered and bruised paradise we inherited and passed on. We need to grow people who see the value in what is left and treasure it, whatever comes. People who love the land and their homeland.

To my mind, the sprawling urban, industrial vision of Pugetopolis is a nightmare—just as my mother warned. I also believe Pugetopia is unattainable. I don't think man's lot is to live in a state of perfection. Nevertheless, we can move forward with hopeful realism knowing that living here well is something that requires commitment and sacrifice. We need to work at breaking the cycle of leaving things worse than when we found them. The first step is to disabuse ourselves of the idea that we can have it all. That is the most dangerous fantasy infecting Pugetopolis today.

The Myth of Seattle Nice

Seattle is a city of postcard appearances: beautiful, fresh, and friendly. But it often succeeds in driving newcomers crazy. It's as if the city lives in two dimensions, but hides a third that is darker and often elusive.

Why do your smiling neighbors never actually talk to you? Why do people look uncomfortable if you try to debate a topic? Why does everyone appear laid-back, yet you often find that "Uptight Seattleite," a *Seattle Weekly* column, is so aptly named?

OK, we're not exactly a Stephen King town where the locals are hiding a creepy secret. More often Seattle suffers from civic self-deception. As a third-generation native, I use this column from time to time to debunk some of the lies we tell ourselves.

The lie I'd like to tackle today is the myth of Seattle nice.

Back in the 1990s a former adman named David Stern ran for mayor. He had one major accomplishment to his name: He was credited with creating the Happy Face. It was a great story and we liked to believe it. What other city—cheery, friendly, home of the kindergarten wisdom of Robert Fulghum—would be more fitting as the source of the international symbol of niceness?

Only it turned out Stern's story wasn't true. Someone else had invented the Happy Face years before, and Stern had been milking the myth. Ironically, the man who defeated Stern was Norm Rice, whose last name and personality gave rise to his nickname, Mayor Nice.

Seattle may not have originated the Happy Face, but it often puts one on. "If you don't have anything nice to say, don't say anything at all" has long been the city's unofficial motto. It is not a plea for civil discussion, but rather a recipe for no discussion at all. This suits Seattle's dominant political styles: consensus (no arguments), back-room dealing (no public arguments), and endless process (no conclusions). Those styles avoid the non-niceties of ever having to decide anything, which is so "noninclusive."

Pitch a proposal in this town—ask for an investment or try selling something—and people will be very reluctant to say "no" or "no thanks." The word "no" is not nice. It's so negative. If a person in Seattle wants to say no, you'll hear "I'll think about it," or "I'll get back to you," or the person will pretend to never have heard you in the first place.

Mayor Greg Nickels embodies this style: He cannot say no to any project. Instead, he has a full-time assistant, Deputy Mayor Tim "The Shark" Ceis, whose job is to say no for the mayor. The Shark usually does this very privately so no one will think the mayor isn't nice.

The voters don't like to say no, either. We voted on the monorail expansion four times before finally saying no. Last November, we held an advisory ballot on the Alaskan Way Viaduct replacement, after which every faction declared victory. *The vote was specifically designed not to decide anything.* In Seattle politics everyone's a winner, just like the Special Olympics.

I have noticed a subtle change in what people mean when they say a person is nice. Nice used to be a judgment that meant you were OK, like wallpaper that doesn't catch the eye.

Back in the '90s, I read David Maraniss's book on Bill Clinton, *The Clinton Enigma*, wherein Maraniss learns that when the president complimented a man by saying "Nice tie," it was really code for—I'll be polite here—"screw off."

The same thing is now happening here in Seattle. Saying someone is nice is often a leadoff into an attack, like saying, "No offense, but . . . " An online critic recently took me to task for a column defending Seattle Center's world's fair legacy. My critic began his tirade using my nickname, saying, "Skip's a nice guy, but he's wack-a-doodle-doo . . . "

The nice-guy preamble was so Seattle. But it wasn't really nice, which gets to my point. Seattle operates under the guise of nice; it tips its hat to nice. But much of the time, we're something the postcard doesn't show: a passive-aggressive, often dysfunctional, conflict-averse town where the sharpest knife leaves its mark in the form of a Happy Face.

Seattle magazine 2007

A Fine Rage, a Fresh Wind

The crown jewel of civilized Seattle—the retail core of big hotels, public-private partnerships, and Planet Hollywood—was transformed. The carless streets were strewn with overturned dumpsters, news boxes, and concrete planters. Each intersection was occupied by the pierced and passionate, many dancing to the rhythms of pounding percussion—drums made of plastic buckets or odd bits of metal. Periodically, a young man with a home-made stovepipe didgeridoo would add the resonant background hum that movie soundtracks use to convince you that something spiritual is about to happen. It was as if Seattle had been conquered by a global tribe of alternative types whose strange rites had yet to be co-opted by frat boys. And I liked it.

It wasn't a city sold out, and shut up, by developers. It wasn't a city too civil to say what was on its mind. It wasn't a city overrun by consensus. It wasn't a city showing off its pretty mountains and tasty coffee confections for the cruise ship crowds. It wasn't a city where the cops, with their new black riot gear and armor, were saying, "Have a nice day."

This was a city that trashed our unofficial motto, "If you don't have anything nice to say, don't say anything at all."

Often what was said was silly. "Fuck you, Nike" or "Capitalism destroys all life" doesn't take you very far. But the honesty that comes with a fine rage is a fresh wind, something to clean out the cobwebs of our stale politics and civic discussions.

Yes, I think the smashing and burning sucked. But long before free-floating anarchists and assholes broke windows, looted Starbucks, or set fire to trash cans, many thousands had made their point and accomplished their goal of shutting down the World Trade Organization while the world watched. And they did it mostly with clever organization and boundless enthusiasm—and a lot of dancing.

I followed the protesters for eight hours, from the pitch-black pissing rain at Victor Steinbrueck Park to the tear-gassed barricades outside the Sheraton at Sixth and Pike. Their props included giant puppets, turtle costumes, a black-clad marching band called the Infernal Noise Brigade, an inflatable blue whale named Flo, and a Macy's parade–style blimp from the Rainforest Action folk. Demonstrators were well organized into "affinity groups" and divided, like smokers and nonsmokers, into "arrest" or "not arrest" contingents. One group I ran into was the Reclaiming Cluster, a collection of eco-feminist pagans from the Bay Area.

As the march progressed toward the Convention Center, groups peeled off to block intersections. By the time they reached the Sheraton, the battle for Seattle was in essence already won: For at least a day, downtown was turned into a giant shopping-free zone, and baffled businessmen from all over the world had to take cover.

The police needed tear gas, pepper spray, and hard rubber pellets to dislodge people. I was gassed twice and took cover in a store entryway as pellets ricocheted through the crowd. Next to me was a Mexican journalist who, eyes red and burning, looked at the police action and said, "This is crazy." We ran, and I found a protester medic to rinse out my eyes.

Seeing clearly, I wandered the streets and watched the crowds, and ran into a friend who summed up the spectacle. He said, "It's nice to see Seattle behaving badly."

Seattle Weekly 1999

Nanny-State Liberals and Neighborhood Creep

People tell me how surprised they are at liberal Seattle's prudish crackdown on strip clubs and lap dancers, but it seems totally in character to me. Five years ago I wrote about Seattle neo-Victorians, the folks who pushed city attorney Mark Sidran's anti-street-people laws (no sitting on the sidewalk!), maintained the teen dance ordinance, and wanted to ban certain legal alcoholic beverages in selected neighborhoods because they attracted the wrong sort of people—a sort of "you are what you drink" form of segregation.

Seattle is a town brimming with nanny-state liberals, Calvinist socialists, and middlebrow public officials who go junketing to Singapore, where law and order is maintained at the end of a brine-soaked cane.

At Expo 2005 in Aichi, Japan, Singapore's pavilion wore a slogan: "A world without walls," it declared. Excuse me, but isn't Singapore the epitome of a walled city, with draconian drug laws and bans against littering, spitting, *Playboy*, protest, "unnatural sex," and gum chewing? It's even illegal not to flush a public toilet. The joke is that Singapore is a "fine" place because there's a fine for everything.

Proponents argue that the laws work, the streets are safe, and such rules are necessary for dealing with high urban density. As Seattle floats atop a real-estate bubble that increasingly makes the city affordable mostly to the affluent, we can probably look forward to more laws intended to make the whole town more like Singapore (recycle or else!). That is part of the price of urban gentrification, the signs of which are everywhere.

I recently completed a long-planned move back to Seattle. I was born and raised here, have lived half of my half century within the city limits, and continued to work in the city most of the years I lived in Kirkland.

I grew up in the Rainier Valley during a time when the economy was in the tank. Our neighborhood was plunging downhill, and the city was depopulating courtesy of white flight and a shrinking Boeing. It seems crazy today to think that for a couple of decades, the city actually lost population. You could get a great house in Mount Baker or Madrona for $25,000. It seems even crazier to be nostalgic for that, but sometimes I am. Not for the time when a friend's dad, a laid-off Boeing worker, was reduced to being a paperboy to feed his family. But for a time when basic middle-class amenities were available to households with one wage earner making a modest income.

Now gentrification is scrambling the old neighborhoods. My partner and I were out to dinner with two real-estate-agent friends, and one half-jokingly said that "White Center is the new Ballard." Apparently, Shoreline used to be the new Ballard, until it got pricey. So first-time single-family home buyers have to go farther afield. It left me wondering: If the old square-head Ballard is gone, and the new affordable Ballard has moved south, what is the current Ballard? The new Laurelhurst?

And new neighborhoods are emerging. A friend who lives near 25th Avenue East and East Madison Street was telling me about the various names being tried out for his neck of the former woods. "Madison Heights" is one, as it rises above the recently gentrified Madison Valley and the old gentry of Madison Park. "The Slope" is another. Or, simply, "The Summit."

Seattle seems to have gone neighborhood crazy, a trend driven by real estate prices. Your neighborhood used to be defined by where you went to high school: Lincoln, Garfield, Roosevelt, Franklin, Nathan Hale—these names told Seattleites everything they needed to know about your race, class, or ethnic background, or at the very least, the milieu you were raised in. That ended with busing and school choice. Now you see neighborhood creep—how desirable places like Ravenna and Leschi have snuck into once-marginal neighborhoods. "Madison Heights" is an easier sell than "North Central Area," I bet.

Seattle—already a pretty suburban city due to fairly low housing densities—has further suburbanized as it has moved upscale, particularly when it comes to retail. In the 1990s, the hallmark of Eastside urbanization was getting a Starbucks. Now the hallmark of Seattle suburbanization is the building and revitalization of in-city malls, from Pacific Place to Northgate. Take University Village. If you shop at U Village, you have no moral authority over anyone who shops at Bellevue Square. Once dominated by a bowling alley and the 1970s low-budget retail icon Lamonts, U Village is now a yuppie fun zone for Pottery Barn shoppers. Both malls have their pluses and minuses, but it's a matter of taste, not values. Bellevue has my permission to wipe that sneer off Seattle's face when it comes to dissing the burbs as morally inferior, at least when it comes to consumerism.

The most rapidly densifying place in King County is not Seattle but downtown Bellevue, which is continuing an inexorable march toward big-city-dom. It makes me think that if Lake Washington weren't there, Seattle and the Eastside would have merged long ago, having met in the middle to become virtually indistinguishable. As it is, the water boundary, even with the bridges, creates a kind of Darwin's finches experiment between how blue cities and red suburbs develop. It seems to me that the dominant regional trend is that the market is driving everyone toward a similar destination: a decentralized urban region for the affluent where everyone is within reach of a Pottery Barn and a PCC.

Seattle Weekly 2005

Bungvilla City

Some years ago, my then-grade-school-aged daughter was trying to figure out where our family fit in the grand scheme of things. "Dad, are we rich?" she asked.

No, I answered. "Are we poor?" No. Her face brightened, and she said happily, "Then we're the 'just right' people!" That's social-class theory according to Goldilocks. In my daughter's eyes, we had attained a kind of secure just-rightness that offers comfort. That value used to personify Seattle, a city that prided itself on being a middle-class, democratic, populist alternative to big Eastern metropolises or sprawling Western ones.

Rich people showed up in Seattle pretty late. The first millionaires were made by the Alaskan gold rush, which ushered in a rum, retail, and real-estate boom. Early labor activism added resistance to the growing influence of the robber barons, and the clash between upper and lower classes evolved a city in which there was little economic difference between union blue-collar workers and Boeing white collars.

In the mid-twentieth century, urban fantasists imagined that the twenty-first century would spawn cities of great equality—"democracity" was one term given to this utopian vision. Seattle, tucked away and doing its own thing in a far corner of America, achieved something a bit like it: a middle-class idyll that embodied the American dream without being a soulless suburb or an economically stratified big city. Was it perfect? Far from it. But there were few rich people, few poor people, and a broad mainstream in between.

Times have changed. In response to my recent column on race, Beacon Hill/Rainier Valley resident Lewis Stockill wrote and described his family of three as "lower- to mid-middle class" with a household income of under

$78,000 per year. That assertion seems astonishing. That much income ought to signal affluence. But then, Mossback's real-estate agent recently sent listings that included a $750,000 bungalow in Fremont. *Uff da!*

The pressure on the middle class isn't just local. George W. Bush's plummet in the polls comes in part because the middle class is being crushed. Under Bush, middle-income wage earners are bearing the brunt of the tax burden, while the wealthiest Americans get the benefits of tax cuts. If the Bush cuts are renewed, by 2009 an estimated 72 percent of the benefits of extending the current tax cuts would flow to households making more than $200,000 per year. Nearly half would go to people earning more than $1 million. More and more middle-income wage earners don't have health insurance. In 2005, 41 percent of Americans earning between $20,000 and $40,000 per year were uninsured. And the disparities between the rich and everyone else are widening dramatically. The liberal Institute for Policy Studies reports the income gap between average wage earners in this country and CEOs was a 42-to-1 ratio in 1980. The current gap is 431 to 1, or $11.8 million to $27,460. So much for letting the spoils trickle down.

Maintaining the middle-class idyll is becoming impossible not as a matter of happenstance but as a matter of policy.

That includes urban policy that promotes dense development in the name of sustainability. This is driving the cost of city living to impossible heights—more so in a city like Seattle that is focused on creating high-wage jobs. If you're employed in high-tech, biotech, or other professional sectors, you may be making out OK. But the majority of folks don't have those kinds of jobs or incomes. They are getting shoved out, bought out, or priced out—at least those who haven't already fled to the exurbs.

Let's go back to the bungalow for a minute. The bungalow appeared in the late nineteenth century as a modern, populist, low-cost alternative to the Victorian megahouses of that era. People of modest means could buy a sensible, one-story, single-family house designed for a small lot and to integrate well with the natural environment. They were easy to build and maintain, and had modern innovations like built-in bookshelves. You could order one from the Sears catalog for $900.

They've long been Seattle's bread-and-butter homes. But rising land prices are changing all that. An article by Christine Palmer in Historic Seattle's online magazine describes the national trend of "bash and build" development, the accelerated destruction of existing small homes and businesses in cities. When the land price exceeds the price of the structure, you've got a teardown—homes are either remodeled to maximize the value or they're scraped off the land and replaced. You see the results all over Seattle as vacant lots and yards disappear and megahouses rise. In Madison Park, you see one-story bungalows raised into three-story bungvillas—mini-skinny towers in search of a lake view. John Chaney, executive director of Historic Seattle, which is dedicated to preserving the city's architectural heritage, describes Seattle's bungalows as "endangered."

If bungalows are the new spotted owl of the urban eco-system, their disappearance, or transformation into housing for the well-off, is a sign of larger problems. To me, preserving local culture and history is the least of it. The disappearance of the bungalow is an indicator of socio-economic trouble ahead that poses a threat to Seattle's "just right" people.

Seattle Weekly 2006

Seattle's Bold Bioneers

Welcome to Biosphere 3, the hermetically sealed city in which citizen explorers engage in strange sustainability experiments.

What are Seattle's brave new bionauts investigating? Cold fusion? Chilly fusion? Pissing-rain-in-the-middle-of-May fusion?

No, what cranks the biofuels of these bioneers is whether it's possible to survive and thrive in Seattle without a car.

(Insert blood-curdling scream here.)

Madness, I know. Fortunately, their experiments are being documented for all to see.

Alan Durning of the nonprofit Sightline Institute (formerly Northwest Environment Watch), a Seattle think tank devoted to promoting sustainability in "Cascadia," is detailing his "year of living car-lessly" on the institute's Web site, www.sightline.org. To be honest, and Durning is, it's not that he's literally carless. It's just that after his eldest teenage son totaled the old family Volvo, Durning decided to go without a car for a year. It's an experiment to see how the family of five (wife, high-schooler, two middle-schoolers) will fare by walking, biking, busing, and mooching.

Yes, mooching, because while the Durnings don't have their own car, they're not above begging some rides from friends and associates who do. Which is a little like saying you've quit smoking because you're no longer *buying* cigarettes, merely bumming other people's. The Durnings also sometimes use cabs and Flexcars, which they calculate into their costs and savings. They ought also to count the gas burned by the Good Samaritans who chauffeur them around. But hey, the researchers inside Biosphere 2 had to pump in outside oxygen to keep from suffocating in their bubble. Since this isn't hard science but a sociological experiment by an eco-advocate, Durning is free to set his own terms.

As any parent knows, raising a family in this day and age without motorized wheels is a challenge—especially with kids of dating age. The modern family, not to mention the modern commuter, isn't rooted to one spot. We live life in wide and complicated orbits that take in the whole sprawling metro region, and we've got technologies (such as cell phones) that encourage movement without loss of productivity. A typical middle-class couple might have jobs on both sides of the lake, yoga practice on Queen Anne Hill, a doctor in Lake City, classes at Cornish, a favorite Mexican joint in White Center—you know the drill. I'll let you figure out the combinations and permutations if you add kids and pets into the mix.

Modern life is full and complex. To some extent, we're experiencing the local version of globalization. We might say we want urban villages, but we're also consumers who demand choice and customization. Being satisfied with what's down the block isn't always going to cut it. We don't all have neighborhood schools or churches or therapists or day cares. Durning says that, using the phone directory, he's identified some 248 businesses within a mile of his Ballard home. A disproportionate number seem to be auto-body shops. Despite the abundance, I'd be surprised if he finds everything his family needs within this so-called walkshed.

What Durning has discovered is that smart carless existence is maybe a little less careless, because everything takes more thought and planning. That "added incremental mindfulness," he writes, is a major bonus.

Another carless chronicler is Carla Saulter, who writes the "Bus Chick, Transit Authority" column for *Real Change* and blogs as "Bus Chick" at the *Seattle Post-Intelligencer*'s Web site. In one column, she accuses Seattle of "carism," as in being too friendly to cars and hostile to walkers, bikers, and bus riders. She, too, admits to cheating, bumming the odd ride here and there (thank goodness a few people are "carists"). But she generally laments the proliferation of strip malls and drive-through windows and the lack of bike lanes and sidewalks.

A real, hard-core bioneer family are the Petersons, featured recently in *The Seattle Times*. These courageous folks are carless, too, and have been since 1987. None of the Petersons even has a driver's license. To make matters more challenging, they live on the Eastside, where it's more acceptable to be gay and married than to be without a car. Mossback is a total defender of parental crackpots. It builds character in kids—at least I sure as hell hope so. But for all the benefits, cost savings, and character-building potential of being carless, how many of us would pay the price dad Kent Peterson does? He commutes by bike *three hours* (round-trip) to his job in Seattle. He's living his work: The *Times* reports his day job is promoting bike commuting for the nonprofit Bicycle Alliance of Washington. But a three-hour daily commute—by any mode—isn't a lifestyle model that's going to convert people.

Even if I could fit inside spandex, I wouldn't spend my time that way.

And time is the precious commodity of modern life. In an op-ed piece about car commuting in an era of $3 gas, author T. C. Boyle wrote in *The New York Times*: "No matter the cost of gas, we need to get to work, and each minute shaved off the commute is a minute—golden and fat and glowing—added to our real lives, the lives that begin after work, at home, in the bars and restaurants, with the children and the bills and the dog."

That is the ultimate challenge for Seattle's carless bio-spheroids: to boldly discover a lifestyle that guzzles neither gas nor time.

The bills and dog await.

Seattle Weekly 2006

Alan Durning took stock at the end of his bioneer family's "carless" year and determined the following: his family had cut its greenhouse emissions by 80 percent; while driving an average of seven miles per day in borrowed or rented vehicles (Flexcar is now called Zipcar, by the way) and carpools, the family still managed to reduce its driving by two-thirds. He estimated the family saved between $1,500 and $4,000, savings that would likely be higher in the era of $4-per-gallon gas. In an honest and detailed appraisal of his experiment, Durning admitted that there were many logistical hassles, and the burden for solving these often fell to his wife. Also, his 19-year-old son, who was living with the family part-time, began driving a friend's pickup truck—his driving was excluded from the final year-end tally. In an update on the Sightline Web site in September 2008, Durning reported that he is still carless. However, he wrote that he and his wife are divorcing. Ever the policy wonk, Durning calculated the impact of the break-up on their carbon footprint and concluded that "divorce boosts resource consumption." That will surprise no one who has already been through it.

2008

The Temple to Tripping

I had a chance to check out the Experience Music Project last week, seeing the blob from the inside out. The staff was busy getting ready for opening night, and the place was filled with workers, guards, PR people, sound and light technicians, caterers, VIPs, and media folk, all trying to stay out of each other's way. Rapper/producer Sir Mix-a-Lot was getting a tour, though it was hard to tell who was the guide since Mix was doing all the talking. Frank Gehry, the building's architect, was climbing a long flight of stairs, trying to explain some of his ideas to a companion. He looked like a tired old Frenchman, kind of like Paul Schell after WTO.

EMP is an incredibly stimulating place. There is a lot to see, and the couple of hours I spent there didn't do it justice. I spent virtually all my time looking at the rock 'n' roll exhibits, important but only one aspect of the place.

And then there's the structure itself, which is a dizzying container for a vast array of, well, stuff. The angles, levels, and fluidity, so evident on the outside, are seen in greater variety and detail inside: the bones and guts of the blob itself, very structural but no less eccentric. EMP has the feel of a fun house inside; not exactly the Fun Forest's old Flight to Mars ride, but more like the kind that features squiggly mirrors and banked walkways. Except here the squiggles aren't images, they are giant steel support beams.

The place contorts reality. I don't think I've heard anyone say this, maybe because it'll scare away the grandmas from Hooper Junction, but EMP is a temple to tripping on acid—if not directly inspired by drugs, then inspired by the music of people who were inspired by drugs. The place is appropriately mind-bending for a rock museum and homage to Seattle's own Jimi Hendrix. Gehry, Allen, and Allen's sister Jody Patton's brilliance is that they didn't shy away from putting the essence of rock 'n' roll into the building itself. There's even sex there, if you scope out the plush lines of some of the contours, not to mention the intense energy in some of the exhibits, music, and videos at play inside.

Standing in front of the exhibits featuring the early days of Northwest rock, I found EMP's senior curator, Peter Blecha, whom I only knew by reputation ("the man who knows everything") and from the liner notes he's written for reissues of various garage band classics. We started chatting about the museum, the collection, and some memories of our own. I told him that the worst crowd I was ever in at a local concert was a crush of fellow teenagers trying to get in to see Don & the Goodtimes during a "Teen Spectaculars" at the Coliseum in about 1966, maybe '67. I was describing the narrow little stage areas the bands were given in what was essentially exhibition space. Blecha said, "Oh, maybe it was like this," we walked a couple of feet, and there on the wall was a photo of Don & the Goodtimes, playing in top hats no less, in front of a '60s crowd, crammed into a space exactly like I was describing.

I don't expect anyone else to give a shit, but I was impressed. A few of you may remember Don & the Goodtimes from hits like "Little Sally Tease," but this band is pretty obscure these days, steamrollered into near-oblivion by groups like Paul Revere and the Raiders. But they were an essential part of the music I was raised on in Seattle, very much a part of the mid- to late-sixties garage and roller-rink bands that inspired me to do very naughty things. "Louie Louie" was a local anthem; the Sonics and Wailers were demon-gods; hell, everyone knew girls who'd slept with the Raiders. All of it was grooming local youth for spending our nights at Eagles Auditorium, Seattle's answer to the Fillmore.

The exhibits at EMP are a little like making a museum out of the crap on any teenager's bedroom floor. Just pick a subculture: early riot grrrl, protopunk, hip-hop, R&B. Because of all the local history in EMP, I don't entirely know what to make of it: How many cities have hometown billionaires who come along and make a museum dedicated to our local teen idols? It is very strange to see old-time KJR deejay Pat O'Day in a fancy museum, for chrissakes.

Is EMP making a mountain out of a molehill, or did the Northwest rock scene really contribute something important? Was it really a player deserving of this treatment? Part of the problem is, like any provincial, I've taken much of our local musical riches for granted. A couple of years ago I took a friend, a transplant from D.C., to see a Wailers reunion show at the Showbox. I had been turning him on to various '60s bands by loaning him CDs, trying to point out early grunge influences in various tracks. Grunge comes from somewhere, I would say. Listen to the Sonics' rendition of "Louie Louie." My pal, who is much more music-literate than I, was watching the multigenerational crowd that was dancing to the Wailers' music: mop-topped pop kids to gray-haired grannies. He said, you don't know how lucky you are to have this kind of local scene, because most places don't—three or four generations of nationally important, regionally generated rock.

EMP takes the Northwest scene and places it into a larger, national and international context that includes both rock history and the joys of making music itself. The building and its exhibits seem to embody that exuberance. And for us locals, it helps us see what we have here in a whole new light. A strobe light at that.

Seattle Weekly 2000

EMP, aka "The Blob," continues to be an attraction at Seattle Center as a museum, concert venue, and architectural curiosity. It now also houses the Science Fiction Museum and Hall of Fame, opened in 2004, which is dedicated to another of Paul Allen's adolescent obsessions. The new museum is packed with books and memorabilia, including movie and TV props like Captain Kirk's chair from Star Trek. The original inspiration for the building was reportedly a pile of trash from an electric guitar shop, but its otherworldly design well serves its new purpose too. On the more practical side, the same year Allen opened his science fiction museum, he also ushered in

These pigs have turned Seattle into the Hanford of whimsy.

KUOW 2002

During Christmas 2007, the downtown retail core was filled with giant Nutcracker soldiers that were dolled up thematically, like the pigs, and guarded the doors of many establishments. They were likely sent down there to augment a busy and under-manned police force. The good thing about Nutcracker cops is they don't charge overtime and demand donuts.

2008

Urban Art in Nature's Gallery

The problem with public art in Seattle is that our natural landscape is tough competition. There is nothing man-made in the city that holds a candle to the awe-inspiring sight of the Cascades at dawn or the Olympics at sunset. A local religious scholar was asked why so few Seattleites go to church. Her reply was that no one had built a cathedral to match Mount Rainier.

So too has public art been outclassed. The city's favorite sculptures have tended to be whimsical populist efforts, like Safeco Field's baseball mitt or Fremont's *Waiting for the Interurban*. Our civic statues have been tucked away, as if we're embarrassed to be giving any single figure much attention: Chief Seattle hides under the monorail, and a statue of Washington's second governor, John McGraw, is dwarfed by vertical sprawl and historical obscurity. Our modern sculpture has often skulked at the base of downtown's skyscrapers.

Successful public art here must generate dialogue with the surroundings. Art may not compete with nature, but it can bounce ideas off nature's backdrops. Isamu Noguchi's *Black Sun*, known colloquially as Volunteer Park's "doughnut," is a first-rate example. It unabashedly blocks one of Seattle's most spectacular views, but offers a new way to see the city and its setting.

It's in this spirit that the Seattle Art Museum's new Olympic Sculpture Park works so well. It's a modern-art playground in the middle of a city whose spirit still flows out of the wilderness. It's a place where modernism's wild things have come out to play.

Before the park opened, I said I would have been happier if the land had been used for something more practical, like a biofuel depot. In my mind, the disappearance of blue-collar Seattle is not to be celebrated. But after half a dozen visits, I am a convert. Not an uncritical one—I think Louise Bourgeois's fountain sculpture *Father and Son* is hilariously bad kitsch—but the park has undeniable magnetism, as evidenced by the curious crowds that are already embracing it. On sunny days, there is a veritable passeggiata of Belltown residents who look like they've tagged the place as home turf.

The Weiss/Manfredi design is as brilliant as advertised, creatively zigzagging visitors on walkways over and alongside swishing cars and rumbling trains. The paths also bring you close to the gargantuan tankers anchored in Elliott Bay. This is no Olmsted-style park cultivating pockets of nature in the city. Rather, it's a celebration of the urban environment in the face of nature, framed by office buildings, condos, and even the brick-and-neon charm of The Old Spaghetti Factory.

Even so, nature is not to be denied, and it frequently upstages the art. Eagles dogfight with seagulls overhead, and the Olympics play peekaboo behind a kimono of clouds. The park offers a west-facing Puget Sound vista unique in the city. Everyone gets a corner office view, thanks to Jon and Mary Shirley and Bagley and Virginia "Jinny" Wright, the millionaires who funded and furnished the park.

Some have criticized the park for lacking artworks by Native American or Asian sculptors, a glaring omission for a Pacific Rim city in a region whose earliest public artworks were waterfront totems. Such sculptures make the Museum of Anthropology at the University of British Columbia in Vancouver one of the best art museums in the Northwest. Others have pointed out that too many of the Olympic sculptures are by older artists such as Alexander Calder, Claes Oldenburg, and Richard Serra. The collection has also been accused of being a hodgepodge. A poster on a blog at Artdish.com called it "Ginny [*sic*] Wright's latest lawn ornament."

But remember, the sculpture park is a work in progress. SAM's modern art curator Michael Darling says new works will be added to the collection and rotating shows will be hosted on the site. He hopes that works by Asian and Indian artists will be among the new pieces included. First, however, the pocketbooks of benefactors need time to recover.

For now, enjoy the art that successfully plays off the location. Calder's *Eagle*—rescued from a plaza in Dallas—is frequently juxtaposed against real bald eagles overhead. Serra's *Wake* captures both the motion of water and the rounded, rusted sensuality of old ships, and is proving irresistible to the touch. And art—modern art at that—finally has an outdoor home in Seattle.

Seattle magazine 2007

How Dense Can We Be?

The folks at the Sightline Institute take great joy in Seattle's skipping gaily over the edge and becoming a dense Pugetopolis. They and most of the environmental community have convinced themselves that growth is good, as long as it is stuffed into high-rise shoeboxes that someone has dubbed "green." Look at Portland's light rail! Praise Vancouver's skinny towers! Envy San Francisco's density!

While Sightline acts as a clearinghouse for new data and ideas of interest to greens, they are ever quick to applaud the urbanization of the region in the guise of "saving" it. One recent blog post cheered the fact that finally, at long last, Seattle has more multifamily housing units than single-family homes. Welcome to the big leagues, New York Alki.

If you'll note, those who express skepticism about growth and development Seattle-style are labeled as gloomsters. I am "sackcloth." The *Seattle Post-Intelligencer*'s Joel Connelly is "ashes." We are not dense enough for Sightline.

The dense ones, however, believe they are on the winning side of history. Time for a "mission accomplished" lap, perhaps, along with the developers and big business interests that greenwash their corporate goals to co-opt labor, enviros, and progressives into supporting urban development policies that roll over the little guy. This is the coalition that powers Greg Nickels's machine, the mayor who can't say no to "more."

We know these green-backed policies are making the city more unaffordable. They are helping to drive the poor out of town. They are displacing long-standing communities. They are changing the scale of a once-egalitarian city that featured few poor people, few rich people, and a lot of folks in between. This old middle-class Seattle is now seen as unsophisticated, not worthy of protection, backward even. Some politicians are finally taking notice: U.S. Senator Patty Murray recently called this economic displacement Seattle's "silent epidemic."

Today's ecotopian vision rejects some of the main tenets of the original Ecotopia, which stood in defiance of the supposedly unstoppable free market. Today's greens don't think small, they think big. They moralize globally while disdaining locally. Sure, buy a locally grown organic parsnip. I do. But if you stand up for tradition and history, you'll be run over by their hybrids. For this new breed of ecotopians, Seattle is a blank slate to be manipulated like a Monopoly board, as if no one really lives here, except the sackcloth-and-ashes mossbacks who haven't seen the new dawn.

And while they're acting as generals on their land of counterpane, they often ignore—or are oblivious to—the downsides of the models they tout so often.

Take Vancouver, the Cascadian city green urbanists most admire. It's a Hong Kong in the making. But wait: Those skinny towers haven't stopped suburban sprawl; the tax policies that created the modern city are likely unsustainable; the cost of living is sky-high; and the boom in condos is making it more difficult to offer the full range of jobs and services a city requires to be healthy. Downtown is so stuffed with rich, idle baby boomers that some critics worry that Vancouver is turning into Canada's Miami Beach.

Portland is delightful in many ways, always a teacher's pet city when it comes to urban instruction. But they've been outed. Their urban planning sparkled because they were able to outsource sprawl across the Columbia River to growth-hungry Vancouver, Washington. On top of that, Portland-style urban planning has worked so well that it's contributed to a statewide backlash. The current property rights rebellion may destroy Oregon. But hey, they have a new tram.

And then there's San Francisco, the city many urbanists yearn for us to be. Which is funny, because I remember author Gore Vidal saying he liked Seattle because "Seattle is the city San Francisco thinks it is, but isn't." And that's true in many ways.

I know San Francisco. I lived in San Francisco. San Francisco was a friend of mine, and Seattle, you're no San Francisco. Which is good.

Don't get me wrong, I loved San Francisco when I lived there in the mid-1970s—the era of Patty Hearst, *Rolling Stone*, Harvey Milk, Herb Caen, and Italian mayors. I love it still when I visit. But what made San Francisco is something you cannot copy. It has to do with when a city is built, by whom, and when it comes of age. It has a unique essence we couldn't replicate if we built a thousand neo-Victorian homes on our hills. Footnote to remember: Most of San Francisco's grand Victorians were built with wood that grew where Seattle now stands. Yes, our forests built their city so we'd have a place to build our city with someone else's forests. And so it goes.

But while many of San Francisco's charms are intact—it was a city built for pleasure, unlike our nanny town—the city of today is less than it once was. Even in the 1970s, natives (the few you could find) complained that it had gone downhill, had lost its neighborly, even small-town, charm. It is not, as Vidal observed, the Seattle it imagined itself to be. Since 1950, San Francisco has not only stolen hearts but robbed bank accounts: Real estate prices have increased at double the national average for the past half century. The new San Francisco is a Golden Gated community. Today's San Francisco is unbelievably expensive. A city for rich people. Its black population all but driven out. Its families headed to the burbs. It's great for tourists—in fact, much of it is designed for them. The working waterfront is a Disneyland for monied visitors seeking things like hand-picked exotic mushrooms and artisanal chocolates. It even has that SoDo new-car smell that comes with taxpayer-funded stadiums and their upscale pubs.

But has San Francisco's density and affluence, its progressive politics, redeemed the Bay Area? Did it save it from becoming a megalopolis? If Seattle doubles its density to match San Francisco's, if we take down the Alaskan Way Viaduct, if we cater to "knowledge workers," can we be assured that central Puget Sound will remain less paved?

The San Francisco experience offers no such assurances. The Bay Area is a sea of sprawl, despite density and despite mass transit (and maybe because of it). The Silicon Valley is ghastly and overpriced, trapped in a tech-boom economy that has turned sleepy towns into vast megacities. San Jose was dead in the mid-1970s, almost a tumbleweed town. Today, it eats the countryside. Same with the East Bay, where the Ken Behring–style megadevelopments of the 1990s are now dwarfed. Yesterday's McMansions are mere bungalows. Sprawl hops the mountains and spreads into once-rural valleys beyond. Mass transit and rail make the commuting easier, but they've greased suburban growth too. And the freeways are still packed.

Yet this ideal is at the core of Mayor Nickels and Governor Chris Gregoire's hype about global competitiveness and the upside of being a sparkling, expensive metropolis instead of a workaday town. Even more strange, it points up how twisted progressives and enviros have become in terms of their priorities. Urbanist Joel Kotkin observes that "the fashionable 'left' defines successful urbanism by its ability to lure the superaffluent, the hypereducated and the avant-garde. . . . One wonders what true progressives like Harry Truman or Fiorello La Guardia would think of such an approach."

Is San Francisco uninhabitable, an unremitting hell-hole? No. Will Seattle be one if it follows its urban footprint? No. Is density itself evil? No. But let's be honest: A bigger, denser Seattle is no panacea for sprawl; it's no assurance that what we love about Seattle today will still be affordable or even available in the future; it means sustaining a vastly larger city in an extremely sensitive ecosystem, Puget Sound, that we're already destroying with our devotion to growth.

Let's admit, too, that you can do real damage if you ignore a city's past, if you threaten a settled urban culture with displacement, if you dismiss experiences and memories as mere obstructionism. You can do irreparable harm if your theories are built on the shaky premise that only elites can save us from global doom. And you disrespect the place you profess to love if your fantasies bloom from urban theories that ignore the roots sunk deeply in the soil of an actual place.

Crosscut 2007

The Latte Tax Is Just a Start

Why stop taxing at espresso, as proposed in Seattle's Initiative 77? Seattle is a wicked, wicked place that can only be whipped into shape with a stiff regimen of luxury and sin taxes. Mossback proposes we make punitive hay from the following new dedicated tax schemes:

Stripper Tax: A ten-cent tax for every dollar stuffed into a G-string goes to fund City Council campaigns.

Windows Tax: A tax requiring that Bill Gates pay $1 every time Windows or Internet Explorer crashes your PC, $10 for every virus attack due to a software vulnerability, and $100 for every piece of incoming spam.

Jet Ski Tax: An $8,000 fee paid on any jet ski operated in King County, with revenue to go to wildlife-breeding programs or public assistance for the deaf.

Boeing Favors Tax: A tax on the salaries of public officials and lobby groups responsible for Boeing giveaways.

The total tax must equal the dollar amount of Boeing's subsidies, tax breaks, and benefits.

Lutefisk Tax: $1,000 to a public food bank for every pound of lutefisk sold in Ballard.

Garlic Fries Tax: $1 of every order goes to help acquire players the Mariners won't trade for but who are needed to win a World Series.

Holmgren Tax: $1 million for every Seahawks loss, to be paid in cash to long-suffering fans who were young men when the Seahawks last won a playoff game.

Rick's Mouth Tax: $100 (retroactive) for every lie told by former Husky football coach Rick Neuheisel. Money will cover the school district's $35 million deficit.

Molester Tax: Churches and nonprofits (such as the Boy Scouts) lose tax exemptions and must pay $1 million for every child molested by a priest, pastor, or Scout leader.

Traffic-Circle and Speed-Bump Tax: To compensate for the artery-clogging garden patches and annoying traffic-calming measures, every residential neighborhood that wants them should pay $25,000 into a Pompeii fund to assist victims of the next natural disaster who won't be able to evacuate the city because the streets weren't wide enough.

Tree Fees: Greenbelts are great, but does every Seattle street have to be a tree-choked boulevard? Saplings grown into mature trees are blocking views and making driving less safe. $1,000 for each view blocker.

Phony Co-ops Tax: A heavy fee for businesses that pass themselves off as consumer cooperatives but in fact just use the label as warm-and-fuzzy gloss to cover their greedy corporate ways.

Signal Fines: Using hidden cameras, fine drivers who don't use their turn signals.

Bikers-Abreast Fines: For cyclists who insist on riding two and three abreast on Lake Washington Boulevard when it's not one of those damnable bicycle weekends.

Yuppie Tax: A countywide fee targeting businesses that are flypaper for yuppies. You know them when you see them (e.g., the new Kirkland wine bar, Purple).

Weather Tax: $6,000 for every TV news anchor who blabs on and on about the great hot weather during droughts and forest-fire season. Funds go to families of firefighters lost in the line of duty.

Phony-Storm Tax: TV stations must also pay $100,000 for every story hyping routine weather such as wind and rain and snow on Snoqualmie Pass in December.

Bad Public Art Tax: To be paid by artists who create awful public art. Tax to be determined by public vote on the artwork and deducted from grants.

The No-Segues Tax: Someday soon, it might be possible to take a ferry from Vashon Island to West Seattle, pedal your bike to Alki, get a water taxi to downtown, grab a horse carriage to Westlake, take the monorail to Seattle Center, hop a trolley to Lake Union, ride light rail to Montlake, and catch a Metro bus across the floating bridge to a Redmond park-and-ride where your vanpool is waiting to whisk you to your job in Bothell. Can we please apply a tax to anyone who suggests any new modes of transportation?

Paul Allen Tax: For every dollar in public subsidy for Vulcan projects, $100 should be paid to the city for low-income housing. Plus free rides on Paul's jet to Trail Blazers games.

Mossback calculates that the sum of the taxes outlined here would generate approximately $67 billion in annual revenue (assuming the Colacurcios report all of their income properly). That's enough to fix all our problems, rebuild Iraq, and still have some left over for quality of life. Which, by the way, ought to be taxed also.

Seattle Weekly 2003

Initiative 77 was defeated by a two-to-one margin, and Seattle lattes remain sin tax free. Even without the tax, people have become touchy about the high price of their morning street drug. In 2008, to fend off competition from McDonald's and Dunkin' Donuts, Starbucks began experimenting with selling coffee for a buck. However, the lutefisk tax idea was unanimously adopted. Unfortunately, it hasn't raised a dime. Why? The last Scandinavian left Ballard to avoid paying such an onerous fee. Lutefisk is now virtually extinct within the city limits.

2008

Paul Allen's Kool-Aid

Recently I took a short trip down to Paul Allen's Discovery Center, the sales showroom for his Vulcan Real Estate holding company on the corner of Westlake Avenue North and Denny Way. It's an architecturally splendid "green" and portable building that sits in a neighborhood once famed for car dealerships. Now they're dealing condos.

Inside, it feels like a world's fair pavilion. As you walk through, there's a timeline and a display of artifacts from the Museum of History & Industry (and from, no kidding, historian Paul Dorpat's basement) that helps visitors track Seattle's boom cycles and puts Allen's South Lake Union plan in historical context. There's a circular minitheater that shows a film about what life in the neighborhood might be like in 2010 if Vulcan's development agenda comes to pass. It's a rosy future: bars, coffeehouses, REI yuppies, trolleys—nothing like we have today, of course. An upbeat newscast from 2010 featuring a hasn't-aged-a-day Joyce Taylor casually refers to the Seattle Mariners being in the hunt for their second consecutive world title, just to remind you this is fantasy.

The pavilion also features scale models of some of the projects Vulcan is developing in the South Lake Union neighborhood, where it owns about 60 acres of property. Prospective condo buyers can come and look at dollhouse layouts complete with miniature furniture, art, and food to help buyers pick out their new in-city dwellings.

The Lilliputians clearly belong to a well-heeled urban gentry—I spotted a tiny table with microscopic sushi on it. It's hard not to envy the invisible urban Mini-Me's who'll be lucky enough to afford these places. A postage stamp studio is the price of a starter home.

But the Discovery Center's centerpiece is a giant scale model of north downtown and South Lake Union. Use of such dioramas was pioneered at world's fairs, like New York's in 1939, where people could tour a miniature World of Tomorrow. Allen's city gives you a God's- or Godzilla's-eye view of Seattle. You press buttons to illuminate lights that indicate amenities such as the proposed trolley line and the monorail. Property owned by Allen is identified. Little models show a mix of existing and proposed buildings. Allentown as a boy's fantasy landscape.

As such, it is an incredibly potent piece of propaganda. The city it shows does not exist. Its blend of fantasy and reality incorporates mere ideas as well as actual drawing-board proposals. In the model Allentown, the so-called Mercer Mess of traffic has been fixed with beautiful tree-lined streets and a street grid completed over a sunken Aurora Avenue North, which, presumably, leads to an underground waterfront "viaduct." You can see where the proposed neighborhood trolley line would run; you can see people enjoying the South Lake Union waterfront park. You can see future biotech research buildings, and you are invited to imagine an urban center built around the so-called life sciences. No price tags, of course.

You are also invited—no, nearly compelled—to use your imagination. Some of the city is rendered realistically, but much is rendered semi-abstractly. And, of course, much is left out. But it is a cleverly crafted slate on which you can co-project the future along with Paul. It exists in a time frame that is unreal—part present, part future, part abstraction. It exerts a weird magic: As you gaze down at it, it takes on the aura of inevitability. It's like a tall drink of Kool-Aid. You like this plan, you want this plan, this *is* the plan. It seems at once grand and doable.

It isn't the only grand plan for Seattle. Greg Nickels has his downtown Manhattan Project. The People's Waterfront Coalition is fleshing out how Seattle would look if the viaduct weren't replaced at all—the kind of dense, sustainable city that could rewire itself after removing an intrusive waterfront highway. And recently, a group of community leaders released the Cascade Agenda, a massive, long-term vision of how to protect rural lands and wilderness in King, Snohomish, Pierce, and, wisely, Kittitas counties. Saving such lands won't be the result of mere densification but of aggressive, expensive efforts to preserve what we are about to lose if we let the market have its way.

But you have to give Paul Allen credit, for while his vision is less bold, it is rendered most tangibly. He has realized that the race to the future will be won by a two-pronged campaign fought in the trenches and in the stars. His staff is fighting for South Lake Union in the streets—lobbying, planning, organizing, co-opting, cajoling, selling. Yet they're also investing in getting their vision out there in three dimensions. No one else has articulated a more compelling alternative that the public can see, feel, and imagine. Is there anyone else who can afford to? While Nickels is talking about more high-rises downtown, it's Allen who is filling the vision vacuum. It's a self-interested vision; the multibillionaire makes no bones that he's in it to make even more money. At Paul's pavilion, you'll get a taste of the good life he's after. But whether you're seduced or repelled by it, you come away thinking that those who have alternative visions must find a way to get them out there in a form as compelling. Otherwise, Allen's future might become ours by default.

Seattle Weekly 2005

The Route of All Evil

You used to see more logging trucks rumbling through downtown on Interstate 5. In recent years, most of the few you've spotted were lugging telephone-pole-sized second-growth timber destined for pulping. But occasionally, you'll see a blast from the past: a truck laden with a couple of massive old-growth cedars the size of sperm whales, trees so impressive you might have thought they'd been smuggled out of some national park. More likely, though, they came from private land where such beauties can still be "harvested."

My first thought when I see such a load is, "Is it still legal to cut those trees?" To me, it's amazing that we are still tossing such rare commodities into buzz saws and turning them into mundane things like shingles and lumber.

I feel similarly when I contemplate the proposed razing of an edifice like Seattle First United Methodist Church, which in Seattle counts as architectural old growth, being a century old. The wonderful sanctuary's fate will be decided shortly. Preservationists are working behind the scenes to find a way the church can be saved, and the congregation relocated to Belltown to continue good works, especially social services.

Thus far, the church has favored a plan in which developer Martin Selig would raze the sanctuary, reasoning that being out from under the burden of maintaining such a white elephant will help them with their Christian mission. A competing plan from developer Nitze-Stagen could accomplish the same thing but also offers a chance to save the church. Preservationists see that as a win-win. The Methodists are thinking it over. God, as they say, is in the details and the bottom line: What will serve the church's financial interests and those of its developer partner?

That the church is in the position of getting in bed with commercial interests bothers activists like Michael Godfried, who is working with a group called Save Our Sanctuary to save the old church. He sent me a quote from the late historian and social critic Christopher Lasch that put what troubles Godfried in a larger, though admittedly rather extreme, context. It's from Lasch's 1995 collection of essays, *The Revolt of the Elites and the Betrayal of Democracy*:

> Individuals cannot learn to speak for them-selves at all, much less come to an intelligent understanding of their happiness and well-being, in a world in which there are no values except those of the market. . . . The market notoriously tends to universalize itself. It does not easily coexist with institutions that operate according to principles antithetical to itself: schools and universities, newspapers and magazines, charities, families. Sooner or later the market tends to absorb them all. It puts an almost irresistible pressure on every activity to justify itself in the only terms it recognizes: to become a business proposition, to pay its own way, to show black ink on the bottom line. It turns news into entertainment, scholarship into professional careerism, social work into the scientific management of pov-erty. Inexorably it remodels every institution in its own image.

It would be unfair to suggest that the Methodists are selling out for filthy lucre, but there is no question that they are making a tough decision in the face of a rap-idly developing, increasingly upscale downtown that is exploding in commercial terms, aided by government that has adopted growth as a good in itself. The dispari-ties being exacerbated between rich and poor are taxing the church's ability to render aid. The value of the land offers a way out but also contributes to a downtown that is more commercial and losing its history.

And we are all facing hard choices as we become prisoners of prosperity. It's a citywide issue that challenges us to redefine what Seattle is. Is it strictly a commercial zone where everything is for sale to the highest bidder? Or are there other community values that need to be asserted? Are we going to let "the market" define us?

A story that slams this home appeared in a recent Sunday issue of *The Seattle Times* that documented how middle-income families are being run out of Seattle and King County. As property values soar and incomes stagnate, fewer and fewer middle-income families can afford single-family homes. The *Times* determined that in 2003 there were only seven neighborhoods in Seattle where an individual or family making the median household income (nearly $58,000) could afford to buy a median-priced home. Today there is, appallingly, only one area in the city left where that is true: the industrial zone that includes Georgetown and South Park. As we contemplate a future in which our kids live in shoeboxes, experts interviewed by the *Times* tell us this is a long-term trend fueled in part by wealthy newcomers, from California and elsewhere, who are equity-rich and driving up home prices.

We can't say we weren't warned. Back in the 1990s, we didn't want to believe creepy Seahawks owner and California developer Ken Behring when he predicted a "tsunami" of growth was headed our way. Well, Behring is gone, but his tsunami arrived, and we're all swimming for our lives, trying to stay afloat as Lasch's "irresistible" market forces wash over us.

This is part of the price we pay for our "world-class" hype; this is part of the price we pay for our politicians junketing around the world promoting growth—as if economic boosterism were job one. It's like growth is the new meth. Somehow, we've got to break the addiction and focus on the kind of city we want to live in, not the city we're left with.

Seattle Weekly 2006

After a full-court press involving preservationists, developers, politicians, and church members, the church and Nitze-Stagen reached a deal in 2007 that appears to work for everyone. Property was found so the Seattle First United Methodist Church could relocate. The historic 100-year-old sanctuary will be preserved and share its site with a new skyscraper. King County councilmember Dow Constantine and Nitze-Stagen's Kevin Daniels won an award in 2008 from the head of the State Department of Archaeology and Historic Preservation for their creative solution.

2008

Race in Seattle: It's Mighty White of Us

Back in the early 1960s, my family's church, Seattle's Mount Baker Presbyterian, gave out buttons that said "I believe it's right." "It" is WASP-speak for something uncomfortable. It's a term you use to approach a subject carefully, to bring up an unpleasantness in an appropriately coded way. "It," for example, can substitute for sex, as in "they did it."

In this case, "it" referred to another unmentionable: race.

The buttons were for supporters of racial equality, civil rights, open housing, and integration, still progressive ideas forty years ago among whites, even in the city's South End. The area was more diverse than most in Seattle and is now a paragon of multiculturalism. But in the early 1960s, when black families began moving south from the Central Area, many of our white Rainier Valley neighbors fled for Bellevue or Seward Park. Apparently not all of them believed "it" was right. But to be honest, none of us wore buttons that proclaimed, "Welcome, Negroes!"

Race is still an "it" word in Seattle. Like rape or incest, race is a charged subject where both perpetrator and victim are tainted. It is bad to be a racist, but almost as bad to be someone who is seen as having race. White Seattle likes to think of itself as color-blind, a place where the unpleasantness of America's racial history was left behind "back East" or "down South." Race is baggage we unloaded along the Oregon Trail, like a too-heavy piano.

Many immigrants of all colors fled here to get away from race's consequences. These included blacks seeking freedom from the Jim Crow South and white supremacists hoping to find a haven for the Anglo-Saxon race (something imagined for the Northwest as far back as the 1850s). While blacks still found bigotry, and the neo-Nazis were (mostly) marginalized to remote compounds, the majority of white Seattle adopted a stance that race did not and should not matter. And it worked for many years in a city that was highly (though not legally) segregated and nearly all white. With the Indians exterminated or removed to reservations, and Asians and blacks economically niched and living in their own enclaves, Seattle's dominant white culture lived with the illusion that it had transcended the great American divide. During the first half of the twentieth century, as the city's African American population grew and concentrated almost exclusively in the Central Area, poverty and isolation worsened, and the city's cluelessness was palpable. As University of Washington professor Quintard Taylor has written in his Seattle history, *The Forging of a Black Community: Seattle's Central District from 1870 through the Civil Rights Era*: "The enemy in Seattle was indifference in the white population, born of its perception that *there was no problem in the city*" (italics mine).

This would seem odd for a city that has made many race headlines. Here's a short list of newsworthy issues and events from over the years: the cheating of the Puget Sound Indians out of their lands; the forced deportation of virtually the entire Chinese population of Seattle in the 1880s; protests over the importation of Japanese and Chinese workers—the "little brown men"—in the early 1900s; the Ku Klux Klan rallies of the 1920s, including one of the largest ever in Issaquah; the mass internment of Japanese Americans during World War II; the Fort Lawton race riot of 1944; twenty years of mandatory busing to integrate Seattle schools; twenty years of resultant white flight to the suburbs; the race riots of 1968; the gunboat diplomacy of the Coast Guard enforcing Indian fishing rights under the Boldt Decision; multiple protests over numerous police killings involving black suspects; racial profiling by the Seattle Police Department; the fatal 2001 Mardi Gras riot; the vandalism of Chief Seattle's grave; the harassment of Muslims and Somali immigrants after 9/11.

Seattle, like most major U.S. cities, has a history of race problems, but we refuse to see these events as part of who we are. They are aberrations or footnotes, not business as usual. This belief is strong in the white community, and it crosses party lines. Over the decades, progressive forces have worked to end both purposeful and de facto segregation and discrimination, and extolled the virtues of a multicultural city. But as evidence of success, the examples cited are usually where race has been transcended: It's mighty white of us, after all, to have elected a black mayor, a black county executive, an Asian governor. We're proud because we voted for Norm Rice, Ron Sims, and Gary Locke not *because* of their race, but *despite* it.

Conservatives have staked out similar ground. In 1998, KVI talk-show host and political activist John Carlson delighted in quoting the Reverend Martin Luther King Jr. while campaigning for Washington's anti-affirmative-action Initiative 200: "I have a dream that my four little children will one day live in a nation where they will not be judged by the color of their skin but by the content of their character." If the legend that Chief Seattle turns in his grave every time his name is spoken is true, then I imagine that Dr. King must be boring a tunnel every time a right-winger sound-bites him to suggest that dealing with the inequities of racism is a kind of racism itself, and by implication, a cure worse than the disease. It is apparently fairer and nobler to ignore injustices and realities than to try to rectify them, even when race is the root cause. In other words, if we simply act as if there is no race, our race problems will be solved. That kind of logic goes down well here. Initiative 200 passed with nearly 60 percent of the statewide vote.

But in denying race for others, we whites also deny race for ourselves. We see ourselves not so much as "white" as clear, transparent like air or glass. Call it the unbearable lightness of being raceless. I remember as a kid I used to think that sense of transparency was the measure of my own racial enlightenment: Going to school on south Beacon Hill, I saw myself and my Asian friends as equally raceless, partly because Asians were better at being white than we were. They excelled at school, assimilation, and the stuff your mom approved of. Blacks, however, were black, not only because they were black, but because they saw me as indelibly white. Being seen as white, I became uncomfortably conscious of my own race for the first time.

And being conscious of race—theirs and mine—forced me to confront an America that was far less benevolent and evolved than the one I wanted to believe in.

This was brought home one day in 1968 when, sometime between Dr. King's assassination and Bobby Kennedy's, a group of young blacks beat me senseless. They were following a few of us home from Asa Mercer Junior High. My chums got scared and ran off. I stayed behind, determined not to fight or flee. They called me names as they beat me. I fell against a rockery, nearly unconscious, then as I slumped to the ground one of the boys kicked me in the forehead as a final coup de grâce. A short while later, a black friend from school found me and helped me to my feet so I could find my way home, black and blue, white and bloody.

It was a hate crime by any contemporary definition, and angry as I was, another part of me understood why they were angry. They hated me because of my skin color, and while my experience was not the black experience, it did serve to remind me that, whatever I thought, I was not clear like glass in their eyes, and my skin would be white in the mirror ever after. For better or worse, I had race, and I'd better get used to it because not having race was an illusion I could no longer afford.

That summer, I participated in a special summer school program sponsored by Lakeside, the tony Seattle private school that was later my high school alma mater (along with Bill Gates, Paul Allen, and a zillion other jillionaires). It was my first real exposure to upper-class Seattle. Promising public schoolers, mostly minority kids, were bused in from the South End to the Great White North. We took classes on the preppy campus, including a math course that taught us how to invest in stocks. Lakeside seniors in button-down sports shirts and Bermuda shorts assisted the teachers, and I was never more aware of my whiteness than in watching these privileged snots deal with minority kids from the "ghetto." I'll never forget when the Harvard-bound scion of one of Seattle's most prominent WASP families was determined not to be shown up by an uppity black student in our class. To put him in his place, the white boy snapped, "OK, smarty, spell 'rococo'." It was an utterly ludicrous scene. I was embarrassed to see this caricature of a clueless WASP make a fool of our race. Like the overamped Chris Farley in the Seattle-set movie *Black Sheep*, I felt like yelling, "Kill whitey!" But my fellow student could take care of himself. Without missing a beat, he correctly spelled the word. If I had trouble seeing whiteness before, I never did again.

Affecting a pose that race is irrelevant comforts whites because it allows us to believe in a hate-free ideal. But it also masks the darker attitudes among our fellow citizens. These include a kind of virulent racism we prefer to associate with the Deep South, but not ourselves. It's safe to say that there's a Northwest racism that is deeply closeted. Earlier this year, state representative Hans Dunshee, a Snohomish County Democrat, in his own words, "opened the closet door."

Dunshee spotted a plaque in Blaine declaring weirdly that State Route 99 was the Jefferson Davis Memorial Highway. Indeed, it was. In the 1920s, the federal government

79

had promoted the naming of national highways—the Abe Lincoln Highway is well known. A Jefferson Davis Highway was designated, linking Virginia with California, and over the years, sections of other highways were added to the system through the lobbying efforts of the United Daughters of the Confederacy. So it came to pass that Highway 99 was named in honor of the president of the Confederate States of America. Dunshee assumed it would be easy to get this forgotten relic from the past removed. "I thought it would be a slam dunk," he reflects. But when he proposed to the legislature that the highway plaque be taken down and the road rededicated to a Snohomish County black settler, he ignited a firestorm of local and national protest. National news stories looked at the dustup as a Confederate flag controversy among the evergreens, and it became a cause célèbre for the so-called neo-Confederates—modern-day Southern sympathizers who range from militia members to coddling pols like John Ashcroft and Trent Lott. The pro-Davis folks considered Dunshee's efforts to be yet another example of politically correct revisionism. Ultimately, Dunshee's proposal never made it out of Olympia, though the Seattle chapter of the NAACP carried on the fight.

The experience opened Dunshee's eyes. "I live my life relatively isolated from racism, in a 99 percent white society," he says. He notes there is a big divide in his district over the perception of race. Almost none of his white constituents thinks race is a problem; virtually all of his minority constituents do. He notes that many of the people who wrote to protest his proposal automatically assumed he was black. The hate in many of the e-mails to Dunshee is notable and reveals a level of rage most of us would find surprising over a little old highway marker with minimal relevance to the history of our state. One correspondent wrote, "You sir, are a liberal, racist piece of trash. I hope your jack boots fit to [sic] tight while you goose step to your NAZI office. Your racist actions WILL be remembered in the next election!"

Ironically, Dunshee wanted to do anything but whitewash history. He hoped the plaque would wind up in a museum with explanatory material telling us about the times when it was erected. Far from hoping people would forget Jefferson Davis, Dunshee wanted him remembered. This kind of honest, contextual exhibit can be done well. At Seattle's Museum of History & Industry there is on display a piece of cannery equipment called the Iron Chink. It was so named—and we're not just talking nickname here; it was actually labeled the Iron Chink—because it effectively replaced thousands of Chinese workers when it was introduced at the turn of the century. It allowed canning companies to lower their costs and assure finicky buyers that the tinned salmon they were buying was "Packed by White Labor Only." Sadly, the company formed by the man who invented this revolutionary machine, Edmund Smith, merged a generation later with a company (now Smith-Berger) founded by my late grandfather. Imagine my delight at discovering my family name connected with this racist past. Nevertheless, it's a personal reminder that you don't have to scratch Seattle's surface very deeply to find a personal link to a disquieting history.

Having looked at a number of the e-mails that flamed Hans Dunshee, I am struck with two common lines of attack, both of which are an attempt to rewrite reality. The first insists the Civil War was not about race or slavery. In this view, Jefferson Davis is in fact a superpatriot more devoted to the Constitution than Dishonest Old Abe. The second is that Dunshee and his ilk are the *real* racists. In getting in touch with their heritage, these neo-Confederates—indeed, many comparatively mainstream conservatives like Pat Buchanan—believe they are fighting a new race war in which whites are the oppressed minority. It is their view that through PC politics and affirmative action they suffer a racism worse than anything our white ancestors may have dished out. One letter writer referred to proposals such as Dunshee's as being nothing less than "a racial jihad."

In February, I went on Seattle's KUOW-FM, the local NPR affiliate, to talk about the Jefferson Davis Highway brouhaha, and an African American caller wanted to know what whites think about other whites who feel this way. "This is a white issue," said Eddie from Monroe, the black caller. And he's right. Not only do whites need to deal with race for the sake of all citizens, but there is a real danger in allowing only a small minority of whites to think and talk about whiteness. The assumption that we whites have nothing to talk about because race is someone else's problem allows us to ignore a festering problem within our own community. Our denial provides cover for toxic mold in the collective psyche. And Dunshee worries that such neglect can lead us to repeat the errors of the past. A new Civil War, anyone?

The lesson is that if we leave race to the racists, only the racists will have race. Our only choice is to deal with "it."

Washington Law & Politics 2002

Despite the threats, representative Hans Dunshee is still in the legislature and reports an interesting end to the Jefferson Davis Memorial Highway controversy. Dundee searched the state archives and found that it turns out that Washington never officially designated the highway in honor of the president of the Confederacy. The two Jefferson Davis markers—one at the north end in Blaine and one in the south end in Vancouver— have been removed. The one in Vancouver is in a private park; the Blaine marker is in a shed waiting to be claimed by the United Daughters of the Confederacy. Without the markers, it's just plain old Highway 99 again.

2008

The Long Boe-Bye: It's Over

Nobody can guarantee jobs and security in
market-based economies.

—Boeing CEO Alan Mulally, *The Seattle Times*, Sept. 15, 2002

Now they tell us. For all the chatter about homeland
security, there apparently is one kind of security we'll
never be able to count on: economic security. While we
poise for a new war in Iraq and build fortress America at
home, within our borders what's doable diminishes. Social
Security? Hah. It won't be there when you retire because
it's been sucked into a black hole of wartime expense
and lower taxes for the wealthy. Your 401(k)? It may
evaporate on Wall Street, or perhaps it's already lining
the pockets of some platinum-parachuted CEO. A decent
job? Dream on. It's an employer's market, and your union
doesn't stand a chance.

As Seattle glides toward becoming the Flint, Michigan,
of aerospace, it seems a good time to review our status as
a company town and ponder where to place our loyalties
in light of Mulally's assessment.

It is hard to overstate the degree to which Boeing has
been part of the fabric of this community. Though over-
shadowed in recent years by the Microsoft boom—a tri-
umph of software over hardware—Microsoft might never
have happened here without Boeing. The aerospace giant
played a huge role in shaping Seattle, creating the kind
of educated, middle-class, tech-friendly community that

would nurture Bill Gates and attract the workers Redmond needs to thrive. Boeing helped seed the Silicon Forest—appropriate for a company that itself had roots in the timber business. It was logging that first brought Bill Boeing to Seattle.

Our modern identity has been built around Boeing's company, whether your dad worked there or not. Our expectations were shaped by it. Boeing's jetliners composed the first Internet—the global connector of every country on earth with every other. It was the model of things to come. Seattle's 1962 Century 21 Exposition was dubbed "America's Space Age World's Fair," and it was tailored to suit Boeing's marketing needs. The company recruited workers there: Come Northwest, young man, and build the future. That, we imagined, was out among the stars. No one foresaw that the Space Age would stall at the moon or devolve to an orbit little higher than space shuttles can fly.

Nor did we imagine that one day, right around the time the twenty-first century actually arrived, the future would be outsourced. Colonies on Mars? Try factories in China.

Whatever you want to call it, however you want to sugarcoat it, Boeing is ditching Seattle. The Machinists Union knows it, which is why the failure of last week's strike vote was devastating: You're damned if you do and double-damned if you don't. The double-damned machinists can hear the giant sucking sound of jobs going elsewhere, and they know it won't stop with them. Boeing is no longer a local citizen but a global entity with its flight deck in Chicago. Boeing helped build a city that it says it can no longer afford; it created an educated workforce it says it can no longer pay; it inspired in us expectations it can no longer fulfill.

Seattle has benefited from Boeing, no question. But also, this city and state have done everything a body politic could do to keep that company happy. Seattle and Washington have molded themselves to suit Boeing's needs: a favorable tax system, a commitment to education, cheap power, and cheaply bought politicians. We didn't just send senators from Boeing to Washington, D.C.—we put their governors in Olympia, their mayors in City Hall, and their engineers on our school boards. We gave the company our children and grandchildren—instilled with loyalty—to work their assembly lines and their drafting tables. We invested heavily in their success, largely because we felt we were them and they were us.

This community couldn't have kissed more Boeing ass if it had Mick Jagger's lips.

Now they tell us that our loyalty was misplaced, because markets rule. This is the bull that corporate America loves to dish out. When it's time to bust a union, lay off workers, ship jobs overseas, shut down factories, or move out of town, they can say, "The market made me do it." But oh, how the CEOs love the protections a loyal (or fearful) community gives them: the favorable tax breaks, the hefty subsidies, the investment in expensive infrastructure like schools and roads. There's nothing free about that market for you and me.

The World Trade Organization—the global capitalist tool—recently approved $4 billion in European Union sanctions against the United States for giving Boeing and other companies what amount to illegal tax breaks. The WTO is policing the market, and now Boeing is squealing.

How are they going to like it out there in the big bad world with their protections stripped away? What are they going to do when there's no place to go home to, no faithful community offering a safe haven in tough times, no pool of loyal workers ready to give its blood, sweat, and tears when they need them?

Ask a machinist whose job has flown out of town on a plane he built.

Seattle Weekly 2002

Sex, Farm Animals, and the City

Seattle is schizophrenic. The evidence mounts on two fronts.

One is nightlife. We're a town founded, like most frontier cities, on sin. But throughout our history we've wrestled with the devil, alternately tolerating and cracking down on drinking, gambling, and sex.

Sometimes that civic struggle has been embodied in a single person. A century ago it was Mayor Hiram Gill, who was elected on a platform of keeping Seattle a wide-open city with a well-managed vice district. That didn't prove popular with the womenfolk. When they got the vote, he was run out of office.

Gill made a comeback as a reformer promising to clean things up. Skeptics weren't sure he'd made a genuine conversion, but he said, "Who knows sin and how to grapple with it better than an old experienced sinner?" Voters bought it, and Gill became mayor again. Later, he was indicted for taking bribes from bootleggers. Old sins and sinners die hard.

Seattle continues to embody mixed messages. We want to be a "world-class city," but we imagine that such a city is without visible vice or mess. The contradiction is personified in those who move to Belltown for urban edge and then complain about the nightclubs. Sex, drugs, noise, boozing: Who said I wanted grit with my granite countertops?

Mayor Greg Nickels and City Attorney Tom Carr are stylistically softer than former City Attorney Mark Sidran, who once sought to sanitize the streets of street people. But these two also want to make Seattle safer for the denizens of the sky-sprawl that the city has promulgated downtown. The nanny agenda: Drive city strip clubs into extinction; expand no-alcohol zones; ban smoking and push bar patrons into the street; slap the nightclub owners around.

The famous Nickels/Carr late-summer nightclub sting ("Operation Sobering Thought") nabbed bartenders and bouncers. What "shocking" truth did the dragnet reveal? No, not that the police could be pounding more useful downtown beats. It was that on any given night, people are getting into clubs with fake IDs!

Every world-class city worth the name throws the book at perps like that. It's a hanging offense in Singapore (but then, so's chewing gum). Predictably, however, our City Council seems to be of two minds about what to do.

The second schizo conflict is over whether Seattle is a city or a farm.

While we aspire to dense Hong Kong–style development, we are also trying to be Green Acres.

The barnyarding of our cities is a hot new trend. Keeping chickens, mainly. And what great timing. Given the threat of a deadly avian flu epidemic—like the one just reported in China—now is the perfect time to address this threat by filling America's cities with tens of thousands of domestic fowl.

Here in Seattle, though, we go one better. City Council member Richard Conlin wanted to make it legal for Seattleites to keep pygmy goats. Not working creatures like the herd that was hired to eat the blackberry bushes at the University of Washington this summer, but pets. Yes, minigoats are the new Labradoodles. The City Council voted 7-0 to give Conlin his wish.

Ah, miniature goats. Now it all begins to make sense. Seattle isn't conflicted by warring dualities but is engaged in a dangerous experiment—dangerous because we know what can happen when you combine sin and farm animals (think Enumclaw and horses).

It is also a visionary urban experiment to forge a unique niche. Our city is well on the path to becoming the first world-class, sinless, suburban, high-rise, gay-friendly goat farm—for millionaires.

What could be more metronatural?

Crosscut 2007

CIVILIZATION

Strait Flush

Spring has sprung, and the giant crap-spewing barges have returned to that Capistrano of the Sound, Elliott Bay. Ah, the cruise ships, part of that so-called clean tourism industry that every year seems to flush more and more tourists into our city. Given the economy, we're supposed to be grateful, and indeed we have spent megamillions to make the tourists happy: new piers, a mall-ified downtown, hotels, trolleys, and restaurants no local would be caught dead in. It creates jobs and keeps some hustle in our bustle. But it costs.

Seattle is a port city, and in that sense the cruise ships are kind of a welcome idea, adding to the diversity of maritime traffic. But these vessels aren't the charming steamers of old. They're not shuttling passengers around the Pacific Rim; they're no mosquito fleet ferrying locals up and down the Sound; they don't have the old-world elegance and scale of, say, the old *Princess Marguerite*, which long carried folks to Victoria.

No, these are floating high-rise cities that lug thousands of tourists at a time through some of the world's most beautiful waterways so they can view the scenery between visits to the onboard casinos.

OK, I'm being a bit unfair, but these tubs are like floating Marriotts, and when they begin to line the seasonal waterfront like pigs at the pastry cart, it's hard not to wonder what the hell people are thinking about this kind of travel. They're tourism's equivalent of the SUV. And

SUVs aren't about enjoying nature, they're about romping around in nature while being utterly oblivious to it. Just check any SUV commercial: The vehicles are shown tearing through, and up, the natural landscape to which they offer "escape."

In a similar way, these cruise ships use the appeal of the wilderness to offer a backdrop to the real experience on board the ships: spas, luxury dining, gambling, karaoke. These diversions keep wilderness at bay and allow everyone to be oblivious to the fact that their very presence is degrading the natural world that supposedly is being celebrated.

The brouhaha over the Norwegian Cruise Line vessel *Norwegian Sun* discharging 16,000 gallons of raw sewage into the Strait of Juan de Fuca should be a reminder that the cruise business, like others, has a downside, and much of that is borne by the natural environments cruises exploit. They can't exactly be honest about it: *Come See the Inside Passage, World's Prettiest Toilet!* But the rest of us don't have to succumb to marketing hype; we can sit here on shore and wonder if this industry is worth it.

For one thing, we need to get over the idea that tourism is inherently clean and that ecotourism is pure. In fact, some of the worst consequences of ecotourism—most of which are unintentional—impact the most distressed environments and species. Take, for instance, the mountain gorillas of Africa, which, thanks to sensitive ecotourism, are now suffering from numerous human-borne diseases, including mange, a malady transmitted by hikers' discarded clothes. In addition, a United Nations report on ecotourism indicated that it actually drives development in sensitive areas.

Too, the Juan de Fuca flush should sensitize us to the problems with our own resident sewage. Just days after the *Sun* discharged into the strait, an overflow problem dumped vastly more raw poop into the Sound: 190,000 gallons into Tacoma's Hylebos Waterway. And Victoria continues to pump millions of gallons of raw or barely treated sewage into the strait every year. There are many potential damaging consequences, some surprising. A new scientific study on the rising mortality rates of California sea otters determined one major factor is that many are being weakened by parasites carried only in the feces of house cats. In other words, all those vegan PETA pet owners who've been flushing Fluffy's dirty litter down the toilet may be killing off wild mammals farther along the chain.

The cruise lines are exacerbating existing problems, which means we need to hold them to high standards while also improving our own behavior. Most of Puget Sound's problems are self-inflicted. The award-winning *Seattle Post-Intelligencer* series, "Our Troubled Sound," did a great job of laying out all the ways we treat this unique inland sea as a toxic dump. It's not the cruise lines' fault that it is deteriorating. In fact, one could argue that Seattle itself is a kind of cruise ship floating in, and soiling, the Northwest environment.

But that only underscores why we need to consider both the cultural and economic aspects of the cruise industry. Is it an industry we want to promote? Is it one around which we want to shape our city's landscape and economy? Do we want to provide safe haven for ships that can legally dump sewage in pristine waters elsewhere, even if not our Sound? It's particularly important because the waters these ships are cruising are among the last of their kind on the planet.

Perhaps it would be wiser to dock the cruise ships in Bremerton and simply show digital IMAX imagery outside their windows to give people the illusion they are cruising remote waters. I have the feeling that if you didn't tell them, many passengers would never know the difference. Gently rock the docked ship and their virtual cruise might be just as pleasant as a real one. And a lot better for nature.

Seattle Weekly 2003

A Luddite Goes on an Electronics Spree

There's nothing more ridiculous than Mossback standing in Fry's Electronics in Renton, a Luddite in the temple of technology. Indeed, one definition of "mossback" is someone deeply set in his ways. I'll say one thing for the place: It's better than that hideous circus that sets up its tents in Renton every summer. There, citizens are exposed to a plague worse than mad cow: mimes and Euro-clowns.

Geeks are much more tolerable. Fry's is a vast Thunderdome of technology—a barn big enough for Boeing filled with everything a techie might want, from computer parts to junk food. This year, I needed to upgrade. My home computer was fried. For months I have been unable to receive spam and hate e-mail at home. What's a columnist to do?

With some reluctance, I headed out to get a new system while my college-age son—my living, breathing IT department—was home for the holidays and could get me all set up. I don't know what people without children do. You must breed to get tech help at home. Without my son, I never would have found the computer assembled in my home office, ready to go, only an hour or so after returning home. All I needed to do to start the thing was push a button a chimp couldn't have missed (once I found it).

My son no longer gets impatient with my technological ignorance. He leads me through the process slowly and kindly, as one would a mentally handicapped child. He tells me from time to time that my confusion over technology is a mental block. That's just what my parents told me about arithmetic. Nevertheless, though Bill Gates and I had the same math and physics teachers, and I was tutored by upperclassmen on the side, I was lucky to receive a charity "D" in algebra, even after being sent back two grades. Gates and I anchored opposite ends of the Lakeside School bell curve. I'll let you guess which ends.

I have a corresponding difficulty with gadgets. Having come from a long line of engineers, surgeons, and craftsmen, it seems odd that I missed the "gear" gene. My grandfather, a large Norwegian engineer, invented heavy logging equipment and winches for use on ships. His factory stood for years on Harbor Island, a monument to man's ingenuity with machines. Whether it's heredity or phobia, I can't say. But I'm a tech klutz and deeply suspicious of new technology. The only aptitude I've ever shown for technology is a knack for breaking it. Nevertheless, life without some tools and toys is untenable, even for the simpleminded.

For me, simply stepping into Fry's was traumatic. I found the presence of all that merchandise overwhelming. Then there's the feeling of high-tech helplessness and inadequacy. To top it off, they were playing over the loudspeakers—I'm not kidding—"It's a Small World," Satan's anthem from that hateful Disney ride that celebrates globalization. Places like this make Bellevue Square seem quaint, old-fashioned, civilized. Yet these big-box retailers work: I was being softened up for a consumer experience, and I bought like a crazy bastard.

It wasn't the first time this season I succumbed. I also visited Costco for the first time in twenty years. I was on another tech mission, escorted by a friend who loves electronics so much he couldn't wait to go shopping with me. I was looking for my first DVD player and bought one. I also gave in to that special kind of Costco consumerism that convinces you life is impossible without also buying six hogsheads of Aplets & Cotlets and a lifetime supply of Kleenex. I showed restraint, however. I only spent double what I intended.

I now see why Costco does so well, even in the shadow of Wal-Mart. Costco has the street appeal of legalized larceny: You feel like you're in New York, buying stuff that fell off the truck at JFK. Who could resist? But I also felt palpably the tension between the personal and the political. Steals at Costco? Cheap stuff at Fry's? Yes, please, but lord knows what sweatshop it's made in to get a price like that. Should I worry about cost or context? In buy mode, you take whatever cost savings you can get and worry about context later (like when writing a column).

Living in this consumer culture, it's hard not to feel split. Was it like this for Thomas Jefferson, who promoted freedom while sleeping with his slaves? I don't like sweatshops, outsourcing, or the gurgling of American jobs draining away. But I don't want to pay a lot for stuff, either. I told myself that my spending spree was helping the economy and defying terrorism, which is good, right?

On the other hand, I was also painfully aware that every piece of merchandise I bought was probably bringing George W. Bush a step closer to reelection. I rationalized my guilt away by promising to do what I could to use my savings and new technology to see him defeated. That way, I could have cool stuff *and* a cleanish conscience.

In sum, my holiday shopping made me feel like I'd just returned from Las Vegas: exhilarated and dirty.

There are worse ways to start the new year.

Seattle Weekly 2004

A Mossback Manifesto

What is a "mossback"? Today, the word is often used to mean people attached to extremely old-fashioned or retro ideas: mossback conservatives on the far political right, for example. An archaic meaning of "mossy" meant dull or stupid. In the *Oxford English Dictionary*, one can follow an interesting trail. In the beginning, the term mossback was applied to fish, called mossybunkers or mossy backs, specimens so old that seaweed adhered to them ("moss," into at least the late nineteenth century, was a poetic name for seaweed). An old bass covered with "moss" was the symbol of antiquity, a place-bound creature of great stubbornness and possessing wily survival skills. In the Northwest, some large old clams are referred to as mossbacks.

During the Civil War, the term took on a more negative connotation: a mossback was a Confederate draft dodger, a fellow who skedaddled to the swamps to escape conscription. It was a term of derision and carried the implication of cowardice—or running away from responsibility. In the late nineteenth century, it was also applied to farmers, homesteaders, and "mossy backed" hermits, particularly those who settled and occupied the West. Herman Melville referred in *Moby-Dick* to a "moss-bearded Daniel Boone." Moss was a consequence of long living in the wilds and forests; it was a sign that the place was growing on you—literally. The *OED* cites the medieval romance "Roberd of Cisyle," which refers to a forest exile: "Fyftene yere he levyd there, wyth rotys, and grasse, and evylle fare, and alle of moss hys clothyng was." Sounds like anyone who has spent a summer camping on the Olympic Peninsula.

The early Northwest pioneers came here and took pride in their suffering. They could have gone to California with its sunshine and gold. Instead, they chose a harsher clime and a more rugged path and they mythologized it. Paul Bunyan, immortalized by Northwest writer James Stevens, hardly leaps from the page as a blossom-sniffing tree hugger. He's a manly reshaper of the land. Northwest author Stewart Holbrook, in his 1953 book *Far Corner*, quotes one prideful old settler giving a speech to the Oregon Pioneer Association: "I say to you that there was no honor in coming to a country already opened up."

Holbrook was writing about life in the region in the early part of the twentieth century, when some of the original settlers were still alive. He describes what he calls the "cult of the pioneer." In these twilight decades, they were honored, lauded, and memorialized incessantly. Their feats along the Oregon Trail were reenacted—as when Washington state pioneer Ezra Meeker, looking like Father Time, retraced his path with oxen and a Conestoga wagon for the newsreels. The pioneers' taming of the wilderness was acknowledged at a thousand luncheons and on a thousand plaques. They represented a rapidly dying culture of people who had lived the frontier experience the rest of us would only read about. They had taken a wilderness and rapidly transformed it into a modern place much like everyplace else—the aged Meeker came out on the Oregon Trail and lived long enough to fly over Puget Sound in an airplane.

But if the old pioneers were honored at the end of their lives, they were not so well-liked in the late nineteenth century when hordes of newcomers arrived. They were often ridiculed by the immigrants who displaced them. The pioneers had bonded through their shared privations on the trails and homesteads, but a new generation was moving in. They poured in via rail and steamship, and most of them couldn't have cared less about the past or the bearded old geezers who were standing in the way of real progress. That displacement resulted in the genesis of the Northwest mossback.

In 1892, *The Tacoma Ledger* held an "Old Settler" contest. It invited readers with firsthand stories of the Northwest's pioneer days to submit them. The entries would be published, and the winning entrant would get two round-trip tickets to see the 1893 World's Columbian Exposition in Chicago, a world's fair celebrating the 400th anniversary of the discovery that started it all. "They came with ox teams but they shall return in palace cars" promised the newspaper. This was a chance for the "pioneer cult" to have its say, and while contributors spun amazing—and mostly true—yarns, a few could not help but sound off about their new, outcast status.

One was Hugh Crockett, who came out by wagon train in 1851:

> The pioneers of this grand state often have their feelings brought to arms by the sneering remark of new comers, who term us

"mossbacks." They tell us how things should be done, and how they are done "back east." Sometimes I feel like telling them to go "back east" and be blessed. The pioneers that laid the foundation for the greatest state in the Union may not just suit the fancy of a "down-easter," but beneath the perhaps rough, uncouth clothing, there beats as true, kind, and loyal a heart as has ever been imported on a palace car.

Another was Martha Ellis, a veteran of the Oregon Trail in 1852 and early resident of Puget Sound country:

Gradually the settlers recovered from the effects of the [1855 Indian] war and have done their best to help the development of their chosen state. Yet the new comers call them 'mossbacks.' I wonder how much more they could have done, with the same hardships to contend with, as the old pioneer.

The pioneers believed that they had earned their right to be here; it was their hard work and sacrifice that gave them the privilege to enjoy the Northwest's bounty. But they could not turn back the tide of change and new generations.

Their feeling of being put upon and displaced by newcomers is still alive today. Growth has made native and longtime Northwesterners feel uneasy. The late *Seattle Times* and *Seattle Post-Intelligencer* columnist Emmett Watson touted the virtues of "Lesser Seattle," an imaginary group with the sole purpose of "keeping the bastards out." In 1960s Oregon, *Oregonian* writer and author Holbrook was chief spokesperson for the James G. Blaine Society, an association that existed mostly as bumper stickers and buttons but was dedicated to fending off prospective newcomers. Though semi-tongue-in-cheek, such groups and their virtual followers embody attitudes that drive the local business lobby crazy. The growth-is-good crowd is quick to blame local not-in-my-backyard types when anything gets off track.

Republican legislators in Washington howled when Boeing announced that it was moving its corporate headquarters, saying selfish NIMBYs (read mossbacks) were ruining the local business climate. The fact that Boeing's decisions were being driven by, say, globalization had nothing to do with it, of course. Today, some developers have gotten a little savvier. They claim, for example, that building skyscrapers and condo towers is in fact good for the environment. They find that a greenwashed message goes down a little easier. Never, of course, do they question growth itself. It is an inevitable tsunami, they say.

Today's mossbacks are no longer pioneers or necessarily even sons and daughters of pioneers; they are people who believe that what makes this region exceptional is not the boom-time hype of snake-oil salesfolk who tout growth as a good in itself, but rather people who put their faith in a more humble and unaffected quality of life. They respect the land and think newcomer pretensions are better left where they came from. They would also say that we now have traditions and habits of life and settlement that ought to be respected rather than run over.

Modern mossbacks—still sneered at by many new-comers and outsiders—are not people who have settled the country but people who have been settled by it. We've been here long enough to put down roots and become part of the modern landscape. "Mossback" is an epithet to embrace with pride.

The mossback spirit is captured in a song that first appeared in Olympia's *Washington Standard* in 1877. The quirky Seattle restaurateur/folksinger Ivar Haglund learned it from his pals Pete Seeger and Woody Guthrie; he played it on his radio show back in the 1940s and on TV commercials in the 1960s. He even named his flag-ship restaurant after it—"Acres of Clams," which is the alternate title of the song. The original title is "The Old Settler," and it records a pioneer's decision to give up the thankless hard work of the mines to eventually find true happiness on Puget Sound. The last verses capture atti-tudes that can still be recognized in "natives" to this day:

I took up a claim in the forest
And sat myself down to hard toil;
For two years I chopped and I struggled;
But I never got down to the soil.

I tried to get out of the country,
But poverty forced me to stay;
Until I became an old settler,
Then nothing could drive me away.

No longer a slave to ambition,
I laugh at the world and its shams,
As I think of my present condition
Surrounded by acres of clams.

And now that I'm used to the climate,
I think that if ever man found
A spot to live easy and happy,
That Eden is on Puget Sound.

In just these four verses you have the classic mossback experience. A newcomer gets a foothold here, doing whatever it takes to stay. But by hanging on when the going gets tough, he finds that the magic and beauty of the place are irresistible. Now he can abandon traditional material values—gaining his freedom from the chains of ambition. He has discovered that the everyday world is a sham. The secret of happiness lies in letting go, getting mellow, and enjoying nature's bounty. Fulfillment is found through simplicity in this rain-nourished land. Or as Seattle historian Murray Morgan once put it, we see this as "a place to live rather than a place to make income from." Puget Sound is a slacker utopia attainable only by hard work and sacrifice. If you want something else, there's always California or New York.

"The Old Settler" also captures the conflict between old-timer and newcomer by raising the issue we still live with: Most of us came here as a result of unprecedented growth and the opportunities it bred. That growth—including immigration—continues unabated. It threatens our quality of life and the classic status mossbacks have enjoyed. In a land of newcomers, the old-timers eventually are overwhelmed and marginalized. The song also hints at a kind of insecurity that comes from leaving the status quo behind. We desire the respect, even the adoration, of an outside world that we've rejected. Yet by seeking validation, we jeopardize what we love by attracting new waves of immigrants and seekers, some of whom are openly exploitive. If people believe in our land's virtues, too many will come and Eden will be overrun; if they come and find us wanting, we are angered by their arrogant outsider ways. We'd rather be worshipped from a safe distance.

I think this insecurity stems in part from what we're doing to the land. We carry a collective guilt about the way we've chosen to live in the Northwest, from nearly eradicating the native peoples to poisoning Puget Sound. Even the original settlers arrived with a mixed sense of awe and mission. The settler's job, as John Quincy Adams once said, was "to make the wilderness blossom as the rose." But in retrospect, we wonder: Did we make the land blossom or did we spoil the garden? As we have seen the forests vanish and salmon stocks dwindle, we feel anger at what is happening and a helplessness to prevent it. For any mossback, even one who has been here only a decade or so, it's easy to see the degradation of the environment and quality of life. We brood on the fact that our mode of living—our technology, our economy, our greed—have trapped us in a cycle that seems destined to destroy what we love because we love it.

That is the mossback dilemma, but there are ways to respond. One is to take pride in place. Another is to try to cut through the hype that sells us stuff we don't need in the currency of our own insecurity. And the last is to recognize a sense of stewardship for land, nature, community, and history.

Crosscut 2007

In Defense of Irrationality

Washington's Defense of Marriage Act might be "rational" in the eyes of the state Supreme Court, as it ruled last week, but as anyone who has been married knows, there is little that is rational about marriage. Few cultural institutions are as emotionally loaded. One reason is that marriage is profoundly symbolic. Throughout the ages, people have been fascinated and moved by the power of uniting opposites: yin and yang, male and female, anima and animus, above and below. There is something magical in combining them into something greater than the sum of their parts. Such pairings can produce children, a sense of wholeness, even enlightenment. The alchemists were obsessed by such imagery and wrote of "chymical weddings" that they believed would produce gold or the philosopher's stone in the womb of an alembic. In modern psychology, Carl Jung described this process as the path to psychic integration.

This is partly why the idea of gay marriage can create an archetypal dissonance even among straight people who are not especially homophobic: A man marrying a man or a woman a woman seems to break the ancient formula that generates some of marriage's psychic fizz.

Marriage is also something we have romantic notions about. We've discarded many of the practical advantages of wedlock, regarding them as outdated, even shameful in our enlightened age. The more pragmatic a marriage is nowadays, the more tainted it seems. Think Anna Nicole Smith and Hollywood prenups.

Arranged marriages have mostly gone by the wayside in Western civilization—the bartering of brides for cattle is a relic. Marrying for social status still flourishes—the Sunday "Style" section of *The New York Times* is living proof that positive eugenics lives (Harvard-educated Wall Street investment banker marries Yale-graduated son of diplomat!). But social status today is less about wealth or heredity than about the possession of cultural signifiers that concretize a "good" match (hip-hop producer weds Hollywood scriptwriter).

Birth control has removed procreation from the equation, the Legislature and the state Supreme Court notwithstanding. It has given individuals much more control over when and with whom to have sex and children. Science has also intervened to allow "sterile" couples to have kids with the help of surrogates and test tubes. Marriage and the biological ability to make children have been forever sundered. And a good thing, too: There are more children in need of parents than parents to go around. Thank goodness some gays and lesbians have come to the rescue by volunteering to be parents.

Marriage gets most of its juju from the illogical and irrational. Love, for example. Marrying for love was still a comparatively radical notion into the early twentieth century, the kind of behavior best indulged in rural communes. It is now de rigueur. Even the seizing of a young trophy bride, say, Katie Holmes, is done under the manic couch-jumping insistence that it's really about love.

People also marry for a sense of completeness, or to achieve "marital bliss." Others marry to gain acceptance in their families and in society; there remains a stigma that attaches to people who go through life without permanent partners. People also marry because they believe it is God's will, that marriage is divinely ordained and sanctified, a religious act.

Today, these motivations are the most powerful and emotional reasons cited for the defense of traditional marriage. Social engineers claim it's about the kids, but the heart wants what it wants.

In considering the rational basis for the Defense of Marriage Act, the Supreme Court was left looking for something that does not exist: a rational justification to match an institution driven by irrationality. The court seized upon the procreative imperative, but it doesn't hold up to scrutiny. If the state really wanted to promote more babies, it might do better to encourage promiscuity, polygamy, and polyandry. And if its goal is raising children in more stable environments, it could encourage practices, especially in light of our high divorce rates, that make it easier for "the village" to raise a child—such as universal day care.

There still are, of course, concrete benefits that come with marriage. There are rights of inheritance and property ownership; there are tax advantages. There is the right to be at the bedside of a dying spouse. These are important and difficult to duplicate outside of marriage without a lot of paperwork.

My longtime partner and I were married earlier this year after consulting with a lawyer about how to do this. We realized marriage was a legal shortcut of practical value. Yes, we mostly married for love; few people marry for the express purpose of being able to one day share a hospice. But deconstructing marriage helped me realize that the legal benefits, while unexciting in themselves, are not inconsequential. We didn't need a piece of paper from the state to make our marriage feel important. But the civil benefits that came with that paper were real.

Such benefits don't justify the special and exalted status that marriage has within our society. But they are valuable enough that denying them to same-sex couples is a form of discrimination that has no rational justification. Marriage as an irrational institution will be largely unaffected if its most pragmatic benefits are shared. The emotional and spiritual benefits are not within the power of the state to bestow, and we ought to rethink the wisdom of asking the state to sanction them at all.

Seattle Weekly 2006

For Whom the School Bell Tolls

Education—compulsory schooling,
compulsory learning—is a tyranny and a crime
against the human mind and spirit. Let all those
escape it who can, any way they can.

—John Holt, author, educator, homeschooling advocate

Do you remember the feeling? Every year, right after Labor Day, the weather suddenly improved. And where were you? Stuck behind a desk in an old brick building, compelled to be there by the state, your teachers, your parents. Meanwhile, fun things were going on down in Puyallup (the fair). And as the September sun flooded your classroom, you could hear a lone plane drone somewhere high overhead. Someone was free, you thought. Someone was flying—maybe even to Puyallup. But you, you were serving the first days of a nine-month sentence in a minimum-security prison. Your crime: being a kid. Your first homework assignment: read *Huckleberry Finn*. Ever notice how little sense of irony there is in schools?

School often feels like punishment. It's a feeling many of us repress as we become our parents and ask our children to do what we once had to do. For their own good. Because it is one of the few nearly universal experiences we have in this country, compulsory education is one of the unexamined questions in the national debate over school performance and reform. School is inherently good, most believe; compulsory education a necessity, otherwise, who would go? (Again, no irony.) And with working parents, who can stay home and watch the kids?

If you want to really push people's buttons, tell them you've taken your kids out of school because you think they will be better off learning at home. Even the most liberal-minded person you know will be antagonized. You have just challenged their own identity and experience; you have just told them they served hard time for nothing; you have just told them, by implication, they are screwing up their own kids. No one wants to hear that.

A few will concede that homeschooling might be OK for you, but *what if everyone did it?*

Most people of all political persuasions agree America's educational system is seriously broken and needs fixing. If we are to discuss serious reform, however, we ought to be willing to at least *discuss* that system's underlying assumptions. Compulsory public education is one of them. The times won't necessarily wait for people to feel good about the discussion before we have it, however.

A growing number of parents are taking on the responsibility of educating their own children or, more radically, allowing their children to take responsibility for their own learning. This is the Shays' Rebellion of education, a grassroots movement that offers an alternative way that isn't theoretical; it actually works. It will become a growing factor in educational debates.

In addition, this is the era of the free market. As we continue to discuss charter schools, the creation of schools run for profit, voucher systems, and schools that compete with one another for students, our notion of the educational system as institution is breaking down. Many of the best reform ideas empower parents and children to choose what is right for them, not accept limited institutional choices. If reformers can crack the institution of public education, more options and escape paths will open up, and the whole notion of "compulsory" will be undermined. Imagine an educational system in which "schools" are oriented toward attracting customers (learners) rather than administering sentences.

Lastly, technology is doing its part. It has the potential to radically change the whole way we learn. Computers eliminate the need for schools to have a physical campus, thus they can be virtual. Students can exercise choice over who teaches them and how they are taught. Internet access significantly increases the gene pool of teachers and fellow students. In fact, the line between teacher and student will fade. We will be students when we ask for help; we will be teachers when others tap us for our knowledge. Cyberspace is the antithesis of compulsory. It is CHOICE in capital letters.

One day, traditional public schools may provide day care or social services to those in need, but education itself will be flourishing elsewhere. A great bell will ring.

Eastsideweek 1995

When my daughter and son—fraternal twins—were in first grade, we sent them to the local elementary school. Shortly thereafter, my son starting doing things that were completely uncharacteristic, like cutting in front of people rudely. When I asked him about it, he said it was OK if he yelled, "I got cuts!"

first. He said he'd learned that when lining up at school. Soon the kids were coming home singing cartoon show jingles. Since their TV watching had been very restricted, their mother asked them how they'd learned songs from TV shows they'd rarely if ever seen. In music class, they said. We assumed they meant from friends, but we soon learned that no, their music teacher was teaching the class songs from Saturday morning TV shows. A few weeks into the school year, there was an open house for parents. I asked their teacher how they planned to encourage creativity and teach art in first grade. She said, oh, we don't teach art until fifth or sixth grade. The first few years they're here, she explained, are designed to teach them how to exist within the institution of school and perform tasks like taking notes home to us parents. We decided days later to homeschool the kids until we could find a better alternative, one that didn't promote rude behavior, fill kids' heads with corporate TV crap, and prioritize the process of creating compliant inmates.

Fortunately, the next year we found that the school district had an excellent alternative grade school that was partly run by the parents. After that, for junior high and high school, the kids attended an experimental, nonschool school called Puget Sound Community School, which at that time was something of a cooperative of homeschooled kids and their parents put together by a brilliant young teacher named Andy Smallman and his wife, Melinda. We pooled resources and knowledge to hire instructors and offer programs that self-motivated kids could pursue. It involved internships and community service as well as voluntary classes, many of which were taught by the kids themselves. The creation of this remarkable nonschool exposed us to the world of people like John Holt, who contended that human beings naturally love to learn but that our schools tend to instill fear and derail our natural learning patterns. He promoted a form of home schooling that was, in effect, self-schooling, or even unschooling. Learning was voluntary, driven by curiosity and desire, rather than coerced. It's a system—or nonsystem—that trusts people will learn what they need to know when they need and want to know it. Andy Smallman not only mentored the students, but he held the hands of us parents as we walked into the educational unknown: Could our kids really teach themselves?

Yes. It wasn't easy and it had its pitfalls, but that's education too. What PSCS did was help my kids develop strong life skills and nourish their independence and love of learning. They are well launched in life, with college educations, good jobs, and fine minds. Interestingly, while they had a freewheeling experience in high school and middle school, they chose fairly traditional programs at large universities for their higher education. But they thrived in both systems because every step of the way, what they did was their choice. Our experience has made me a big believer in the power of free-range education.

Homeschooling has been a growing trend for a small percentage of parents. It still gets a bad rap as something engaged in by cultists or control freaks. When we got involved, most of the parents involved were either old hippies or religious conservatives. What we seemed to have in common was a critique of our educational system that was more complicated than arguments about curriculum, WASL tests, teacher pay, or whether recess is racist or not. At root, it often had to do with values: What kind of people were we teaching our kids to be, and how empowered would they be within this society?

Homeschooling isn't for everyone, but among homeschoolers you run into all kinds of educational philosophies and approaches, like the guy who told us that all you need to teach your kid is Latin and geometry and the rest will take care of itself. Because of that diversity, you can learn a lot. Everyone, parents and kids, gets a chance to think—and learn—outside the box.

2008

What I Learned as a Boy Scout

A Scout is: Trustworthy. Loyal. Helpful. Friendly. Courteous. Kind. Obedient. Cheerful. Thrifty. Brave. Clean. Reverent.

I was a lousy Boy Scout—literally a Second Class one—but I can still recite that bit of code from memory.

But they left one thing off the list: A Scout is *not* queer.

The U.S. Supreme Court is deciding that matter right now, whether it's possible to be gay and "morally straight" and "clean" as the Scout code demands. The Boy Scouts of America says that to be gay is to be immoral—in effect, unclean—and therefore at odds with the definition of scouthood. Their lawyer, George Davidson, told the Supremes, "The Boy Scouts are so closely identified with traditional moral values that the phrase 'He's a real Boy Scout' has entered the language." Arguing the other side before the court was the lawyer for James Dale, the gay Eagle Scout and assistant scoutmaster who was expelled from the organization once his sexual orientation was published in a newspaper. Dale's attorney says that to equate the scoutmaster's mere existence with an assumed moral message is "identity-based discrimination," pure and simple.

Of course, nowhere in the Scout laws does it specify that you can't be gay; it's supposed to be self-evident, I guess, because the morality of the Scouts is eternal. But let's look at how the Scouts themselves measure up, from my personal experience as a Scout in Seattle in the mid-'60s when I was a member of a troop I'll call Troop XXX.

Troop XXX met at a local church. The fathers who ran it had all obviously been buck privates during WWII, and they were determined to treat us like they'd been treated in boot camp. The head scoutmaster was Homer Simpson with hair, with the dull eyes to match. He never looked at us kids, instead addressing us while staring offstage for the other fathers' approval. He thought it was funny to require that we wear our summer uniforms year round, no matter how cold or wet it was. A bunch of freezing boys in shorts and kneesocks did something for him, I guess.

Occasionally we would be visited by another Scout dad whose flamboyant fashion sense would have done Reich Marshal Hermann Göring proud: He was covered in medals and patches, wore a big Smokey Bear–type hat, and carried a staff. No doubt he was an Order of the Arrow guy, a member of Scouting's answer to Skull and Bones: a cult for the über-pricks. Did I mention he also wore an enormous red Superman cape? Most of us found him pathetic, because he obviously expected this roomful of adolescent boys to be impressed with his martial strutting. The other dads seemed eager to please him, though: When he was around, they became extra tough, like General Patton on little sleep. We were ordered to do special drills, practice holding and folding the flag properly, and our patrol units were inspected most thoroughly by the assistant scoutmasters. You'd better not have a garter out of place.

I had joined expecting the Scouts to offer some fun in the great outdoors and lessons in Indian-style woodcraft. But for the most part we were like a poorly run right-wing militia: chores, inspections, various intertroop competitions. Week to week, the guys who did the grunt work of running the show were older teens, a few of whom seemed to be out-and-out sadists. They were indifferent instructors; mostly they enjoyed barking orders and humiliating and hazing the younger Scouts—and occasionally hurting them. We learned to resist work and discipline.

Weekend campouts at Camp XXX were a cross between *Animal House* and *Lord of the Flies*. The fathers would hole up in a small cabin and drink and smoke. We Scouts would hole up in our tents and drink and smoke. We'd go for days without visible adult supervision. So when I was supposed to be learning how to read a compass or tie knots, I was in fact learning skills that would be useful if I were joining the Viet Cong. Like how to place a can of Sterno in the campfire so that when it exploded it would send debris into the laps of unsuspecting fellow Scouts. Like how plastic tarps when melted make a kind of napalm that when dripped onto human skin won't come off. Like how every tribal group needs one person to be the butt of every cruel prank, and how a sane person will do anything not to be that person.

I learned that some of my fellow Scouts were sexually excitable. One would carve voluptuous votive objects out of candle wax. One night, he also attacked me in a kind of hysterical, giggling sexual frenzy. He got hold of some vital parts of my anatomy and wouldn't let go, even as I beat him repeatedly over the head with one of those special Scout flashlights that looks like a small periscope. In fact, he laughed and squeezed harder the more I hit him, which everyone else found hilarious. Do they give S and M merit badges?

One weekend at Camp XXX, a group of Scouts went nuts. They shed their clothes, then attacked other campsites with rocks and spears. They captured and dragged several other Scouts into the woods and roughed them up. The night filled with screams. They killed a squirrel and set it on fire on a stump they'd converted to a pagan altar. While it burned, they chanted and danced. All the while, the dads were sleeping it off in their little cabin, oblivious or uncaring: Boys will be boys.

One Scout's experience, yes, but I've talked to dozens of others who tell similar stories.

What is it about organizations that are always standing up to enforce traditional moral values? Why is it that we're always safer when we keep our distance from them?

We shouldn't be trying to get gays *into* Scouting. We ought to be trying to get everyone else out.

Seattle Weekly 2000

Who Would Jesus Punch for an Xbox?

The holiday season has officially begun with widespread reports of near rioting at various big-box retailers, including the Wal-Mart in Renton, where the police had to be called in to quell crowds driven to a frenzy over the chance to buy laptop computers at a deep discount.

So-called Black Friday—as in black ink the day after Thanksgiving and the official start of the annual retail binge that's become Christmas—has become a rite akin to the annual running of the bulls in Pamplona. We are treated to film footage and video accounts of rabid consumers kicking, punching, goring, and trampling each other for—well, it doesn't matter what it's for. Stuff.

Forgive me if I have an Andy Rooney moment, but remember when Black Friday wasn't a story? Remember when Christmas wasn't used as just another economic marker, a kind of rectal-temperature-taking of the national well-being? Remember when shopping was either a pleasure or a private anguish, not a public spectacle, let alone a trauma? Remember when we didn't keep score, we merely did the best we could as individuals and families?

I see two distressing trends here. One is that our media have become obsessed with quantifying everything, from holiday sales figures to athletes' salaries to movie box-office receipts. For the sake of injecting a competitive or disaster angle into everything, we now track the fiscal ups and downs of every move. The meaning of everything is determined by the bottom line. We've become a bar chart society, and we track metrics like commodities traders.

Second, both news and entertainment have begun fusing into a variant of reality TV. Our entertainment is not great films or literature about conflict, it is conflict itself, delivered by ubiquitous minicams. It's the difference between reading Shakespeare or Dickens and watching cockfights or *Survivor*. Our tales of retail madness around the holidays feed our taste for turning everything into Darwinian blood sport. We're happy to watch real children and families being abused on network nanny shows or made a spectacle of on Dr. Phil's stage; we watch attention-starved anorexics duke it out to be the next top model or next year's second-rate Vegas act. We're like the Romans in the Colosseum for whom the equivalent of must-see TV was watching what a pride of lions could do to a bunch of unarmed slaves. We care little about plot; it's the abuse that exhilarates. "News" events like Black Friday mania are effectively manufactured for our entertainment.

The sad accounts of holiday shopping insanity appeal in part because we spectators can take solace in the fact that there is someone out there—maybe lots of someones—more desperate, more willing to be humiliated, more pathetic, more deserving of scorn than we are. Better to be a fan in the stands than to be struggling in the arena yourself, right?

Watching people duke it out over Christmas gifts distracts us from the fact that we're all suffering from diminishment. We can roll our eyes over their foolishness without thinking about the bigger picture, that these foolish shoppers paid $2.50 a gallon for gas to drive miles and miles to fight with their neighbors over electronic merchandise—which they'll buy on credit—that was made by foreign workers in countries where their living-wage jobs wound up. We're getting desperate because we're being drained.

If people thought about the real context, maybe there'd be real riots.

With this general bankruptcy of spirit, it's no wonder the religious right is up in arms over the desecration of Christmas, the turning of a sacred season into a pie chart supervised by politically correct bureaucrats and retail-industry consultants. Evangelical preacher Jerry Falwell is upset because a Christmas tree in Boston was renamed a "holiday tree," which, he says, is part of a concerted effort to "steal" Christmas. Even as a heathen, I join Falwell in fury. A Christmas tree is a Christmas tree. Are we also going to refer to menorahs as "holiday menorahs" to disguise their association with Jews and Hanukkah? If you strip Christmas of its religious and symbolic meaning, you're left with nothing but the emptiness exemplified by the few things you can still talk about, like sales figures and shopping riots. Who would Jesus punch for an Xbox? This is a concept of Christmas that would make Scrooge, the Grinch, and Mr. Potter all happy.

The spiritual umbrella provided by the American celebration of Christmas also shelters non-Christians, including those who celebrate Hanukkah, Kwanzaa, the pagan yule, or some solo, secular creation that allows us to exist, for a few days, nights, or weeks, in a sacred zone where the last thing on our minds or in our hearts is the latest sales figures for Wal-Mart or Target.

We seem to be living in the dystopia that Jimmy Stewart was trapped in during *It's a Wonderful Life*, only there are no angels to snap their fingers and wake us from the nightmare. No angels, that is, except—as Lincoln phrased it—the better angels of our nature.

It's time for them to earn their wings.

Seattle Weekly 2005

Onward, Secular Soldiers!

American politics is possessed by religious mania. One by one, our leaders and their constituencies are seized by the modern equivalent of Saint Vitus's dance.

They're in a frenzied whirlwind to prove they—and their politics—are right with God.

What else explains the long, lavish, unrelenting coverage of the death of one pope and the installation of another? Pageantry and history are worth an appreciative look, just as many of us were momentarily mesmerized by the wedding and funeral of Princess Diana. One shouldn't be surprised that the Catholic cardinals chose a conservative leader in Benedict XVI: You don't keep institutions like this running for millennia (sixteen Benedicts alone!) by letting open-minded liberals lead them.

But the length and intensity of the coverage suggests there was more at work than televising a colorful medieval pageant. The media whipped it to the level of religious pornography, not to mention unabashed idolatry, which is what TV, in particular, does best (see *American Idol*). It had resonance as religious propaganda for the fact that it became a stage on which people—including some very powerful people—could demonstrate their religiosity.

On paper, the Vatican, a sovereign state, is the word's smallest country. It is also one of the least democratic. Its form of government is ecclesiastical; the only people who can vote are a couple of hundred handpicked elderly men. It is an absolute monarchy, the kind our foreign policy purports to oppose. According to the philosophy of George W. Bush, democracy's evangelist in chief, the Vatican should look less like an institution deserving homage than a state ripe for invasion and democratization. During the president's visit for Pope John Paul II's funeral, a few Marines could easily have shocked and awed the

Swiss Guard and freed the oppressed. The Papal State still awaits liberation.

When the Bushes and Bill Clinton went on their pilgrimage to the funeral, they took advantage of the chance to be seen kneeling in a holy space before God. Republican and Democrat, our political ebony and ivory, brought together by a common deity. There was a time in this democracy when no president would be seen kneeling or bowing before a foreign monarch, alive or dead, lest he risk impeachment.

Not long after the funeral, members of America's religious right hosted their own nationally televised service to bash federal court nominees who dare follow and vote their conscience. James Dobson, the chairman of Focus on the Family, was quoted in *The Washington Post*, speaking from the pulpit: "The court's majority, Dobson said, 'are unelected and unaccountable and arrogant and imperious and determined to redesign the culture according to their own biases and values, and they're out of control.'" He could also have been talking about the Catholic Church. Or he could have been describing his own religious right, a group of unelected fundamentalist fanatics determined to impose their narrow version of Christianity on the rest of us. You know the biblical adage about casting stones? The religious right has learned that you don't get anywhere without casting the first stones hard and fast. If you smite (I'm in biblical mode here) your enemy, your own hypocrisy doesn't matter because your glass house is standing and your enemy's isn't.

While Dobson is casting stones at our constitutional courts, liberals are playing catch-up. There is much talk from the "religious left" about taking back God and the Bible. Jim Wallis, the liberal evangelical Christian author of *God's Politics: Why the Right Gets It Wrong and the Left Doesn't Get It,* makes a passionate case for lefty, God-driven politics that claims Martin Luther King Jr. as patron saint. It's a politics that tends to focus on the compassionate Christ of the Gospels rather than the wrathful demiurge of the Old Testament. But while Wallis's interpretation of Christianity might be more inclusive and tolerant than most of his fundie brethren, it's still a fight against secularism. It's a fight over who owns the Bible. "Conventional wisdom suggests that the antidote to religious fundamentalism is more secularism. But that is a very big mistake," he writes. "The best response to bad religion is better religion, not secularism." For non-Christians (and non-Jews and non-Muslims), the meaning is clear: All the rest of you can exit the public square while we battle over God's messengers and messages.

That doesn't get us anywhere. The problem with the monotheists is that only one of them can be right. But that isn't true in a genuine democracy under which there can be more than one right answer. And a key element to an open society is the ability of those in power to be held accountable for mistakes. Infallibility is not a virtue in democratic leadership.

The blithe dismissal of secularism by both right and left is worrisome. I'm not saying people shouldn't be informed by the gods or spirits that move them. I certainly am. But democracy works best when minds are open to change, to ideas, and to reason.

While so-called secular liberals have become the punching bags for Christians right and left, let me ask for the secular *right* to start stepping forward to call an end to the extreme nonsense on their side. Libertarians, scientists, economic and Wall Street realists, and old-school flag-waving conservatives who agree with Barry Goldwater that religion should butt out of politics need to join the secular center and the secular left to speak up against the religious takeover of America.

Unless, of course, they want our country run like the Vatican.

Seattle Weekly 2005

Stumped in Puget Sound

Ever since white man first set foot here, he has waged eco-war. The early traders rewarded the Indians for the slaughter of the sea otter, paying them with guns and rum. The Hudson's Bay Company, which ruled the Pacific Northwest for decades, devoted itself to the extermination of the beaver—not just for commercial gain, but also to make an "invasion" of British territory less appealing to American settlers by laying waste to a potential resource.

Native American tribes were threatened with extermination if they did not become a part of this new economy: Unscrupulous traders often held them hostage with a "smallpox bottle," a vial said to contain the disease that was already eradicating the tribes. Cooperate with us or else, our ancestors said.

As a result, we stripped away the ancient forests, polluted the depths of the lakes and seas, rendered the wild salmon extinct, and emptied Puget Sound of much of its life. Creatures that had existed here in abundance for millennia were gone in fewer than 200 years.

We're here now, surrounded by the vestiges of these things. On a clear day, you can still see the wild Olympic Mountains, which are federally protected, and the Cascades, many of which are too. Lake Washington is cleaner than it used to be, and air pollution isn't as bad on its worst days as it was back in the early 1970s.

Read the history of this region and you are struck by the dissonance between what we said about it and what we did with it. The early British looked upon the landscape surrounding Puget Sound and found it lovely, reminiscent of the English countryside. They marveled at how it provided for the needs of its native inhabitants. They were awestruck by the scale and magnificence of its beauty. They took cuttings of plants back to improve their gardens. Later, the settlers referred to it as "God's Country," a sacred land of abundance. These impressions were immediately followed by plans for exploitation.

Some early settlers cut down huge old-growth trees—so large their stumps were big enough for houses. They cut them down and moved in. You see wonderful old photos of these stump dwellers, troll-like pioneers standing stiffly by their stump homes: log cabins built, in essence, with one log. They've added doors, windows, even chimneys to make their stumps habitable. Even so, you cannot help but see that they're living in hollowed-out shells.

This dichotomy lives within us. It's not simply a case of loving a place to death; it's a case of loving a place without accommodating any of its needs.

For one thing, we refuse to acknowledge that growth will continue to erode the very qualities we love unless and until we find a different way of relating to—and living in—this land. We must limit the number of people who live here or we must change the way we live here. Unfortunately, all the momentum seems to be in favor of further erosion.

The road builders are one species in ascendance. Traffic congestion is becoming everyone's number-one concern. But even on this one highly controllable issue, we will not change our collective habits, and we will not provide reasonable alternatives. We passed I-695 to shave the cost of owning our cars and as a result necessitated deep cuts in bus and ferry funding. Another initiative by the same author proposed that even more money be spent expanding roads at the expense of transportation alternatives. In Olympia and King County, some lawmakers want to take back the HOV lanes for single-occupant cars, and they're also considering more money for road-building—despite the fact that the department responsible for the roads is one of the worst-managed in state government.

That department just conducted a $500,000 study to show how a new highway, I-605, would ease congestion. This hypothetical highway would slice through the Snoqualmie Valley, the saving of which was once considered the sine qua non of growth-management and open-space initiatives. It lies on the "rural" side of the "urban/rural" line that was to be unbreachable. That such a route is even being considered is an example of how far the road-building forces are willing to go: all the way to the Cascade foothills.

Recently in a *New York Times* story about highway improvements in the suburbs, officials in these outliers said they had realized that decades of road-building had only made matters worse, and they had aerial photography to prove it. Building new roads to ease congestion is like buying bigger pants to deal with a weight problem, one said. Building new roads and highways and bridges doesn't ease congestion; it eats the land. What is so hard for people to understand about this?

Washington state's Growth Management Act is itself under attack. The builders and developers argue that people are being priced out of the region because they cannot buy affordable homes, this because of the artificial scarcity that has been created by the GMA. And while it's true that affordability is a huge problem, we cannot build our way out of it. The Silicon Forest can learn from the Silicon Valley, where one-room Palo Alto bungalows sell for up to $700,000. The Valley has taken massive growth in the last 30 years, and the San Francisco peninsula—the entire Bay Area, in fact—is now bay-to-mountain sprawl.

The price of bungalows has never gone down. Those "little boxes" on the hillsides of Daly City that Pete Seeger sang about? You couldn't afford one. That's the legacy of their high-tech boom economy.

The challenge for us is to find a way to treat the land more respectfully and reshape our priorities. Or be content to continue as stump dwellers, living well in a land we've impoverished.

Seattle Weekly 2000

The Future Ain't What It Used to Be

A few months ago, I went out to Lakeside School to hear Bill Gates talk about the future. It promised to be a grand evening, with students, parents, alums, and friends eager for a sneak peek at the twenty-first century given by the man who is driving us there. No waiting for the book.

The evening seemed ripe with meaning: Here was Lakeside's favorite son, returning with wealth and laurels to preach to an audience of the successful and privileged from his own vantage point as America's richest man. There was a symbolic torch-passing too, as one member of the audience was Wilber Huston (class of '29). Huston, a rocket scientist, won an MIT scholarship back then and was dubbed by Thomas Edison himself as the "smartest boy in America." On this night, he seemed a living link between Edison and the still-boyish Gates (whom Edison no doubt would anoint were he alive today).

Gates, backed by all the electronic gadgets he could muster, painted a picture of the electronic world over the next decade. The presentation included a film set in the year 2004 featuring a day in the life of a boy. The lad's homework was a multimedia presentation, though still offered up in a twentieth-century classroom; his mother interacted with her TV set, though the programming was still *Good Morning America*–style dross. The world was a little flashier, but fundamentally familiar.

Of course, the glitz and rhetoric surrounding these high-tech visions nearly always imply that we are in the midst of a millennial revolution. Recently a *New York Times Magazine* piece on the online magazine *HotWired* quoted a staffer claiming the cyber age is evolving humankind into nothing less than *a new species*.

Gates's bottom line was more mundane: Technology and the software that runs it will make the near future an incrementally more convenient place to live and give us a skosh more leisure time.

That's the problem with the future these days: It ain't what it used to be. Shining cities on the hill have been replaced by cell phones and CD-ROMs. We're told a Brave New World is upon us, but is Windows 95 really the window on that world? The hype is hyper, the reality lacks imagination.

What happened to the future that once lay glistening in the distance?

The answer is suggested by computer science professor David Gelernter, a man with unique credentials. He is the author of an important book on computers, *The Muse in the Machine*; he was nearly blown to bits by the neo-Luddite Unabomber, who apparently misread Gelernter's book as an apology for technology; and he has just published a new book about America's loss of faith in the future, *1939: The Lost World of the Fair*. It is a social history of the late 1930s built around the moment when the future was alive and flourishing at the New York World's Fair of 1939–40.

What Gelernter describes is an era when popular culture was much more sophisticated than it is now, filled with subtlety and taste: pop music by Gershwin, industrial design by Bel Geddes, modern art by Picasso, science by Einstein, and government by Roosevelt. It was an age of faith in authority; a time when science and technology collaborated with the arts to produce imaginative visions of tomorrow (superhighways, suburbs, skyscrapers, appliances, electricity, and a car in every garage). The fair was the era's (and the future's) ultimate expression, and those visitors who walked away wearing their "I Have Seen the Future" buttons could truly say they had. In the late 1930s, he writes, "the future was a tangible, tasteable, nearly corporeal presence in your life."

But today, the future lacks credibility and we lack subtlety and vision. Instead of Bel Geddes and Gershwin, we have Beavis and Butt-head. Nuance and style are dead.

Art and science ignore one another. There is little collaborative creativity binding commerce, technology, and the spirit.

The future of 1939 actually came to pass, but it did not make us happy. Its bright hopes were discarded like a spoiled child's Christmas toy.

Worst of all, like those who have lost religious faith and cannot see God, Gelernter says we have lost civic faith and cannot see the future any more.

We have not lost the desire to look ahead, as evidenced by the turnout at Lakeside to hear Gates. But until we better ourselves, our multimedia visions will fail to inspire. The future lies within.

Eastsideweek 1995

My Summer's Page-Burners

Why are people so afraid of burning books? I agree that censorship is a bad thing: there should be no restraint on what we publish, what we buy, and what we read. And I oppose the banning of books from schools and libraries, where the highest degree of tolerance and broad-mindedness should be the norm. But the symbolic statement made by tossing a book into a bonfire seems quite powerful. We defend our right to burn the flag, but burn a book and suddenly we're Nazi Germany.

Let me make a distinction. I oppose the wholesale, systematic burning of books, libraries, or collections. But you have to agree that selective book burning makes a potent political statement, and as such should be a kind of protected speech—it's certainly less malicious than trashing a Starbucks.

One of the favorite targets of book burners in recent years has been Harry Potter. In just the last year, Harry Potter bonfires have blazed in New Mexico and Pennsylvania. The Reverend George Bender of the Harvest Assembly of God Church in suburban Pittsburgh hosted one such bonfire. He said: "We believe that Harry Potter promotes sorcery, witchcraft-type things, the paranormal, things that are against God. That is really bad." I certainly agree with the first part of Reverend Bender's statement. In fact, it is undeniable: Harry Potter glamorizes practices that many Christians have condemned for centuries. I disagree with the second part: that promoting witchcraft is a bad thing. But let's be clear: It is not witches that are being burned here, only books. Burning a few Harry Potters— even a lot of Harry Potters—isn't going to make a dent in the book's popularity or availability. Just as burning an American flag isn't going to lead to the burning of all American flags.

I must confess that after seeing that dreadful Harry Potter movie—the movie seems not so much guilty of promoting witchcraft but of encouraging a pernicious narcissism that is far more corrosive of the human soul than a little sorcery—consigning a few Harry Potters to the flames doesn't strike me as such a bad idea.

I recently read a book that is also ripe for a weenie roast: Pat Buchanan's new polemic, *The Death of the West*. It is a racist, xenophobic diatribe by a so-called mainstream conservative commentator who essentially defines Western civilization as a white people's culture, one that is under threat because whites aren't breeding fast enough to outrun a tidal wave of dark-skinned people who will soon conquer the earth. Turning a millennium of history on its head, Buchanan concludes that it is whites who are the poor oppressed minority on this planet, and it's time for white people to breed or buy guns. Which is what white supremacists have been arguing for years, only the Ku Klux Klan doesn't have any books on the *New York Times* best-seller list. Last I checked, Pat Buchanan's book was number five.

So after you read it—which I recommend, because it's always good to know what the enemy is up to—merely tossing this book across the room may not be enough. If you burn only one book this year, let it be Pat Buchanan's.

KUOW 2001

Dead-End America

National Geographic recently ran satellite images of suburban sprawl in America. From high above, the cameras captured a network of lights that fill the highway corridors and river valleys with tendrils reaching onto the plains and deserts where once there was only darkness. From the sky, the settlement pattern looks like microbes taking over a petri dish. Let's hope it's not anthrax.

America is becoming The Suburban Nation. Once there were cities, villages, farms, and wild lands. Today, most Americans live in sprawl. It is not by accident but by design. Suburbs were invented alongside the second Industrial Revolution of the mid-1800s as a place for home and family. A successful man wanted to protect his loved ones from the filth of factories, muddy streets, saloons, and madding crowds, so he built his castle on the quiet tree-lined lane of a town at the end of the Interurban line. In the twentieth century, some modern thinkers such as Frank Lloyd Wright imagined a populist landscape where every American lived in equality in vast low-density grids covering the prairies. At the New York World's Fair of 1939, visitors were told that the "world of tomorrow" was a sprawling blanket of modern subdivisions linked by commodious freeways. After World War II, Americans began building and populating exactly that landscape— and on it goes.

The suburbs are still popular, largely because they are safe. Safety, in fact, is their greatest commodity. Gated developments protect against the outside world; covenanted communities offer the security of neighbors willing to conform, who will mow their lawns and won't paint their homes an unsettling shade of gamboge. SUVs and minivans protect families who travel that paved Möbius strip that leads to an infinity of soccer matches. Suburbs are monuments to defensive living: life without surprise, without risk, without variety.

The War Against Terrorism will complete the process of shaping The Suburban Nation. The events of September 11 have emphasized for many people the danger inherent in cities: Despite Mayor Rudy Giuliani cleaning up the streets of New York—some would say suburbanizing them—the nation's best big-city mayor couldn't make the world safe for skyscrapers, nor for the people who work in them. USA Today estimated that 81 percent of the World Trade Center victims were men, median age 39. They were largely suburban dads who rode the Interurban every day to do their duty in the dangerous city. If the city isn't safe for dads, it isn't safe for anyone.

The values that have caused the suburbs to blossom have seized the national consciousness. People are staying home, turning inward, and renting from Blockbuster. Polls show we are willing to surrender our individual rights for the promise of protection. We will carry national ID cards and support the detention and deportation of suspicious aliens and strangers. Senators call for a Homeland Security force to patrol our streets. Others call for us to spy on one another. We demand more border guards and tougher immigration laws.

America once welcomed the tired, poor, huddled masses yearning to breathe free; now we are accelerating the process of becoming the world's premier gated community. Forget making the world safe for democracy, we must make America safe. Period.

But there is danger in allowing fear to become our driving force, in making America as sterile as a strip-mall Starbucks. The Suburban Nation ought to remember that "cul-de-sac" is just a fancy word for "dead end."

KUOW 2001

No More Free Ride

I've recently been on a road trip, enjoying the freedom of the American West. When I returned, I realized that the future of our system of open roads is as endangered as the nonchain diner. Just as the range was fenced off, we in the auto age are now facing a future that comes with more toll gates, private roads, and high-tech tracking and surveillance technology. Eventually, our every move will become somebody else's business. In states like ours, we've taken for granted that road travel is free. We pay for gas, gas taxes, and license fees (often reluctantly), but where we go—and when—has been our business. Roads have been part of the commonweal, a benefit for all.

Unlike the East Coast, with its pay-as-you-go turn-pikes, in the West modern roads are rarely tolled. Yes, we have ferries and a few toll bridges, but our tradition has generally been that tolls come off once a bridge is paid for. That was the case with both Lake Washington float-ing bridges. Generally, the state has been a part-time toll taker, and the people regard free access to the roads as a basic right.

But all that is changing. Tolls are being considered again for both Lake Washington bridges, Snoqualmie Pass, stretches of I-5 in southwest Washington, even major roads in Greater Seattle. It's a profound change in the way we think about transportation, taxation, and freedom of movement. And the politics are interesting because they jump traditional ideological barriers.

The romance of driving has been replaced by alarm over global warming. Urban planners want to make cit-ies greener and commuters want less congestion. While there are still those who say we can build our way out of gridlock with more freeways—a policy which, if it worked, would make Los Angeles our least gridlocked city—many policymakers are focusing on getting people to drive less and at different times. The Puget Sound Regional Council completed a massive study that looks at charging fees on every freeway and major arterial in Greater Seattle. A transponder in your car would send a record of your travels to a computer and you would be billed for use. You would be charged little or nothing if you drive late at night and much more if you travel at peak commute hours.

The council's findings projected that with the right financial incentives and disincentives, people would drive less and the program could generate as much as $1.5 billion to $2 billion per year—if enough roads were tolled so that drivers become captive to the user-fee system. It would get enough people off the roads to relieve congestion and, unlike most transportation projects, generate revenue without enormous new capital investments—revenue that could be spent on anything, including transportation projects.

And that's another reason politicians are warming to road pricing: It gets into the taxpayer's pocket without having to raise taxes per se—a neat way to wire around Tim Eyman. Bonding capacity is getting tapped out, and there's a growing consensus that continuing to raise the gas tax is untenable when gas is more than $3 per gallon and oil supplies are likely to diminish.

Since the 2007 Minnesota bridge disaster, there's been a focus on the nation's aging infrastructure—how to pay to fix and replace it. Federal funds have about run out (the federal Highway Trust Fund is expected to hit a negative balance in 2009), and the public is skeptical of tax increases. Tolling offers a ray of hope, and the Bush administration has been pushing it with incentives. Washington was awarded a $138 million federal grant for transportation improvements contingent on tolling State Highway 520.

Privatization of roads is another Bush administration favorite. Across the country, there has been a trend toward turning formerly public toll roads, such as in Chicago and

Indiana, over to private companies that lease and operate the roads, replacing public tolling authorities. This raises immediate revenues for local governments through upfront lease payments. The private companies can often cut maintenance expenses (by dumping union workers, for example), and they can jack up toll rates to levels that would be impossible for a public agency to justify.

Privatization is not a popular concept in Washington state—liberal powerhouses like state House Speaker Frank Chopp and King County Executive Ron Sims oppose it—but it was proposed for the new Tacoma Narrows Bridge, and a bipartisan group has suggested private investment for a new downtown Seattle tunnel.

Despite assurances that privatization is off the table, in the longer term road-pricing schemes and public-private partnerships will prove tempting to private investment funds that are targeting infrastructure projects. They love those revenue streams.

The new driver of all this is technology: the ability to use radio-frequency identification chips and transponders to scan moving vehicles and eliminate the manned tollbooth. In addition, many cities—famously London, but also New York and others that plan to rely increasingly on road tolling—are installing extensive networks of surveillance cameras to monitor traffic and catch scofflaws. We are rapidly approaching a point where a citizen's every move in an automobile can be recorded and tracked, not to mention monetized.

Such tracking has other privacy implications: On the East Coast, electronic tolling records have been used in criminal and divorce cases to track cheating spouses. Here, the state Legislature has yet to pass any laws to protect the public's privacy when it comes to such radio-frequency ID technology, even though it is already being used on the Tacoma Narrows Bridge and is planned for a State Highway 167 high-occupancy toll lane between Auburn and Renton. It's also in the state's new "enhanced" driver's licenses, which drivers can now purchase as part of a special ID program. It will get you easy access into Canada. And it's a pilot for a mandatory federal program down the road. So Big Brother is already hitching a ride with many state drivers.

This year saw the fiftieth anniversary of Jack Kerouac's beat classic *On the Road*, a tribute to the frenzied freedom and individualism of the postwar car years. Such freewheeling may soon be a bygone era. The Kerouacs and commuters of America, like cowboys, are about to find themselves electronically fenced in as a last bastion of liberty gives way to economic convenience.

Washington Law & Politics 2008

NATURE

Jet Ski Jackass

It was a gloomy fall day. It wasn't raining, but the light was thin and the air was thick. I was walking alone around the northern tip of Seward Park in South Seattle, and I had the place nearly all to myself. Just offshore, I noticed a great blue heron perched on a white buoy. Its head was down and its shoulders were hunched, like a vulture guarding the entrance to some godforsaken realm.

Seward Park is a great place for watching birds. This peninsula pokes into Lake Washington like a crooked finger tickling an invisible chin. You can follow trails through its thick groves of old trees, stroll its open fields, or follow a paved perimeter that traces the water's edge for a couple of miles. From this trail—a stretch of which is an old road that was once a popular high-school cruising corridor back when it was open to cars—you can gaze across the lake at a number of vistas. On a clear day, the massive flanks of Mount Rainier are to the south, and on almost any day, you can eyeball the gold-coast compounds of Mercer Island to the east.

But a real attraction here is the bird life. I'm no bird nut, but there often is so much drama acted out in front of your eyes, it is impossible to ignore.

Earlier this year, a friend and I watched a bald eagle attack a formation of black, blunt-beaked coots that had bunched themselves into a kind of protective oil slick on the water. As the eagle dived, the water birds called out in a chorus and beat their wings to turn away the predator, something that seemed as effective as threatening to slap-box an armed mugger. After several dives, the eagle easily snatched one bird and injured another. The survivors swam off quickly in their feathered flotilla, leaving their crippled colleague behind, the proverbial sitting duck for when the predator returned for a second course.

And then there is the small flock of bright green and red tropical parrots who live in the park. How miserable they look in wet winter weather, clinging to the drooping Doug fir branches, their gorgeous feathers made the color of dark mildew by the damp. My bird book says such exotics—often escaped pets—never breed, but this population does. Somehow they've survived both the cold and the harassing crows. When I first saw the parrots, I took them to be the squawking harbingers of climate change. I wonder if they're at all happier during this weirdly warm and dry fall, or if they've lived here long enough to have the same sense I do, that things are slightly off.

Another day, I stumbled onto the roundup of Canada geese by government wildlife workers who are trying to thin the population of this once-rare (around here, anyway) bird that many people think has overstayed its welcome and become a pooping public nuisance. I watched as a couple of dozen were herded into a cage, then stuffed into the back of a pickup truck that had been turned into a mobile gas chamber. I will never forget the sound of those geese dying in the back of that truck, the muffled thumps as they threw their bodies against the metal walls to escape, the panicked honking that faded to silence as the gas did its work.

That wasn't the only time that man has been part of the dramas I've witnessed, nor was it the creepiest. Which brings me back to the great blue heron. As I rounded the point closer to the bird, I heard the buzz of a jet ski. I saw it racing toward the buoy. I couldn't make out who was driving it, just that it was a wet-suited stick figure of a man. He almost rammed the buoy, and the giant gray bird lurched from its perch in fright. The jet skier turned sharply—almost 90 degrees—and began chasing the heron close on its hanging heels.

Herons are huge solitary birds known mostly for their stillness. In flight, they help you better imagine what living with pterodactyls would have been like. They fly in a slow, graceful motion on wide prehistoric wings. This heron was barely able to outrun the jet ski and seemed to have trouble gaining altitude. The boater chased it around the lake, turning to follow every time the heron changed course. The bird finally got high enough off the water so that it would not be run down, but it soon looked like it might collapse from exhaustion. The jet skier persisted in chasing it for at least a quarter of an hour. At one point, the panicked bird turned back toward shore. As they came near, I heard a sound over the noise of the engine. It was the tormentor imitating the terrified bird: "Caaaaawwww, caaaaawwww," he mocked.

Eventually he gave up, and the heron escaped. I felt incredibly helpless standing on that shore with no bird cop to call, no boat of my own to give chase. All I could do was imagine being a bald eagle to that jet skier's coot, piercing his sadistic little heart with my fierce talons. Then one bird drama would have had a happy ending.

Seattle Weekly 2002

Golden Shower

Last weekend, a group of us bundled into a car at 1 a.m. and drove east to get a look at the Leonid meteor shower. The shower is an annual event, but it was more spectacular than usual this year because the earth is passing through a particularly debris-thick section of a comet's tail, meaning there's lots of stuff to burn up as it enters the atmosphere. Amazingly, the skies cleared for a little while between our November storm fronts, so the show was actually visible here in the Northwest, a place where even our August meteor showers are often blocked by clouds.

You have to drive far east these days to find darkness. A couple of years ago, my son and I set out on a similar late-night mission to see the Northern Lights—we got as far as Snohomish and still could not get far enough away from the light pollution of city and sprawl. On this night, though, we headed east toward Snoqualmie Pass to find an expanse of dark, open sky above the thickening valley mists. We pulled off I-90 past North Bend and turned onto a dark side road where other sky watchers were parked in the dark. Some of them leaned against their cars looking skyward; others watched cocooned inside big blobs of sleeping bags on the roadside.

The view of Leonid was spectacular—shooting stars from every direction every few seconds, often several at once. Not the kind that quickly flashes in your peripheral vision, but some bright and long with glittering tails that hung in the air for a few moments after the meteor had vanished. It looked as if invisible hands were striking matches against the slate-black butt of the heavens.

As I stood there, I thought about the scientific theory of panspermia, the idea that life on earth came from elsewhere in the cosmos. While many scientists believe that life originated here on earth and emerged from some ancient ooze, recent discoveries support the idea that some microbes could survive the extreme conditions of space. Researchers are finding such life forms here on earth, so-called extremophiles. They include bacteria that can live in deep-sea volcanic vents, or beneath Antarctic ice, or be revived after millions of years trapped in amber. Some microbes don't require air or food as we know it but survive by eating and digesting minerals. Some scientists believe there is fossilized evidence of such life in meteorites from Mars. There are many ways such life could arrive here. Perhaps riding piggyback on a comet or even floating down from the void of space like a soft, invisible, life-giving rain.

Too often today people don't think of life when they look at the heavens. They think of death. The Bush administration wants to militarize space; others cringe at the idea of earth-smacking asteroids that will do in humans like they did in the dinosaurs. But looking up at the shooting stars of Leonid, I felt like I was witnessing some ancient, procreative rite, watching the skies seed the egg of the earth as part of a rhythm of life that we are way too young to understand.

KUOW 2001

Sharks and Spiders and Chimps, Oh MY!

Huge black widows are on the rampage in Kazakhstan. A new species of poisonous spider has been found under the Queen Mum's home at Windsor Castle. Sharks swarm off the coast of Florida and the Bahamas, turning surfers, swimmers, and stockbrokers into aquatic Kibbles 'n Bits. A man in New Zealand mysteriously drowns in his cat's water dish. A bald eagle attacks beachcombers in New Hampshire. A chimpanzee is discovered to be making crank calls on a cell phone. In downtown Vienna, a crocodile is fished out of the Danube Canal. A snake that can only be seen by women—and disappears when it strikes—has been attacking and killing Nigerian housewives.

All these stories have been reported in recent weeks. Dog bites man, that's not news. Man bites dog, that's yesterday's news. Shark munches moronic surfer dude: that's a headline, and astonishingly, we're expected to sympathize with the surfer.

In ancient and medieval times, even later, the learned might pore over such stories looking for signs and portents, just as the ancient Etruscans sought to see the future in animal entrails, a common enough practice that there remains a word even today for a person who reads critter guts: a haruspex. Do we still find meaning in the weirdness of the animal world? Do these stories of ominous animal bizarreness reveal anything about the state of humans and nature?

Somewhere along the line we began to see ourselves as special, even divine—the animal world became our eternal Other. In Eden, we imagined that we once lived happily with other creatures. Many Northwest Indian myths tell of a time "when animals and people were one." But today, we seem obsessed by the idea that nature has turned against us. It is as if there had been a mutiny on Noah's Ark, and we, like the captain in *The Caine Mutiny*, rage like paranoids, holed up in our little cabin, imagining that everything is about us, and against us. Through the media we project our own worst attributes and fears onto the animal kingdom. Wasn't the message of the recent remake of *Planet of the Apes* that gorillas make even worse humans than we humans do?

Once upon a time, we reveled in fantasies of exploring the stars. Now we contemplate space weapons to shoot down asteroids and cower in fear of space bacteria. Once, we worshipped the sun. Today, we block it lest it cover us in cancerous lesions. Once, we hunted and gathered. Now, we genetically modify our crops as liberally as we salt our food. Once, lovers were advised to "let nature take its course." Now, nature can no longer be trusted: we must clone.

This isn't to say that human science and invention is bad, just that it is often in the hands of people who have decided that Earth isn't big enough for the both of us; that in some ultimate, impending smackdown between humans and nature, there can be only one champ. And it won't be a chimp. Even a chimp with a cell phone.

KUOW 2001

Bitch-Slapping Bears, Bigfoot, and Mystery Moss

Things have quieted down on the local bear-attack front, which Mossback has covered on a regular basis. The Boeing software developer who was recently attacked on his bike in a Kitsap County park by a bear finally described his painful ordeal to the press. The bear, however, was never caught, and officials now seem rather laid-back about bear sightings, saying that other than this one near-fatal encounter, they are at normal levels. Nevertheless, the *Kitsap Sun* warned readers in a headline: "Garbage Cans, Bird Feeders a Buffet for Bears." So, homeowners in Poulsbo: Be on the watch for smorgasbears.

Things may be dormant here, but human/bear mayhem continues unabated elsewhere:

- In Snowmass, Colorado, a man fought "a mature male, weighing approximately 350 pounds" in his garage (sounds like it could have been one of his couch-potato buddies).

- In Hickory Run State Park, Pennsylvania, a Boy Scout fought off a furry attacker (and no, it wasn't his scoutmaster).

- At Yellowstone National Park, a wide receiver for Montana's Carroll College Fighting Saints football team was chomped on by a devilish grizzly who seemed to know exactly where the player's hamstring was. The rumor is he's on the training staff of archrival Montana Tech Orediggers.

- In Aspen, Colorado, a woman was bitch-slapped by a bruin in her own condo kitchen. Apparently the leftovers were cold.

- And in peace-loving Sweden, where attacks of any kind are rare, no one is safe these days. Apparently, local bears have found that hunters go well with lingonberries, just like meatballs.

Meanwhile, there is no shortage of animal enigmas to keep us hopping in the Northwest:

- This month, scientists determined that a giant fungus in eastern Oregon's Blue Mountains is the largest living organism on earth. It is 2,200 acres in size, more than 2,400 years old, and produces honey mushrooms. Now if you could only combine its DNA with Bill Gates's, you'd have the world's biggest, oldest, and richest living organism.

- Of special interest to Mossback, scientists have also been poking around on the bottom of Oregon's Crater Lake, examining an ancient, oozing, smelly "mystery moss" that's growing there and might hold secrets about the lake's pristine waters. Maybe they'd be more pristine without ancient clots of rotting moss, is my first thought. But nature works in mysterious ways.

- In Willow Creek, California, Bigfoot failed to show up for Bigfoot Day in the "Bigfoot capital of the world." But that doesn't mean the big fella wasn't there. A native guide in British Columbia told a writer for the *Toronto Star* that the creatures are real, but, "Sasquatch is a slalocum. These supernatural beings can shape-shift into anything. Sasquatch has the ability to walk the two realms, both the physical and spiritual. . . . I've seen their footprints but I've never seen a Sasquatch. Because they can transform themselves into anything they want, they can never be caught." So, at Bigfoot Day, the guy in the giant Winnebago could have been . . .

Finally, we can be thankful that bears, Bigfeet, and giant fungi are all we have to worry about in the Great Nearby. At least we don't have—and folks, this is not science fiction—vampire dogs like they do in Texas, or amoebas who feed on human brains like they do in Arizona, or deputy-mayor-killing monkey gangs like they do in Delhi.

Crosscut 2007

In early 2008, NASA released a photograph taken on Mars showing an unidentified figure that looked remarkably like a striding Bigfoot. The image suggests that instead of shape-shifting, the Northwest enigma may be shuttling between planets. That could account for why he was a no-show on Bigfoot Day.

2008

Mist and the Muse

Now's the time of year Tim Egan gets the calls. The Northwest's *New York Times* correspondent and author of *The Good Rain* picks up the phone: "Hey, Egan, what the hell's so good about it?" callers ask. Some claim their paperback editions have swollen to twice their normal size with the humidity, creating a special expanded

Northwest edition of Egan's look at life in this far corner. "It's a freeze-dried book," Egan explains.

Despite their rain-weary whining, Egan is chipper. He relishes 4 p.m. sunsets and a December gloom that could crack the psyche of Poe's raven, because he is a member of the Clan of the Cave Bear: writers who find inspiration in the wet dark. "It forces you to go inward," he says, "to be more creative—to go into caves and tell stories."

Or something else. Another friend of mine insists winter is the "love season" in the Northwest. Sure, our month of summer is sexy, when almost everyone strips down, but in the winter, she says, we build nests, start deeper relationships, find love. Perhaps it's just another manifestation of Egan's muse: a roll in the hay with moist Gaia.

Or perhaps it's simply delusional.

Another pal, a Microsoft editor and newcomer, says, "Anyone who's proud of this rain should be shot. There's a lot of Stockholm syndrome going on." We believe we love it because it holds us hostage, he maintains. Its power over us forces us to see the world on its terms, to sympathize with it, to submit. The rain is our Cinque and we are its Patty Hearst. He points out that Northwesterners don't seek out the rain on vacations; they look for sun. If it's so nurturing, how come the little rainbirds fly off to Palm Springs, Maui, Cabo? Perhaps Egan's mood and this Microsoft cynic's case are bolstered by the fact that Egan will soon be off to sunny Tuscany to write a book: hardly a place of damp, creative caves (unless he takes up residence in an Etruscan tomb). It has produced, however, more than its fair share of love and literature.

The rain has left its mark on all of us. It used to separate the men from the boys in pioneer times. When the Oregon Trail split, the wimps went south to California and the Norse went North. They became known as "mossbacks" and took pride in their toughness. They gave up the easy life in the land of milk and honey to live in hollowed-out stumps and chase clams on the tide flats. The Northwest rain took its toll, however. It is said that Ulysses S. Grant's drinking problems started here, stemming from a stretch at Fort Vancouver. His papers and letters of that time (1853) describe unrelenting rains, floods, crop failure, colds, and cramps that wouldn't go away. He stayed indoors for months at a time. "I have suffered so much," he wrote, "that I walk like an old man of 80." His worst complaint: He couldn't get dry.

That's one characteristic of our rain that seems to be unique. My Microsoft friend describes it as "background" rain: It doesn't pour, it's simply there. A scholar at the local library describes the phenomenon as "Seattle-ing," as in, "Look, it's Seattle-ing outside." That's when you peer out the window, see that everything is wet, but you can't quite see the rain. Walk a few blocks, you're soaked.

The Puget Sound Indians have a name for this heavy "misting," roughly pronounced (and forget even trying to spell it): *chu-bash*. They also had a name for "rain that lets up a little but keeps on raining": *kat-cil*. In fact, the natives had many words for rain, wet, and water, often describing how it behaves: rain that starts, rain that lets up. No one knows the origin of the Chinook jargon word for rain: *snass* (with a short "a"). It's not Chinook, Salish,

English, or French, some of the usual contributors to the local trade patois. Perhaps it was onomatopoeic, inspired by the sound of drops hitting the top of an overturned canoe.

While researching this question, the librarian came across this phrase in Lushootseed, the language of several regional tribes. Perhaps it is onomatopoeic too, and therefore universal. The Indian phrase for "I got caught in the rain" translates as: *ukle-bitch-chug.*

"That's what I said this morning when I got to work," the librarian told me one day last week. Man, I hear you. I must have said it a hundred times myself.

Eastsideweek 1996

Weather Wimps

It's a Seattle tradition to complain about the weather, but it's also becoming a custom to complain about the way that weather is covered by local media. So let me indulge.

Why are winter "storms" newsworthy? Wind and rain hit the Washington coast! Film at 11! Snow in the passes—in December! When a couple of fronts came through last week, KING-TV quickly dispatched a reporter for a live remote from Burlington, where the intrepid journalist found just enough breeze to muss her hair. Another

reporter was sent to Westport to point out waves crashing on the beaches—oh, the humanity!—and to warn that
rogue driftwood was a threat.

Dog biting man, in the form of raindrops hitting
human heads, now seems to be breaking news. How did
we get to be such weather wimps? What kind of sissified
Seattleites have we become that we cower at the threat of
a seasonal shower? Or is there something more to it?

Our relationship with rain does seem to be changing.
This year has been uncommonly dry. Our autumn just
plain made me feel uneasy. My laden landmark poplars
weren't ready to do their big annual leaf dump until
well past Halloween. The mountains were naked. And
the poor cedars were drooping and turning brown until
the rain began falling earlier this month. Only now are
the Olympics finally looking Olympian, showing off their
ermine mantle; only now are the cedars perking up. The
Seattle Post-Intelligencer last week examined the Northwest's shrinking glaciers. Drier, warmer weather and its
long-term consequences are really the weather story we
ought to be thinking and talking about. That's much more
newsworthy than another Snoqualmie River flood watch
where moo cows might get their tootsies wet.

This points up the other huge local weather-reporting
problem—the big disconnect between long-term reality
and short-term benefit. Of course, this isn't only a weather
problem. It shows up in how, as a culture, we're always
more excited by today's benefit than the price we pay for
it tomorrow. Taxes, social security, transportation, even
war: What it means to us today is what matters; what

it means to us tomorrow is just the boring stuff. It's the Eyman and Enron mind-set.

Thus, we sit at home while the TV anchors squeal with delight because tomorrow is another sunny day, even if it's one step closer to a drought that's going to kill the fish, dry up our reservoirs, and drive up our electric bills. This is the world where every sunny day is a "nice" day or a "beautiful" day, even if it's also a day that's slowly sucking us dry of the vital, life-giving fluid that makes the Pacific Northwest what it is. Wake up, people. Water is good. Rain is good, as Tim Egan reminded us in *The Good Rain*.

It would be easy to blame it on the Californication of the local populace. Once upon a time, the people who ventured up this way were, well, a little weird. One pioneer, C. B. Talbot, came here via the Oregon Trail at the time of the California gold rush in 1849. He described the decision every pioneer family had to make about whether to continue on to California or take the fork up to the Oregon Country:

> When the Oregon road was reached nearly every man who started therein was marked down as a simpleton or an idiot, or, in some cases, not in the best state of mind, since a man who would go to a place where there was no gold—when on the other road was heaven and heaps of yellow ore—certainly a man was not right who would do such a thing. Yet the Oregonian here left the road to 'bright jewels and the mine' and went down the middle of the other to the perfume of the apple and the pine.

Imagine that. Passing by the chance for sunshine and riches for the mere scent of apple blossoms and pine needles. OK, they were going to get free land, too, but it was hardly a picnic. Anyone who thinks the Northwest Indians or the early pioneers had it easy has never spent a Northwest backpacking expedition in a rain-soaked tent. The message is clear: The greedy softies went south, the tough-ass idealists headed north. Now, either we've gone soft, or we've been invaded by Californians who've fled their smog-choked paradise to re-create it up here. These are people for whom global warming is just a way to bring the world a little more sunshine.

Yes, the weather can drive you crazy. But to move here and especially to stay here, you had to be a bit crazy to begin with. And whether or not you want to consider embracing the rain as a manifestation of Stockholm syndrome, the lousy weather is not only an integral part of our experience, it is also a force that shapes us. We can live in houses, we can shop in malls, we can drive SUVs, but the Northwest weather cannot be controlled. It will not accommodate us; we must accommodate it.

Which goes back to why a gentle breeze at Alki Point tops Eyewitless News: because it is. Even mild weather is still something demonstrably beyond our control. And in a modern world where we seek to control everything completely, even a raindrop is a headline.

We should be grateful for that still.

Seattle Weekly 2002

How Green Is Our City?

My nominee for Best Off-the-Radar-Screen Initiative is the development of a city forest management plan now being crafted as part of Mayor Greg Nickels's green agenda. In the next few weeks, the city will receive some new laser radar (LIDAR) satellite data that will help generate a three-dimensional picture of our city's green areas and how they're doing. The study will help the city identify what kind of greenery we have left and where it is.

Why does a city of concrete need a forest plan? Seattle has an estimated 1.2 million trees, and the canopy of that "forest" covers some 25 percent of the city—not untypical given our size. Still, being typical is not as good as you'd expect of an environmentally conscious city built in the middle of a vast forest.

On the other hand, the first thing our founders did after landing was put up a sawmill, so we shouldn't be surprised if we're a bit naked. Nevertheless, it's understood that trees improve the health of a city. Not only do they prettify a place, they clean the air, reduce noise, improve water quality, and prevent runoff and erosion. The city roughly estimates the value of these functions alone at more than $1 billion per year. It's probably much more. In aesthetic, spiritual, romantic, and recreational terms, it's incalculable.

But getting a handle on what's happening with our trees and habitats isn't easy. To my eye, parts of Seattle seem much greener than when I was growing up. Stretches of Rainier Avenue South evoke a tree-lined boulevard, and some avenues have "Olmsteded" nicely, in keeping with the vision of our turn-of-the-century planners. Even buzz-cut Ballard, which was cleared by Mossback's ax-wielding Scandinavian kinfolk—people who saw trees as a challenging grass to be mowed—seems to be sprouting more leaves of late.

The old growth is mostly gone, though some survives in pockets. The most impressive is in Seward Park, the city's biggest and oldest stand of original coniferous forest. The city's forester, Mark Mead, says there are trees in the park more than 200 feet tall (the LIDAR data will be more exact), and he estimates some could be as old as 600 years. They include the city's biggest Doug fir and some impressive cedars. The whole ecosystem, small and isolated, is essentially intact. What was once an island in Lake Washington is now an oasis of ancient memory in an increasingly urbanized terrain.

Old growth was still being cut in Seattle (Carkeek Park) as late as the 1940s, partly due to World War II timber shortages. Despite aggressive neighborhood planting, we're still losing trees and urban wildlife habitat to development. A consequence of density and infill is that we've been building in greenbelts and vacant lots, and the size of yards is shrinking. It would be convenient to blame chain saw–crazy judges for our vanishing trees, but development is the main culprit.

It's hard to mitigate those changes on the fly. As older trees are cut, thousands of young ones are planted, but the loss of older trees has an impact. Fewer trees are capable of hosting an eagle's nest, for example—eagles demand high-rise aeries. Fast-growing parking-strip saplings don't make up for the loss of mature trees reaching the natural end of their life cycles, any more than tree farms replace old growth. Maintaining and nurturing an urban forest requires information, management, patience, and a plan. It also requires cooperation between city departments and from private property owners. The city is working to develop a forest management plan to keep our trees healthy and to identify and improve key habitats. It will also help steer development.

Urban forest health is affected by what happens beyond the city limits. While no one I talked to is sure how the city's forest is doing overall, it's dead certain that the forest of the metro region has shrunk. Suburban sprawl is chomping away, like an infestation of caterpillars. Yet the health of these lands is important to the quality of life in Seattle. Our city's official bird is the great blue heron. Many of these birds nest and breed at the Black River wildlife refuge in Renton, according to Alex Morgan, conservation coordinator for Seattle Audubon. If we want to preserve healthy and happy herons in Seattle, we need to keep them safe in the Black River region, too.

Dennis Paulson, director of the Slater Museum of Natural History at the University of Puget Sound, is an avid Audubon birder. He's been counting birds in Seattle for 35 years. When he first moved to his current home 11 years ago, he said, he did all the things you're supposed to do to make it more bird friendly: install feeders, dig ponds, plant trees. Sadly, he's concluded that it hasn't made a bit of difference. What's happening in the larger region matters even more.

While the city's forest plan won't address regional problems per se, it will help us better understand our piece of the ecological puzzle. The new satellite data can inform city planning and yield a detailed inventory of our green spaces. That will provide the basis for knowing better how our policies affect the quality of life for everyone in Seattle, including trees, frogs, eagles, robins, otters, and beavers. They don't get to vote, but the mayor has rightly recognized an important constituency.

Seattle Weekly 2003

The city of Seattle released its Urban Forest Management Plan in April 2007. The study revealed that the city's forest canopy was actually only about 18 percent, less than half the canopy coverage (40 percent) that is recommended for cities like Seattle. A comparison of the new LIDAR data with older satellite photos suggests to Mark Mead and others that the canopy in the Greater Seattle area has been reduced by as much as half since the early 1970s, though that's not a strict apples-to-apples comparison. Most of that decline is due to tree loss on private property (more development, vanishing of greenbelts and vacant lots, more megahouses, smaller yards, etc.). The new estimate is that there are approximately 1.4 million trees in Seattle proper, and that one million have been lost in recent decades. To turn that trend around, the city plans a more detailed inventory of what's on the ground, and the mayor suggests an active tree planting program of up to 650,000 trees over the next 30 years. Tree canopy targets have been set for the city as a whole and for various neighborhoods. In addition, there's a growing realization that current regulations protecting existing trees need to offer more protection, especially under the pressure of densification. The city council has adopted new rules to protecting tree groves. Without them, the so-called Emerald City will continue to be deforested and will have to be renick-named "Clearcut City."

2008

Tragedy's Sacred Space

On the Monday before 9/11, I was hiking on Mount Rainier. It was warm and sunny and, it being a post–Labor Day weekday, I had the trails nearly all to myself. In the morning, I walked along the Ohanapecosh River to the Grove of the Patriarchs, a small biological island where 1,000-year-old trees make their home, cedars and Doug firs that have survived a millennium of fires, eruptions, and logging. In the afternoon, I walked on trails winding through alpine meadows that were still decked with fragrant wildflowers and covered with lush grass. Speckled blue grouse pecked for insects; an invisible pileated woodpecker thumped against a tall pine somewhere. At a viewpoint I watched the milky melt gush from the foot of the Nisqually Glacier, birthing a river from ice that has oozed up and down the mountain's flanks for centuries. The glacier's dirty, fragmented back resembled the spine of a massive dinosaur lying half-buried in the debris formed by its burrowing.

Some years ago, a religious fanatic decided that each of Mount Rainier's glaciers was a gate to Heaven. What with global warming, these glaciers are now all in retreat: the gates of heaven receding from us. On that day, at a place named Paradise, it was not hard to feel as if those trails led somewhere very much like bliss—or were bliss itself. I stood there feeling my size and taking comfort in it. Back at the visitor center, I'd read a quote attributed to John Muir, who had climbed the mountain early in the last century. It went something like this: When a man says he's conquered a mountain by climbing it, it's like a fly saying he's conquered your head by landing on it. This day, I took joy in being an unconquering fly.

I left Rainier that evening and drove home, determined to hang on to this day—to nourish myself on it as I returned to daily life.

On Tuesday, like everyone else, I woke to a very different reality: unspeakable tragedy, destruction, death, and sadness. I felt anger, incomprehension, fear, and grief, and still do. For solace, there are candlelight vigils, religious services, and public memorials. But these leave me cold: Churches and their preachers, and politicians and their posturing are not where I go for comfort. There is some reassurance in merely knowing the facts—perhaps that is the journalist in me. But as the days and media coverage draw on, the facts become fewer and fewer and the propaganda, scapegoating, and saber-rattling get louder and louder.

Tragedies do, for a time, create a kind of sacred space—forcing the world to stand still, giving us all an opportunity to observe life's enormous forces and take stock of our flylike scale. Markets close. Airplanes don't fly. Everyday life halts, and we wander a landscape that is uncommon. Here, that landscape is anchored by both a real and metaphysical Mount Rainier, a reminder of the power and beauty of life and its persistence through time and disaster. It also reminds us that even we flies can find bliss, if only for a moment.

KUOW 2001

Gassing Geese

I was going for a walk in Seward Park on Tuesday, late morning. As I drove in, I saw a police car and some official-looking vehicles near one of the beaches. My first thought was that it was a crime scene—I could see the silhouettes of uniformed people bent over looking at the ground. I parked and went over, curious.

What I found was a bunch of pickup trucks, a Seattle police car, and a group of men and women in blue jeans and uniform gray shirts. They had set up a kind of walkway out of mesh netting and were herding a large flock of Canada geese through it. I realized this must be part of the government's program of rounding up wild geese and gassing them. Officials say there are too many. They poop on our lawns. They contribute to swimmer's itch. This once-endangered species is now considered a nuisance, in part because it has thrived in the environment we shaped.

The uniformed folk were from the Department of Agriculture. They worked with incredible speed and stealth, like the Impossible Missions Force. They had soon herded the geese—twenty or thirty or so—into a wood-framed wire cage. The terrified geese huddled in one corner. The uniforms then backed a pickup truck up to the cage. A man entered the enclosure, wearing gloves. He began picking up the large birds by the backs of their wings, awkwardly handing them to another man who stuffed them into the truck. When there were just a few left, the last ones began hurling themselves at the wire walls to try to escape. Soon, they were all in the truck.

While the crew rapidly dismantled the cage, I noticed it wasn't an everyday truck. The bed of the pickup was carrying what looked like a large pizza oven—a large, low metal box that inconspicuously filled the truck bed. With the tailgate up, you wouldn't know it was there. It wasn't even tall enough for the geese to stand, but that was where they had been stuffed. Someone ran over with a red gas canister. And then I realized: This was a mobile gas chamber, and they were going to kill the geese right there.

Someone turned on the gas, and within the truck, you could hear the geese beating against the metal walls as the gas poured in, their panicked honks muffled. Thump. Honk. Thump-thump. Honk. I overheard one of the crew say that it wouldn't be long, and after a few minutes everything went silent. I heard someone else compliment the crew on their efficiency. A man replied that things were a lot easier when protesters weren't around.

I continued on my walk around the park. About fifty yards away, I passed another flock of Canadas. A little farther on, I came within a few feet of a beautiful flicker. Frequently I see bald eagles and herons, too. Oh, we love species when they are endangered, I thought, and we do our best to save them. But if they flourish, like the Canada geese, we treat them like weeds that need pulling. I tried imagining the mass gassing of flickers and eagles and herons, to think of these animals as pests or crops.

It is so easy to love wildlife, as long as it doesn't inconvenience us. As long as it is not truly wild.

KUOW 2001

Love and Loss in the San Juan Islands

Shaw Island sits at the center of the small spiral galaxy that forms the San Juan Archipelago. The larger islands—Orcas, Lopez, and San Juan—float gracefully around its axis.

Of the four islands that have regular ferry service, Shaw is the smallest and, despite its location, the most isolated. Orcas has many resorts; San Juan hosts the county seat, Friday Harbor; and Lopez is noted for its bikeable roads and B&Bs.

Only Shaw has resisted the outside world. For nearly thirty years, from the late 1970s until 2004, an order of Franciscan nuns ran the island's general store and ferry dock. Those nuns were the face of the island for hundreds of thousands of ferry passengers and became emblematic of Shaw's difference: Unlike the other ferry islands, Shaw was a place that could do without tourists. Shaw has no B&Bs, no amenities, no mountaintop viewpoints, no condos. It's an island without a welcome mat.

The San Juans have always attracted those seeking isolation. Most of the islands have no regular ferry service—they are private hideaways for people with boats or planes. The islands used to have a population of hermits too, people who sought escape and self-sufficiency. As a child, I remember going to visit a widow who lived all by herself on Yellow Island, now a wildlife refuge under the care of The Nature Conservancy. Her name was Elizabeth "Tib" Dodd, and she lived in storybook coziness in a driftwood cottage where her main companion was a well-thumbed set of Charles Dickens's works.

In the late 1950s and early '60s, more and more city folk from Seattle began buying summer property in the islands. Seattle is famous for its livable neighborhoods, but it was not uncommon for middle—even lower-middle—class people of that era to have a vacation home, too. It's unimaginable now, but back then a Boeing salaryman could support his family, buy a house, put his kids through college, and have a nice little cabin on Hood Canal or Shaw, all paid for with a single income.

Why would people in Seattle need to get away? Clamming, fishing, hiking, beachcombing, boating: Many of these pleasures can be found within the city limits. The real appeal was a chance to shed "the world and its shams," as the lyrics of the old Puget Sound settler's song "Acres of Clams" go. To get away and live, if only for a weekend, like the Tib Dodds of the world.

In the 1960s, Shaw Island was that place for our family. We had been visiting the islands for years. My mother's cousin and her husband, both artists, had retired and built a home on Shaw. One day, while we were vacationing on Orcas, they picked us up in their boat and took us to their property on Shaw's Neck Point. That outing changed our lives.

We fell in love with Shaw Island, all the more so because it was small and private and unglamorous. The inhabitants then were mostly fishermen or small ranchers, summer folk, even a ferry captain or two. There was a one-room schoolhouse (now expanded to two) and no social scene. Even the ferry service was irregular: Shaw Islanders needed to raise a wooden "flag" to get the ferry to stop, but sometimes on busy summer holidays, the homebound ferry would skip the island and leave us stranded. Not that we minded.

My parents ended up buying an excruciatingly beautiful, yet affordable, piece of waterfront property with hard basalt bluffs softened by thick moss. The madronas and Doug fir, old and sometimes wind-twisted, had so much personality they felt like individuals, and eventually friends. We built a prefab A-frame cabin and moved in, at least when we could get time away from work and school. We were newcomers, but we adopted the local ethic of leaving things be. Like other part-time islanders, we were eager to pull up the drawbridge behind us.

Our summers became Shaw Island summers. We spent days exploring the coastline in a skiff, walking the woods, collecting old fishing floats on the beaches. Our only social life consisted in hanging out with my mother's cousin and her husband. Margaret "Babs" Cameron was an artist who made sensuous wildlife sculptures in soapstone. Her husband, Malcolm, was an illustrator and architect who built wooden steamboats for fun. He also carved Shaw's road signs with a distinctive hand. The Camerons weren't hermits, but on Shaw they found the isolation they needed for their art.

My parents, part-time artists too, found the place stimulating. My dad began experimenting with found-object sculptures and tapped out a suspense novel, and my mother found inspiration for her poetry.

In the mid-1970s, my parents decided to retire on Bainbridge Island and sell Shaw. When my aunt died, our last link with the island disappeared. Property prices sky-rocketed. The Franciscan nuns moved to Shaw in the late '70s (eventually there were three separate orders on the island), and they represented an alienation I felt: They were guardians of a place to which I no longer had a key.

I have been back to Shaw a couple of times in the last thirty years, to my aunt's funeral and for a speaking engagement at an island writers' conference. This winter, I took my mother there for a brief visit for her ninetieth birthday. On a blustery day we drove off the ferry and across the island to our old property. We were both stunned at how little the island had changed. So often these days, development has obliterated the landscape of one's personal past. But Shaw is remarkably preserved: narrow roads, no commercialization, few people.

It's not by accident. Much of the island has been bought up by very wealthy individuals who value Shaw's low-key life. Some of the land is protected in trust. While it doesn't look like a gated community, essentially that's what it is: a place where Seattle millionaires can get away from it all.

Families like mine are priced out now. That's bittersweet, because as much as I hate the idea that I can never go back, I find solace in the fact that the island I remember endures. My mother recently told me that she would like her ashes scattered to the wind on a certain point on Shaw.

Maybe that's the only way any of us exiles can return.

Seattle magazine 2007

The Inconvenient Truth About Our National Parks

A rches National Park in southern Utah worked its late-afternoon magic on me. The sun lit the sculpted red rock a brilliant crimson, and in the glare and shadows the weird sandstone formations looked almost manmade. The arches are the least of it: There are towering megaliths that resemble the remnants of Egyptian statues, mushroom-shaped formations that look like hobbit villages. The whole place could be the sculpture park of an ancient abstract-art-loving civilization—one whose grand monuments were later blasted by the Taliban's guns.

The formula for a great national park or monument in the western United States seems to be this:

$$C \text{ (cataclysm)} + T \text{ (time)} = B \text{ (beauty)}$$

The worse the cataclysm and the longer the geological forces have had to work, the more wondrous the place seems to be. Turn an inland sea into a Sahara-scale desert, add two million years of sandblasting and erosion, and ta-da! Nature at her best.

We protect the parks for environmental reasons, but most are poster children for eco-devastation. The world was fully capable of destroying itself before we came along. In the Northwest, many of our sacred parks and monuments are the sites of volcanoes and the surrounding landscape they have annihilated repeatedly over the millennia.

Many of our parks are testaments to disasters, albeit ancient or slow-moving ones. See enough of them and you begin to root for catastrophe: meteor strikes, epic floods, volcanic eruptions, mass extinctions, earthquakes that thrust mountain ranges into the sky in a single upheaval—all leavened by wind, fire, rain, and drought. Who knew that millenarian prophecy could be so cool?

In fact, if you visit enough parks you begin to see the bright side of global warming: It might wipe out civilization as we know it, but in a few million years, the cockroaches that survive are going to have some awesome campgrounds. (Note to survivors: Be sure to book ahead on busy summer weekends.)

Gazing out at the Grand Canyon from the North Rim, you can't help but feel that Al Gore's hand-wringing over climate change is a little silly. The Grand Canyon took a billion or more years to build up, and scientists say it took a mere 750,000 or so years for the river to carve the canyon. In geologic terms, that's a flash flood. From our perspective now, the Grand Canyon is a national treasure, but it's really a monument to nature's poor land-use practices. How's that for an inconvenient truth?

Speaking of what scientists say, this brings me to another impression: Creationism makes as much sense as some of the scientific explanations you get for these landscapes.

Take Petrified Forest National Park in Arizona. According to science, hundreds of millions of years ago there was a tropical paradise near the equator that was dominated by giant alligators. Somewhere along the line, ancient forests were buried on a flood plain, infused with minerals, and turned into agates of sparkling jasper and crystal the size of old-growth logs. Then this landmass migrated from the equator to Arizona.

I like this story because it makes the border-obsessed state of Arizona itself an illegal immigrant from Latin America. But delicious irony aside, be honest: Is this account any more believable on its face than the idea that a god flicked his wrist for six days and created the world as we find it? It makes intelligent design seem like a less ridiculous explanation.

No wonder creationists are using places like the Grand Canyon for biblical accounts. To bolster their argument, read the Bible yourself. It records that the Judeo-Christian God's favorite MO was bringing down disasters of, well, biblical proportions—floods, famines, droughts, plagues, locusts—and it promises more apocalyptic destruction. Evidence of all this is enshrined in our National Park System and presented as wholesome family entertainment. God's country, indeed.

Pondering the flood damage of ancient seas in Utah, Arizona, and New Mexico, one begins to wonder if the best chance for a New Orleans recovery would be to turn the place into Katrina National Park. Forget FEMA. The government should send in rangers to maintain order and build a grand lodge so we can view the destruction in comfort. Surely it will also seem more beautiful if we give it a little time.

Say, a million years or so.

Crosscut 2007

PEOPLE

PEOPLE

The Gambler

I don't have a horse in this race. Mossback is neither Husky nor Cougar. Yes, you guessed it, I'm 100 percent pure Geoduck. I went to The Evergreen State College, where the only organized sport was stoner Frisbee.

But I have to confess some sympathy for Rick Neuheisel, the University of Washington's overpaid jerk football coach who is being run out of town on a rail for being the overpaid jerk he was hired to be.

His next coaching stop might be at Gambling State or Bill Bennett Bible College. But why are people so worked up about his apparent transgression of NCAA rules regarding gambling? For those who haven't been following the brouhaha, Neuheisel got together with a few millionaire pals and plunked a few harmless Gs down in a college basketball betting pool. The bets were substantial in laypeople's terms: Estimates are he put down about $6,400 and won $12,100, according to the *Seattle Post-Intelligencer*'s story. That bet for Neuheisel, who earns about $1.4 million per year, is in proportion to a person who makes $50,000 a year placing a $129 bet, according to the *P-I*. In other words, essentially peanuts (or about the cost of a bag of Safeco Field peanuts).

This is hardly indicative of a gambling problem, especially in a state where casino gambling is booming on reservations, where the politicians have been considering allowing big-time gambling off-reservation, and where we've come to depend on the stupidity of people (like me) who throw hard-earned cash at Lotto tickets. (I like to tell myself it's for the kids, since our school systems would be nearly bankrupt without the filthy lucre of legal gambling.)

Education in this state is partly funded by gambling revenue. Yet the highest-paid public employee in the state, who works for our most highly regarded educational institution, is dinged for betting his own money on his own time.

Some people think his gambling is unseemly; others object to the large amounts bet by Neuheisel and his friends. But if we're making this guy a millionaire for coaching a kids' game, why punish him for behaving like a millionaire kid? This is the Rick Neuheisel we hired; this is the Rick Neuheisel we overpay. Let's not punish him for having a little fun, let alone for being who he is—or being who we are.

Is he a role model? Well, he's reflecting what most contemporary adult sports fans do themselves. Just check the sports pages or sports radio stations for gambling info. It's in with the box scores. You can't avoid it whether you gamble or not.

Betting on your own sport or being involved with professional gamblers is something else entirely. Be clear: Neuheisel is no Pete Rose.

One question raised is whether the coach knew if this type of gambling activity was forbidden. Apparently, the rules were enough to confuse even Dana Richardson, the UW's person in charge of reading and interpreting NCAA regulations for the school, who apparently cleared gambling in private pools. That was wrong, and ignorance of the law is no excuse. The NCAA says the coach should have known. Plus, he has a track record of breaking or stretching the rules. He was hired to be what they call aggressive. He's been that.

And coaches *should* be aggressive, because football, after all, is a living testament to testosterone-fueled primitive violence, but in a controlled setting. Which is why Mossback likes to watch football and why football needs to be coached by people who are not necessarily people of great character. Mike Price, the former head Don't-Call-It-Wazzu football coach, lost his job at Alabama because of character issues—if you call getting sloshed in a strip bar and waking up with strange women in your room a character problem. As a Clinton lover, I do not. I call it presidential.

Nevertheless, the rules of football do not necessarily translate well into the outside world, except in war or on Wall Street. Take Howell Raines, the deposed executive editor of *The New York Times*. His hero was legendary Alabama football coach Bear Bryant (which almost rhymes with *tyrant*). Yet when Raines brought Bear's bully-boy values to the most vaunted newsroom in America, disaster resulted. Raines's reign of terror ended quickly, despite the fact that the *Times* won *seven* Pulitzer prizes last year. His biggest crime: modeling himself on the kind of jerk that wins a lot of football games.

Despite the PR job we get from boosters, alums, fan groups, and some sportswriters, what makes a good coach—or a good player—is not necessarily what makes a good citizen. We don't want to be entertained by good citizens. If we did, *Survivor* and *7th Heaven* wouldn't be TV hits. And our gladiator sports, like football, wouldn't be such big moneymakers. And yes, that includes highly lucrative college football. If a guy or gal commits a crime, as many Husky players have, fine. Punish them with the full force of the law. But if a coach breaks a rule to do something he is legally entitled to do, well, slap his wrist or even fire his butt— but please spare us the moralizing about money, gambling, millionaires, and bad behavior.

Seattle Weekly 2003

Rick Neuheisel sued UW and the NCAA, who agreed just before closing arguments in trial to settle with the fired coach for $4.7 million. In late 2007 "Slick Rick" was named the new head coach of the UCLA Bruins after a stint as offensive coordinator for the NFL's Baltimore Ravens. His salary was announced as $1.25 million per year, plus up to $500,000 in incentives. In early 2008, The Seattle Times ran a series called "Victory and Ruins" about the misconduct and criminal activities of a number of players on the Neuheisel-coached 2000 Husky Rose Bowl team. The series raised serious questions about the role and management of the university's football program and underscored the fact that winning teams are not necessarily teams of great moral character. At the same time, the UW requested $150 million in public funds as part of a planned $300 million renovation of Husky Stadium, reminding everyone that college sports and big money are inextricably tied together.

2008

John Q. Liar

In a democracy everybody has a right to be
represented, including the jerks.

—Christopher Patten, the last British governor of Hong Kong

The stumble, slide, and possible fall of Tim Eyman is one
of the most closely watched political stories of the year.
The mainstream pundits love an unmitigated collapse,
and Eyman's confession that he was taking initiative
campaign money and feathering his own nest while righ-
teously denying he was doing any such thing has made
him an irresistible target. After all, it's a man-bites-dog
story when the leader of a lynch mob hangs himself.

Editorialists have written lengthy obits declaring that
it was "ego," "greed," "hubris," and the "cult of personality" that brought about Eyman's downfall. Floyd McKay,
chair of the journalism department at Western Washington University, wrote that Eyman was a "secular Elmer
Gantry, promising salvation for the folks while lining his
own pockets and looking for ways to advance his career."
Eyman more modestly explained that he was akin to a
"Greek god."

Of course, if "ego," "greed," "hubris," and the "cult of
personality" are always a bad thing in politics, then Washington state—indeed all of America—is headed toward
doomsday on a greased luge. Certainly the corridors of
power are slippery with the stuff. Our civic monuments
are designed to look like classical temples, home to the

demigods of democracy. Tim Eyman has no corner on ego, greed, and hubris.

Nor is he the only liar in politics, which hardly needs saying.

What Eyman may have lost, perhaps fatally, is the Fear Factor. Before he became another truth-challenged politician with his hands in someone else's pocket, he was regarded by friends and enemies alike with a kind of awe—like a swaggering warlord who'd moved into the neighborhood. It's fair to say that Tim Eyman was at one point Washington's de facto governor, busily running the state while Gary Locke posed with Mona and the kids for another photo op.

The Eyman story offers a look at the perils and problems facing the modern populist. The Eymans of the world have particular, often self-imposed, burdens to bear. Their base is usually not a party or a system, so they operate without a political safety net: Fall and you fall hard. Their popularity is based upon exposing the lies of more professional liars, which makes them targets for attack. They can't deflect such assaults with armor, but they can quickly don the sackcloth of martyrdom, which is often just as effective.

Populists almost always annoy the establishment—particularly the media—because they haven't been preapproved for public consumption. Writing about Eyman's tumble in *The Seattle Times*, former editorial page editor Mindy Cameron feigned a forgiving tone but said, "What I can't do, and suggest voters of Washington state should not do, is welcome him back into the folds and creases of civic life." Of course, Cameron never welcomed Eyman in the first place, calling him a "self-empowered charlatan" back in 1999, so she can hardly pronounce his exile. Eyman's power was never conferred by the pages of *The Seattle Times* or any other newspaper. Eyman wanted their attention but never needed their approval.

The main asset of the populist, popularity, is an ephemeral thing, even more so in this age of channel surfing, speed dialing, and nanotrends. In this post-Warhol world, the torches of a peasant rebellion burn not for fifteen minutes but fifteen seconds, which is one reason why, in Eyman's hands, the initiative has become such an effective tool: It embodies point-and-click politics.

Anger is populism's fuel, but for the attention-deprived it is difficult to sustain. Nowadays, people get mad but are soon distracted by the modern world's shiny new toys. Grudges are out (think Bosnia); road rage is in (think your commute). That Eyman barnstormed the state in an SUV paid for with other people's money is an apt symbol for his road-rage-style campaigns.

Oddly, the kind of situational anger represented by Eyman's initiatives exposes a schizophrenia in the electorate that should make the Democrats pause in celebrating Eyman's demise. During the Eyman era, Democrats have begun to retake lost ground in the Legislature and have been winning in suburban swing districts. I suspect this is partly due to the fact that voters vented their rage by punching ballots hard for Eyman's initiatives—the $30 license tab makes an appealing bull's-eye—then settled down to vote for the nicer folks listed below. If Eyman sinks into oblivion, will the disaffected voters who spoke so dramatically and angrily for the GOP in 1994 make a return appearance at the polls? Eyman's initiatives seem to have been a safety valve that has taken some steam out of the Republicans.

The last point about our divided mind is that there are no populists without a following. Eyman was popular because We the People made him popular. OK, right, not you—the other guy. Nevertheless, statewide majorities gave him their votes because he offered simple solutions that promised us something for nothing. And we believed him even though the press diligently reported the flaws in Eyman's initiatives and the lies he told in selling them. By supporting Tim Eyman, his lies became our own. So as long as we're pointing fingers at liars, we must point a finger at ourselves.

Washington Law & Politics 2002

Like Mark Twain's death, Tim Eyman's political demise continues to be greatly exaggerated. His more or less permanent initiative campaign operation has indeed become the opposition party in Washington. In recent years he has scored a number of victories, including passage of an initiative (with some rare bipartisan support) to require performance audits of public agencies and also legislative passage of a law that limits property tax increases. Also, thanks to another Eyman measure, it is now more difficult for the legislature to raise taxes in general. Pretty good for a guy who sometimes shows up in public wearing a gorilla suit.

2008

Mayor Munchkin

Several decades ago, the old *Seattle* magazine ran a cover story about then-mayor Wes Uhlmann. The cover featured just the top of the politician's head and in the vast white space above it asked: "Will this man grow up to be president?" At the time the cover was provocative, but somehow in the late '60s it seemed possible that a young, growing, visionary city like Seattle could give birth to a new kind of progressive politics—one that could capture the imagination of a nation. Tacoma may have snagged the slogan "City of Destiny," but people here have always scoffed at that, as if Wazzu described itself as "Harvard of the West." Here in our "most livable, world-class city," we prefer to believe in our own hype and our own destiny.

Wes Uhlmann did not grow up to be president. Or vice president. Or postmaster general. He didn't become governor, senator, or congressman. Nor did he become lieutenant governor or even dogcatcher. Nor has any other former Seattle mayor since. Being mayor of Seattle just isn't a stepping-stone to anywhere important in politics. In fact, it leads to political oblivion—a realm opening its arms to Paul Schell right about now.

If you don't believe this, consider if the new *Seattle* magazine ran a cover featuring Greg Nickels with the "Will this man grow up to be president?" headline. Such a cover would be laughed off the newsstands—even in an era with another Bush in the White House.

So why does the Emerald City elect munchkins? Partly it is because cities—which were once a fount of new civic ideas—are no longer seen as a source of solutions. And cities have become balkanized, with no strong central leadership. Political sausage is made in the neighborhoods, way off most peoples' radar screens. Another problem is that the actual city no longer reflects the *real* city. The *real* city of Seattle is a metro area that includes most of King County, from watershed to waterfront. The Seattle mayor is just a bit player in this real city, whose sprawling, divided nature makes solving regional problems—and city problems—like transportation nearly impossible. Political leadership has shrunk as the scope of the challenge has grown, and accountability has nearly evaporated. As a result, many of the voters have become Tim Eymanized, having no faith in any government they pay for.

These are the systemic problems, but Seattle also has a particular fondness for hearing what it wants to hear, and Greg Nickels is just the man for that job. It's the "Seattle Way" he's always talking about. Greg Nickels is not a young man in a hurry, not an ambitious dynamo, not a visionary, not a sexy ex–TV commentator, not a tough-love doer. No, he is a man representative of the soft mediocrity that Seattle is always willing to settle for, a man whose vision seems to be one of endless meetings, commitment to PC process, a belief in everything lest he displease anyone. His Seattle Way embraces telling soft white lies instead of hard truths; it embraces limbo rather than leadership. He'd rather be nice than be right. He's a man tailor-made for the dead-end job of Seattle mayor.

KUOW 2002

Mayor Greg Nickels has not disappointed in the arena of general mediocrity, but he has also proven to be no softy. From early in his administration, he has fought for, and gained, more power. Born in Chicago, Nickels seemed to interpret the "Seattle Way" as being "My Way." He may be a munchkin, but he's the strongest munchkin in Munchkin Land.

2008

Brian Derdowski, Cul-de-Sacked

A Sammamish Plateau Republican once called Brian Derdowski the "John the Baptist of the slow-growth movement." Well, guess whose head's on a plate.

The King County Council member was defeated in last week's GOP primary by Dave Irons Jr. The race was filled with ironies, including this: In 1989, The Derd defeated longtime GOP council incumbent Bill Reams, a relatively moderate Republican in all things except his love of developers, over the issue of building a road across the Sammamish Plateau. Reams wanted it built but was defeated by a grassroots coalition of suburban NIMBYs and Snoqualmie Valley hippies who supported the "sensible growth" movement Derdowski led. The Derd promised he would stop such road-building nonsense, and he did.

A decade later, the issue was once again roads, with Dave Irons Jr. claiming that Derdowski had failed because the plateau was underserved. Gridlocked commuters who listened to that message played a major part in defeating Derdowski for doing what he set out to do a decade ago. Of course, he also set out to slow down the tsunami of growth the Seattle metro area has experienced in the last decade, roads or no roads. Ken Behring, the creepy California developer and Seahawks owner we all loved to hate, used to say you can't stop growth, and he planned megadevelopments like the plateau's Grand Ridge to accommodate it. But he was right: While Grand Ridge was scaled back, in part because Behring made such a perfect poster child for the Demonic Developers Fund, there were too many cracks in the growth management system to slow things down, especially in the booming economy of the last few years. Even cities designed to absorb major growth, like Redmond and Kirkland, have been choked, forced to swallow decades' worth of condos, office parks, and subdivisions in just a few years. Of course, it turns out it wasn't just the economy: A streamlined process for approving projects and a rigged county computer system did the developers as many favors as old Bill Reams (who, in the meantime, had slipped off to Olympia to work with the Republican majority in gutting the enforcement of environmental laws).

For a while, it seemed like Derdowski would succeed in his broader plan: to slow growth down to a manageable, sustainable pace. In the early '90s, other Eastside communities began to elect citizens, supported by Derdowski, who were growth skeptics: The late Georgia Zumdieck, who opposed downtown development, won a seat on the Bellevue City Council; slow-growther Rosemarie Ives was elected mayor of Redmond. On the Eastside, at least, mainstream politicians had to take "sensible growth" seriously. Concern about quality of life transcended party, and many Republicans grew to hate sprawl as they saw their suburban villages and rural landscapes gobbled up by the Ken Behrings and Weyerhaeusers of the world.

But that's an old-world memory, isn't it? By definition, growth is bringing new people—people who sign the community covenant papers and buy the cookie-cutter homes of Klahanie or one of its less charming clones. They don't remember the looping country roads, the berry farms, the horse pastures, the feed stores, the salmon streams. All they know is they're bumper-to-bumper and someone didn't build the schools and amenities fast enough to suit them. They arrived yesterday, but want a perfect place to live today.

Derdowski had seen this firsthand elsewhere. He was a child of Southern California, where the paradise of his youth was paved into a parking lot. He's among those immigrants who came here, put down roots, and decided to help create a better outcome than Seattle becoming Greater Los Angeles.

So he came as part of a tide he tried to stem, then got Californicated himself, falling victim to the new arrivals, folks living in a landscape that gives them little sense of place or context. People who take the surviving trees for granted, as if Derdowski and his followers hadn't fought for them. People who think the salmon are healthy because Issaquah still celebrates Salmon Days (might as well be Spotted Owl Week). People who've never heard of Harvey Manning and who must think the Issaquah Alps saved themselves. People who really could not care less about what is disappearing—they just want to get to Costco on time.

Derdowski's defeat should be a wake-up call for county greens. Where were they on primary day? Paul Carkeek, a Preston activist and a longtime Derdowski supporter, believes environmentalists were asleep at the switch or too preoccupied with big-picture issues. He says they often disdain the dirty trench warfare required in fighting unglamorous local battles. "The cashmere commies really screwed up big time, too full of Brie," he says. He also criticizes himself for not working hard enough. But how much could he do? In Carkeek's neighborhood, 75 percent of his neighbors voted for Derdowski—a total of 75 people. He describes The Derd's loss as "a scalding-hot mocha in the face."

Bob Simmons, who has covered the county growth wars for *Seattle Weekly* and *Eastsideweek* and is now on the board of 1,000 Friends of Washington, agrees that Derdowski's defeat "really shows the disarray and weakness of the environmental community." He's incredulous: "They couldn't round up 500 votes to save The Derd's ass?"

In some ways, it's a miracle Derdowski's ass survived as long as it did. His quirky motormouth style and *Twin Peaks*ian weirdness (harassment allegations, messy divorce, mysterious "FBI investigations") plagued him all his political years. A Derd campaign was always filled with accusations, last-minute hit attacks from opponents, ugly rumors. Additionally, he was a political platypus produced by a populist movement: a coalition that included greens, property rights folks, Democrats, Republicans, and neighborhood activists. How stable a base is that? Even his friends and allies disagreed with him half the time. His fellow Council members mostly hated his guts for his changeable positions, stalling tactics, and down-the-rabbit-hole escapades. But somehow, Derdowski made it work, and he scored many successes.

The Derd became an important part of this county's political ecosystem. He played a critical role in providing some environmental balance in the County Council, delivering key swing votes that tended to keep his colleagues from running rampant on behalf of their developer funders. In addition, though his focus was always local, his understanding of the big picture and how sensible growth cannot be disconnected from economic and cultural forces is almost unique among local politicians. He's a visionary in the genuine sense, which is why his current work against the World Trade Organization is entirely consistent with his world view and strong environmental principles. He believes those principles—which honor localism and the crafting of communities—have a power to effect positive change beyond Issaquah, Sammamish, or Maple Valley. Perhaps Derdowski, who "failed" on the plateau, can join the battle against growth at all costs on a bigger stage.

Seattle Weekly 1999

Brian Derdowski switched parties and became a Democrat. He attempted to retake his King County Council seat and failed. He now practices as a public interest consultant, sharing what he knows about grassroots organizing and "localism" with clients. He's still a part of the region's political ecosystem, albeit a much less visible one. Needless to say, the issues he raised about the consequences of growth are now front and center throughout the region.

2008

The Jerry Falwell of the Left

Scarcely had Ralph Nader left the KUOW studios last week than the producer of *Weekday* forwarded me an e-mail that read: "How long will I have to wait for Knute Berger to deliver a hypocritical condemnation of Nader's appearance on your program?"

The correspondent need wait no longer.

I would like Ralph Nader if I subscribed to the old dictum, "The enemy of my enemy is my friend." Nader has many of the right enemies, particularly corporate scumbags and their apologists who rape the environment, loot the public treasury, and screw the unwitting consumer. And I respect his desire to inject real alternatives into the political debate.

That said, Ralph Nader drives me nuts because he is a sanctimonious liar and pretends not to be. In that, he is no different from most politicians and righteous windbags who have spent 30 years in Washington, D.C., but it bugs me no end because Nader so adamantly denies that he is any such thing. He's the Jerry Falwell of the left.

Take the title of his book: *Crashing the Party: How to Tell the Truth and Still Run for President.* I find it amusing because Nader's 2000 presidential campaign was based on a Big Lie. He said there was no meaningful difference between George W. Bush and Al Gore—or their parties, which he calls the DemReps. Of course, the vast majority of voters disagreed with him. Die-hard Republicans knew there was a difference and voted for Bush; five Supreme Court justices damn well knew there was a difference and voted for Bush too. And on the other side, the vast majority of liberals, gays, blacks, women, pro-choice advocates, and union members knew there was a difference and voted for Gore. Hell, the majority of all voters knew there was a difference, and they picked Gore. But just enough did believe the lie, and Florida was lost.

The American house we live in is on fire. Gore offered us a fire hose, albeit a small one; Bush offered a can of gasoline. And Nader just screamed, "Fire!"

Like a typical politician, Nader dodges blame for his actions and says it's all for our own good anyway. It would be more honest for him to say, yes, I screwed the Democrats and I'm proud of it.

Instead, he wants their gratitude. In Nader's world, his voters didn't contribute to Gore's defeat, but they do get the credit for electing Senator Maria Cantwell over Slade Gorton. He sniffs that he hasn't received a thank-you note from the Democrats for that. But if Nader really believes there is no difference between the DemReps, why would he want thanks? Isn't Cantwell just Gorton in a skirt?

Of course she's not. She's a senator with a fire hose, not a can of gasoline. And Nader knows it, but his ego won't allow him to admit it.

Thanks for providing us with such a righteous alternative, Ralph.

KUOW 2001

Bill Clinton's War Wound

In the fall of 1972, I sat before my draft board to defend my request for conscientious objector (CO) status. One of the board members, an immigrant from Eastern Europe, leaned across the table and folded his huge, working-class hands. He was the very picture of an up-by-your-bootstraps blue-collar guy who had escaped the harsh realities of his country yet was still bewildered by some of the freedoms granted by ours, such as the right of a young man to appeal a decision by the Selective Service.

"Are you prepared," he asked, "to accept that if you are granted your request for CO status you will be marked

for the rest of your life?" To him, C and O were scarlet
letters. That I would ask for such a brand seemed to him
inconceivable.

I had applied to be a CO when I registered for the
draft as a high school senior at age 18. Shortly after, my
lottery number came up low and I was classified 1A. I
appealed, showed up for my preinduction physical, then
appeared before the board to make my case. I was willing
to do alternative service, prepared to go to jail if drafted.
I did neither. My CO status was granted, but before I was
called to build trails or empty bedpans, President Nixon
"froze" the draft. Those of us born in 1953 were the Vietnam War's last class of nonvolunteers, though few of us
were required to serve.

At the time I received my scarlet letters, I considered
my CO status to be a red badge of courage, a young man's
reward for a passionate fight for moral principles and
against an immoral war. I had marched against the war
since 1968 as a freshman at Overlake; I was perhaps the
youngest delegate to the King County Democratic convention in 1972 (we eighteen-year-olds had just received
the vote and were still a novelty) and supported an anti–
Scoop Jackson, antiwar slate. I volunteered for George
McGovern in the Oregon primary, doorbelling blue-collar
suburbs on his behalf.

At eighteen, circumstance demanded that I look within
and answer some of the deepest moral questions one can
face. Is it right to kill? If yes, who and under what cir-
cumstances? How does one best serve one's country? By
serving unquestioningly, by serving as asked but with reservations, or by refusing, as conscience dictates? What

were the principles on which I had been raised? Did they make me inferior, equal, or superior to my peers? To be a CO in 1972 was less an issue of religious upbringing than a question of what you believed and how passionately you believed it.

As anyone who lived through the Vietnam era knows, it was a time of soul-searching and extremes. Every value seemed to be up for grabs, every convention in need of challenge, every decision ultimate and defining, every stand a moral one. It was a chaotic and intolerant time, and life was full of "edge." I have friends who miss it very much, but I do not.

I am not comfortable today with some of the answers I found back then. Just as many Vietnam vets reappraised their sacrifices, so, too, have many antiwar activists reappraised the conclusions they reached on the moral battlegrounds of the home front. While I still believe the war was wrong, I would no longer describe myself as a conscientious objector. The teenager of 1972 is now 20 years older and a father who understands why his own father was driven to distraction by his son's moral certainty about every issue raised on the evening news. In the intervening years, my red badge has faded as I have worried that my evolving views have been a betrayal of genuine values and therefore, in retrospect, that my CO now stands for "cop-out."

The "revelations" about Bill Clinton's draft status raised last week* have brought so much back. As I listen to the media grill and the candidate squirm and explain, I am struck by how so few seem to remember how it was for thoughtful young men of that time. As I heard ABC's

Ted Koppel read the candidate's letter of 1969, I admired how Clinton had groped to articulate his thoughts, his feelings, and how he came by them. I admired the clear-headedness of a young man who could see the issues so fairly and could express his conflicts over them so well.

Before Bill Clinton's letter was made public, I liked his prospects, politics, and style. But like most people, I was unsure how much of the candidate was manufactured, where "Slick Willy" ended and the real Bill Clinton began. I still don't know for certain. But I do know he did not dodge or avoid anything. Bill Clinton wrestled with the central moral issues of his time and is doing so now in the glare of a national presidential campaign. I also know that a letter leaked to the press to demonstrate his lack of character has, for me, proved that he has one.

Eastsideweek 1992

*Clinton had agreed to join an Army ROTC unit at the University of Arkansas, but never attended the university or joined after he drew a high draft lottery number that made his induction unlikely.

Bones and Blonds

It's been a bad couple of weeks for Aryans. The news from their favorite obsessions—archaeology and genetics—hasn't been good.

First there is the conclusion of researchers that Kennewick Man was not a white man. Scientists examining K-Man's 9,000-year-old remains at Seattle's Burke Museum put that notion to bed.

The racial identity of Kennewick Man has been central to his celebrity and controversy. When two college students found the skeleton by the bank of the Columbia River in Kennewick in 1996, he was claimed by local Native Americans, who believed him to be a sacred ancestor.

That became a contentious issue when the first archaeologist to examine him, James Chatters, mistook his skull for that of a white settler and later announced that it had "Caucasoid" characteristics, which many translated as Caucasian. This "white" identity firmly lodged in the public imagination when Chatters and a sculptor created a "forensic reconstruction" from K-Man's skull that had him looking like Jean-Luc Picard, the *Next Generation* captain of the starship *Enterprise*.

The importance of this was in the projection we whites could make upon the bones: What if history could be turned on its head and we discovered that North America's real "first people" were white?

When the government sought to turn over K-Man's remains to the tribes for burial, scientists sued, claiming that his bones were so old it was unlikely that he had any connection with local tribes. And while the litigants didn't claim that K-Man was a white man, the burden of proof shifted to the Indians to prove he was one of theirs. They didn't succeed in court, so finally the scientists were able to examine the bones at the Burke.

They've announced that they don't believe he was white—or connected to local tribes. More likely, they concluded, he closely resembles a Polynesian or immigrants from Asia and Siberia, like the Ainu of northern Japan.

That meant that K-Man needed a public makeover. So this week, *TIME* magazine stepped up with a cover image depicting him as a pan-Asian androgyne. You might even mistake him for a young Sulu, *Star Trek*'s original *Enterprise* helmsman.

At least we now know that K-Man could fly a starship.

The two Kennewick Man portraits demonstrate that much of this "science" is projection—what we want to see in his bones. At least one of these portraits, if not both, must be total nonsense. They're also indicative of our continued fixation on race and the huge importance we attach to characteristics that are now known to be genetically insignificant and ephemeral.

Which brings us to the second bit of bad news for Aryans. *The Times* of London reports that evolutionary scientists have concluded that blond hair evolved rather quickly over a very short period in what is now northern Europe about 10,000 years ago. It was a rare mutation that was a sexual turn-on for male ice age hunters, who were in short supply because of their nasty, brutish, and short lives. Blond hair and blue eyes gave some cave gals an unfair advantage in finding rare male mates, and soon the mutation spread. (Aren't you glad science is so free of male fantasies?)

The bad news: If blond hair evolved quickly, it can also presumably disappear quickly.

To add perspective, albeit extreme perspective, I recommend a recent book by science writer and British Columbia resident Heather Pringle. *The Master Plan: Himmler's Scholars and the Holocaust* is a chilling take on the Third Reich's corruption of science.

The book tells the history of the Ahnenerbe, the SS-run institute that supervised research into the Aryan and Jewish "races" under Heinrich Himmler. Their purpose was to prove the crackpot theories of the Nazis—Himmler believed that the blond, blue-eyed Aryans came from Atlantis—by engaging in anthropological, ethnic, medical, and archaeological studies around the globe. The SS sent scholars to Tibet, Finland, and Iraq in an effort to define racial groups, search for evidence of Aryanism in other peoples, and recover artifacts that would help tell the story of the by-then-faded master race. And you thought Indiana Jones was make-believe. The Germans planned to restore the Aryan "race" through eugenic breeding and mass murder. Some of the Ahnenerbe scholars were legit but all too eager to twist their work for a research grant or to prove their own Nazi prejudices; others were crazies with the full power of the Third Reich behind them.

You can always leave it to the Nazis to provide a reminder of the hideous extremes to which some humans will go in the pursuit of an agenda. But closer to home, in more innocent quarters, *The Master Plan* also reminds us how misguided it can be to confuse our fantasies for science. And how important it is to be skeptical of both.

Seattle Weekly 2006

Kennewick Man's remains remain at the Burke Museum, where his bones have been examined by scientists. The debate over the "ownership" of ancient remains in general continues at the federal level. As to the origin of blue eyes, a paper published in the journal Human Genetics *in 2008 suggests that all blue-eyed people are descended from a single common ancestor who lived in the northwest part of the Black Sea region some 6,000 to 10,000 years ago. That means that Brad Pitt and Mossback come from the same stock, which should be obvious to anyone with eyes.*

2008

Good Men Dying

If you've lived here for a while, you know it is not uncommon to publicly mourn the loss of mountaineers. The Mount Everest deaths last month of Seattle's Scott Fischer and another local climber, while momentarily shocking, easily slide into a Northwest ritual in which we recognize the life-death cycle of those who faces nature's extremes.

Those who die on the high peaks, distant or close to home, may not always have our total approval as they take what seem to the gravity-bound to be unnecessary risks, but their deaths reaffirm something of our sense of nature and ourselves: We're proud to live in a place that produces or attracts men and women tough enough to risk everything in the wild.

But while the professional mountaineers die dramatically and make headlines, another important Northwest breed is dying off quietly.

A few weeks ago, I sat in the old Mount Baker Community Club in Seattle, attending the memorial service of an old family friend, an activist attorney named John J. "Jack" Sullivan. Jack was a local boy (Garfield High), a World War II bomber pilot, a no-apologies liberal (president of the local ACLU in 1963), and an instructor at the University of Washington School of Law where he taught would-be lawyers the art of persuasion (he headed the trial advocacy program).

Jack was a dynamic man with a huge smile. He always seemed larger than life. His motto was "Anything worth doing is worth overdoing." Jack was a man of enthusiasms.

My earliest memory of him is from 1960. The Sullivans were major Democrats, and they had a huge poster of Jack Kennedy over their front porch. I was six years old and kept hearing how "Jack" was running for president. Jack Sullivan was charismatic and proud of his Irish heritage. He had a zest for life and a big, beautiful family.

I confess that for a time I thought Jack Sullivan and Jack Kennedy were the same man; I couldn't understand why, if Jack Sullivan was running for president, my folks were for Nixon.

Jack also had a quality that was common to his generation: a love of the outdoors. Baby boomers and Gen Xers love the outdoors too, but often as a place to test endurance or conspicuously consume. Yuppies pay $60,000 a head to climb Everest with pros like Scott Fischer to prove something to themselves and to gain a trophy few will ever possess. Slackers seem to regard nature as one big Mountain Dew commercial.

But Jack had this old Northwesty cornball style of enjoying the outdoors: a cabin on the Sound at Redondo Beach, a love of campfires and campfire songs, and a habit of wearing certain grubby, Huck Finn–style clothes when enjoying the beach or backcountry.

What occurred to me as I sat at Jack's service was that he was not alone in these traits. These last few years I have attended the memorial services of a number of wonderful men who shared them: local roots, life-defining WWII service, social activism, and a love of roughing it. Guys who didn't give a damn about climbing Everest but loved to chop wood, build fires, haul driftwood, or go gunkholing. Guys who camped with army surplus stuff and who appreciated this peaceful use of wartime gear.

I think of the late Harry Truman (not the former president or the Mount St. Helens character), a big, beardless Paul Bunyan of a man who started Hidden Valley Camp near Granite Falls. He and his wife, Imogene, were well-known Seattle activists who founded what is now a Northwest institution that has introduced several generations of local kids to woodcraft and the folk music of Woody Guthrie. And I think of my late father-in-law, Bill Terry, a product of Madison Park (when it was working-class) and Garfield. He served in the 10th Mountain Division. He was active politically and an inveterate sailor who had explored much of Puget Sound by the age when today's boys are taking up skateboards.

If you're lucky, you too have known men like these, men who helped build a better Northwest without pretensions, men who loved this place like boys, not hip consumers. They are old-growth guys of a generation that can't be replanted.

Eastsideweek 1996

The Passion of Peter Steinbrueck

It's a funny thing to watch the kids you went to high school with grow up and, in some cases, become important people. In December they had a good-bye party at City Hall for Peter Steinbrueck, who is wrapping up a decade on the Seattle City Council. He chose not to seek reelection. Peter will be diving back into his first passion: He'll be teaching this winter at the University of

Washington's College of Architecture and Urban Planning and hanging out his shingle as a consultant in sustainable urban design. He also plans to write and do radio commentary.

I first got to know Peter when we were students at Lakeside, the North End prep school famously known as Bill Gates's alma mater. In that era, we were explicitly told that Lakeside was charged with grooming the next generation of civic leaders. There's an apocryphal story about Lakeside kids cheering at a basketball game they were losing: "That's all right, that's OK, you'll all work for us someday!"

That wasn't hard to believe when classmates and alums had names like Pigott, Weyerhaeuser, Blethen, and Nordstrom. Peter's dad, Victor, was famous too, but he wasn't a timber or retail baron; he was a well-known troublemaker, the guy credited with mounting the citizen insurgency that saved the Pike Place Market. Peter was not a trust-fund kid but a classic long-haired, surly, smart, funny, and angry young man. You'd hardly have picked him for the guy who'd be most likely to look good in a suit and tie accepting a plaque for a decade of City Council service.

But there he was. Handsome in a dark suit, a man who looked younger than he should at 50. The hippie bangs that used to fall over his face were long gone. A sign on the wall posted by his family declared, "Welcome back, Dad." His wife and kids were there, his two teenage sons providing the evening's musical entertainment, one in a jazz combo and the other giving the crowd of well-wishers a brief Beethoven piano recital. No one seemed like a political prop: You sensed that here was a bright, loving family that was happy to celebrate Dad's return from politics.

Despite the picture of respectability, Peter has never really lost his edge, his ability to piss people off, his concern for the homeless, for affordable housing, for the environment, for building a city that is not only beautiful and green, but socially just. Never considered a team player on the council, Peter often angered his fellow council members by going his own way. As council mates Nick Licata, Jan Drago, Richard Conlin, and staffers and associates stepped up to the microphone to pay tribute, the word they all seemed to use was "passion." Though Peter can cite the details of the city's land use code, he isn't really a wonk. He's a guy driven by deep feeling about what kind of city Seattle ought to be.

That city, he suggests, is not unlike the Pike Place Market, which is now inextricably tied to the Steinbrueck name. Both father and son have saved it from ruin, Victor from the city fathers who sought to tear it down and Peter from the New York investors who planned to carve it up. Seattle can be vibrant, diverse, habitable for rich and poor, deeply rooted in history and unabashedly urban. The market isn't just the soul of the city but a road map of how we can once again become a city for all people, how we can grow without losing our essential character. Some of Peter's greatest work on the council—fighting over building heights or to preserve industrial lands or working for affordable housing or pushing for an eco-friendly comprehensive plan—all come back to this vision.

In that, he may have been unique on the council, not simply for having such a clear vision for the city but also the training, as an architect, to see how it could all come together, one saved landmark, one low-income apartment, one line of code at a time. I asked City Council President Nick Licata who will take Steinbrueck's place in the council ecosystem. No one, he answered. Peter's departure, he said, will "shift the ecosystem."

So, too, the ecosystem of Steinbrueck's life. Peter told us that he had a dream that he was floating on a river through a complex urban landscape, whooshing and bouncing along as he pointed out various buildings and landmarks. He suddenly plunged into a watery abyss. When he landed, he was floating in a beautiful, natural pool surrounded by forest. He felt calm and at peace.

The wild ride, he said, was a metaphor for Wild Waves (every parent knows Wild Waves), and Wild Waves symbolized his City Council career. He's had a wild ride and is now headed for a pleasant respite from the rapids and whirlpools of city politics—features that are nicely represented, by the way, in the man-made creeks and fountains of the new City Hall, which gush and crash through their courses, much like the waters on Madison Street during last year's 100-year storm.

Given his youth, energy, and passion, I don't think anyone thought they were saying good-bye to Peter. In fact, he says emphatically, "I do not plan to 'retire' in any way from civic life, ever!" He's still a maverick, but now one with ten years of training in the ways of city government, an outsider with insider's savvy. As such, Peter Steinbrueck leaves the council more dangerous than when he joined—and that's a good thing. He can now pick and choose his battles (he's committed, for example, to making sure the waterfront becomes viaduct-free). He can help rejuvenate the city's activist corps, and he has the résumé (and suits) for a credible establishment takeover. Many of Steinbrueck's political friends believe he's still the best alternative to another Greg Nickels mayoral term or is at the very least well-positioned for the post-Nickels scramble, whenever that occurs.

He won't float in that sylvan pool forever.

Crosscut 2007

POLITICS

POLITICS

Kids Just Love Trains

Now that so many other columnists around town are calling for a quick mercy killing of the People's Boondoggle (aka the Seattle Monorail Project), Mossback can turn to the bigger picture.

Recently I noted in this column that *The New York Times* has reported that Seattle is the second most childless city in America. But I now think the reporter got it all wrong—Seattle is the city with the fewest adults.

Our whimsical obsessions were a lot more charming when we were younger and could do less damage. *Waiting for the Interurban* never hurt a soul. But now the city of Peter Pans has morphed into a lummox of a child, not a nine-hundred-pound gorilla but a nine-hundred-pound Baby Huey doing billions of dollars of damage to itself because it will not be denied its whims, including a monorail—even at $14 billion and counting.

Personally, I'd like one question answered: Who gave Baby Huey the credit card and the freaking car keys? Doesn't that qualify as reckless endangerment? Is someone going to call the Department of Social and Health Services? Our civic inner child needs a foster home.

In answer to the first question, I do have a list of prime suspects.

One is Mayor Greg Nickels, a guy who just can't say no. The mayor likes all big projects and thinks there's magic money to pay for them—even when Aunt Patty Murray, our senior U.S. senator, has to slap naughty

Greg's wrist and tell him "No!" when he begs for $1 billion in federal funds to bury the Alaskan Way Viaduct in a tunnel. Greg, the Mom in Tennis Shoes knows that when you're around, she's got to lock up the pork rinds! Nickels has redefined the "Seattle Way" as "My Way," and his way features an endless appetite. In short, he's a role model for irresponsible excess.

Another group of suspects is the Seattle City Council, which considers Dr. Spock a civic role model. (That's *Dr. Benjamin* Spock, not *Mr.* Spock, though I guess either would work. One is the baby-care guru blamed for spoiling a generation of baby boomers; the other is a guy who will do anything for Vulcan.)

The City Council is chock-full of poster children for *Who Wants to Be a Gutless Wonder?* Even those on the council who claim to be holding Seattle accountable find a way to cave when it counts. Last week, council member Richard McIver was quoted in *The Seattle Times*: "Councilman Richard McIver, a monorail skeptic, called the latest [monorail cost] figures 'extremely disturbing.' But McIver said he would respect the will of the voters, as long as the city is not held liable for any monorail problems. 'It's not my place to overturn the votes. I'm not going to lay my body across the track.'"

What kind of leadership is it to say: OK, kid, go kill yourself, just don't spatter your brains on my carpet?

The City Council is specifically tasked with reviewing the viability and sanity of the monorail project before allowing it to eat up the public rights of way. It is the job of the reluctant McIver and his colleagues to throw themselves on the tracks if it will save us from a multibillion-dollar boondoggle. But if so-called critics like McIver aren't willing to make any political sacrifice to save the city, the fight is already lost.

Another group of suspects is the Seattle Monorail Project (SMP) board, the people specifically charged with keeping the project on track. They've already signed off on the Kool-Aid–stained bidding process. SMP head Joel Horn says they can pull the plug, but does anyone think they'll have the nerve to kill the thing they love? Did Dr. Frankenstein?

Let's look at their record. According to the SMP Web site, the board adopted the following goals: to make sure the project was on time and under budget, would break even on operations, would have excellent design, would remain true to its grassroots history, and would be transparent and accountable to the public.

What we have is a project that, by SMP's own admission, will be years late; will cost billions; is already millions of dollars over budget; will indenture our children and grandchildren; offers clumsy, stripped-down design; and whose accountability and transparency have been in question since day one. Can we really expect more excellence from their oversight?

It should also be pointed out that part of Seattle civic parenting now routinely includes "outsourcing" responsibility for major projects by creating separate public "authorities" to oversee them. It allows the mayor and City Council to run for cover when things go bad with the baseball or football stadium, the Port, public transportation, the monorail, the Pike Place Market, or the Seattle Center. Hey, not my department, they can say. They've outsourced accountability until there is none.

Lastly, as Edgar Allan Poe wrote, there are "the people, ah the people / they that dwell up in the steeple . . . they are neither brute nor human / they are Ghouls!" As a devoted Hobbesian, Mossback agrees: The people are incorrigible. But they are also crying for help. They are desperate for some good old-fashioned parenting, and they are begging for leadership that offers common sense, direction, discipline, and progress. The state is undertaking an intervention as state Treasurer Mike Murphy and state Auditor Brian Sonntag step in to get hold of the runaway monorail. But we need full-time parents, not state-appointed babysitters.

Has the last adult left Seattle? Did he or she leave a night-light on? Or is Seattle truly, finally, actually a "Kid's Place" at last?

Seattle Weekly 2005

The Monofail

The Seattle Monorail Project teeters on the brink of collapse. The long-negotiated plan is discredited; the financing options are a nonstarter; the chief proponents, executive director Joel Horn and SMP board chair Tom Weeks, have resigned in disgrace—exposed as the premier flimflam men of River City on the Sound.

The best SMP has been able to do, despite Herculean efforts, is offer a single-bidder project scaled back, bulked up, $400 million over budget, years late, and based on an already onerous tax that is insufficient. We faced the prospect of paying, when all the borrowing was done, more than $11 billion for a $2 billion system. That was the downplayed official estimate. A more realistic projection would put the cost at more than $14 billion. None of that included the operating expenses of a train that, like every other transit system in the country, would be unlikely ever to pay its own way.

SMP has turned a populist dream into a giant turd in Seattle's punch bowl.

Not everyone sees it that way. As we speak, people are mobilizing to save the new monorail. They are fighting among themselves. A Kool-Aid hangover is wicked, and the recriminations are spilling out on the bulletin boards and e-mail lists run by the faithful. Some support a re-vote. Others demand a re-bid. Others suggest fixes, minor and major: Raise the motor vehicle excise tax to eliminate the need for high-interest bonds, or reshuffle the elected and appointed monorail board.

And some, like the recently departed Weeks and Horn, seem to be in deep denial that there is anything wrong with the rejected financing plan. They see themselves as the victims of the lies and spin of monorail opponents who have exaggerated the problems. By the monorail dreamer's usual ever-optimistic logic, this disastrous plan

221

is the best of all possible plans. The dream is within reach, and they see SMP's troubles as merely a public relations problem.

And that's been the problem with monorail leadership all along: an inability to distinguish engineering from spin, public policy from flackery. This project of steel and concrete has been built by top management and its enablers on the SMP board over a foundation of hot air. And they've been rewarded for it.

No wonder Horn says he went into the Fourth of July weekend intending to stay on. No wonder Weeks has been surprised by the near-universal opposition to the plan. After months of feeding us bullshit, why wouldn't they believe Seattleites would swallow the last big dose? The monorail board seems stunned by the turn of events, clueless about public outrage and about fundamentals of the project. They are a group that has reveled in ignorance and rewarded the men who've kept them in the dark. The only mass transit they should be involved in is a mass resignation. It is unfair for Horn and Weeks to take the fall for the whole gang.

The monorail could be saved, but it would take some doing on the part of true believers: a plan and budget for a city- or region-wide, publicly-owned-and-operated system; a robust design for truly rapid transit (a maglev train?); a longer, more realistic time frame; a new and sound tax proposal; a revamped board and oversight, and perhaps a merger with an existing transit agency; adjustments to the route (like ditching the insane shortcut through Seattle Center); a budget that includes ample contingency and mitigation money; and a way to preserve and incorporate the current (and historic) Alweg line into the system. Such a plan would also have to be judged in light of the city's other pressing needs, but if it had all of the above, proponents might be able to make a reasonable case for a $14 billion (or more) project. Despite what some are saying, the problems with SMP and the Green Line can't be fixed with a re-bid and a sharpened pencil, let alone a board that's asleep at the switch.

The more sensible solution, though, is to close up shop. Now. Let this be a $100–200 million lesson, instead of a multibillion-dollar folly.

Realized or not, the monorail will be one of those moments that define the city. If the project gets back on track, it will transform Seattle culture and politics forever. Whether a success or a boondoggle, the impact will be felt for generations—like the regrading of Denny Hill or the digging of the Lake Washington Ship Canal.

If the monorail project crashes and burns, that impact, too, will be felt for decades to come. This moment will be remembered either as a time when the city came to its senses or missed a New York–Alki opportunity to catapult Seattle to a higher level. The Green Line could go down in civic history as one of the great might-have-beens, like the voter-rejected Bogue Plan that was to remake downtown or the R. H. Thomson Expressway's ramps to nowhere.

Despite the quirky, populist origins and impetus of the monorail movement, both friends and foes admit the vision's power. And both reserve the right to say, "I told you so."

Seattle Weekly 2005

The Little Landmark That Could

November was April for monorails—the cruelest month. On November 8, Seattle voters euthanized the bungled Green Line, ending the rise-above-it-all dreams of a new generation of monomaniacs. Then, on November 26, the venerable—and sometimes venerated—historic Seattle Center Alweg monorail trains crashed, a seemingly impossible feat given that they run on separate tracks.

The collision appeared to be operator error. The folks who run the Seattle Center monorail have known for seventeen years of a design flaw that put the two tracks too close together when a stretch was rebuilt in the 1980s to accommodate Westlake Mall. I know, I know, it's hard to believe that any project in Seattle would compromise its integrity to cater to commercial interests, but there you are.

The monorail's operators have successfully worked with the flaw for nearly half of the monorail's life (it's been running since the 1962 Seattle World's Fair) by making sure the trains never passed each other on the narrowed stretch near Westlake. Until now.

After this latest accident, some of the monorail's weaknesses have become a hot topic. While inspections of current damage continue, it turns out that Seattle Monorail Services, the private company that runs the line, is suing its previous insurance company over an earlier incident—the 2004 mechanical failure that resulted in an onboard fire and shut the system down for many months. That breakdown cost the operators more than $4 million in repairs and lost revenue, according to insurance claims.

Two accidents—both requiring evacuations—a design flaw, and an aging infrastructure have raised concerns.

For some, the latest crack-up is the final straw. *Seattle Times* columnist Nicole Brodeur became unhinged at the menace hanging over our heads. In a recent column, she described the fortysomething monorail as "decrepit" and worthy of having life support pulled. "Instead of putting more money into resuscitating the monorail," she wrote, "the city should expand the streetcar line," by which she means new streetcars that South Lake Union property owner Paul Allen and developers are getting in that part of town.

Longtime anti–Green Line activist Geof Logan fired off a letter to the Seattle City Council questioning the monorail's "costly pattern . . . of breakdowns," saying the train has "clearly exceeded its optimal lifespan." His main concern is that the city will throw money at the monorail based on sentimentality instead of a hard-nosed look at the future. One of Logan's fears appears to be that the Green Line monomaniacs might begin to lobby for upgrades and expansion of the Seattle Center line as a way to get a city-wide system back on track.

Ironically, it is the death of the proposed Green Line from Ballard to West Seattle that has given a new lease on life to the Seattle Center monorail, which would have been disassembled and replaced upon completion of the new system. Seattle's love for the old monorail was used by Green Line backers to get support for their project, which they sold as an expansion of the original. But the city's love was conditional. Seattle was willing to dispose of the older icon if, in return, it got a shiny new system. Now that it turns out we can't afford the new model, the Alweg continues in the role of providing rapid transportation between Seattle Center and the downtown retail core for 2.5 million passengers a year.

But can we afford even that?

Seattle Monorail Services (SMS) partner Stuart Rolfe is adamant that we can. What does he say to suggestions that we tear down the Alweg? "It's completely asinine."

Rolfe argues that the city isn't being stuck with repair bills—SMS is covered by insurance, and the profit the system generates for the operator and the city, which amounts to about $800,000 per year, is divided equally.

"They're not making sense," Rolfe says of critics. "It's an asset of tremendous value to the city, one of the few transit systems that makes money." He points out that despite the two recent accidents, there's been no death or major injury on the system, something virtually no other municipal transit system can claim. SMS can make safety improvements to the line—perhaps even install a kind of fail-safe system that would prevent future collisions along the too-close sections of parallel track. Even without that, they've moved millions of passengers on tens of thousands of trips over four decades without many incidents.

As to the general condition of the trains, Seattle Center spokesperson Perry Cooper claims that up to the time of the latest accident, they were in the best condition ever.

After the 2004 fire, the trains were significantly upgraded and made safer, at substantial cost. Someday, we might be asked to invest more in the line, especially now that we know it's going to be the city's only monorail. Logan's right that we have to ask tough questions, but the starting assumption should be that preserving the monorail is a priority, not a burden. It's an important landmark, part of the civic ecosystem that includes the Space Needle and Seattle Center. It's not a derelict or a relic. It continues to serve a real public service, and it mostly pays its own way.

There aren't a lot of landmarks that can claim that.

Seattle Weekly 2005

In January 2008, after selling its properties, disposing of its signs on eBay, and paying its debts, the agency that would have built the Green Line officially went out of business. Its last act was to send King County a check for more than $400,000 to help pay for transit in the Ballard–West Seattle corridor, which the monorail would have served. Meanwhile, the aging 1962 Alweg keeps chugging along, though with continued service interruptions and long-term maintenance needs. It is still the critical link between downtown and Seattle Center.

Mass transit in Seattle is making slow progress. The most recent addition is the South Lake Union Streetcar, more popularly known as the SLUT (South Lake Union Trolley). It takes people from downtown and drops them off at the end of the line near Hooters. There is talk of expanding the streetcar to perhaps serve a more useful purpose, if one can be found.

2008

Republicans in the Rain: Don't Dissolve Just Yet

Tucked under the lanky mushroom we call the Space Needle is a waterlogged shire packed with hobbits who mostly vote Democrat. Seattleites, in fact, are among the most liberal in America: George W. Bush won nearly half the national popular vote posing as a "compassionate conservative" but garnered a measly 20 percent in Seattle. Republican state party chair Chris Vance says Seattle is populated by "limousine liberals . . . intellectually committed to left-wing ideas."

But is Seattle really unassailable? Is the region's political and financial capital doomed to be a one-party town, a Berkeley with rain?

I say "doomed" because no major American city ought to run without a mainstream party of opposition to keep it honest. Even in Democratic strongholds such as Los Angeles and New York, citizens have found ways to elect candidates who buck the status quo. If biodiversity is essential in nature, why not also in politics?

In that light, the 2001 mayoral race between Greg Nickels and Mark Sidran offered a look at the form a successful opposition party could take; Republicans especially should pay attention.

Though officially nonpartisan, the mayor's contest nevertheless matched men with differences that often distinguish conservative and liberal candidates. Sidran, the city attorney, was known for being big on enforced "civility," at least as defined by his readiness to roust street people and prosecute WTO miscreants. His major campaign issue was criticizing the region's current public boondoggle, Sound Transit, a well-meaning megaproject troubled by mismanagement and cost overruns.

In contrast, Greg Nickels loves Sound Transit as he loves almost every other public project. The longtime Democratic King County Council member embodies the city's liberal status quo. He promised to manage according to the "Seattle Way," which presumably involves saying yes a lot more than sourpuss Sidran would.

Sidran's tough-guy reputation gained him a name but also big negatives. Many social activists had him tagged as "Satan" or "Seattle's Giuliani," back when that was a bad thing. During the campaign, one Web site portrayed the Jewish Sidran with a swastika over his face. Worse, he was accused of being a closet Republican. Proof lay in prominent GOP supporters and donors, including developer Kemper Freeman Jr.; former Governor John Spellman; and Mike McKay, deputy chair of George W.'s state campaign. Sidran denied being a Republican, and his Democratic supporters came to his defense. State Representative Ed Murray, a gay Democrat who endorsed Sidran, defended the candidate, saying, "Only in Seattle would a pro-choice, pro-gay-rights Democrat be accused of being a right-wing Republican."

Still, that "right-wing Republican" came within 3,000 votes of getting elected, taking home 49 percent of the vote.

So could another "Sidran" do better? One with similar ideas but more charisma?

Yes, particularly if you believe politics is cyclical. Once upon a time, Republicans were *the* progressive force in Seattle—back when Jean Godden was in pigtails and our rivers writhed with salmon. The local GOP could still be revived if it were to capitalize on several factors.

First, the gentrification of the city, its affluence, and the aging of its large base of homeowners bode well for candidates representing so-called traditional values.

Second, the city's devotion to neighborhood rule is inherently conservative, seeking to move control to the local level (liberals call it "empowerment"). In fact—and the hobbits won't like to hear this—it's the domestic version of Pat Buchanan's foreign policy.

Third, Seattle has more than a little Singapore in its soul. Paul Schell's inability to keep things under control during Mardi Gras and the Battle in Seattle did him in. Public safety will continue to be a major concern, and electable law-and-order types, like King County Sheriff Dave Reichert, remain popular.

Fourth, a successful Republican-style candidate would have to have "a strong, decisive leadership style but not be dragged down with ideological baggage," says John Arthur Wilson of Pacific Public Affairs, a Sidran campaign adviser. That could mean one of those now-rare birds—a Dan Evans–style liberal Republican. But it could also mean a maverick whose character transcends category. A very enthusiastic crowd greeted John McCain when he toured Puget Sound with Edith

Williams, Teddy Roosevelt's granddaughter, during the 2000 primary campaign.

Fifth, Seattle's GOP used to be the party of reform. In the late 1960s and early '70s, those reformers included prosecutor Chris Bayley and city attorney Doug Jewett cleaning up police corruption, state legislator Joel Pritchard leading the fight to liberalize Washington's abortion laws, and a City Council stocked with promising young Turks ready to shake up City Hall. Seattle still needs plenty of reforming and watchdogging.

Of course, independent money would help, as it did in the case of Michael Bloomberg, who spent nearly $70 million of his own stash to become GOP mayor of New York. Decades ago, large fortunes were rare in Seattle; today, many potential war chests sit in the vaults of the Midas class.

Chris Vance is already combing the shire for candidates. "A major party should never concede anything," he says, promising to field Republicans in every Seattle legislative race next time around. He hopes to recruit blacks, Asians, and Hispanics, and he swears the Big Tent party still lives. "One mistake is we forget sometimes that all politics are local, and that Ballard is different from Yakima." In the future, the litmus test for Seattle Republicans may be not whether they are true believers, but whether they're creative enough to find a way to win in a hometown where they're no longer entirely at home.

Washington Law & Politics 2002

If anything, Seattle is more of a one-party town than ever. Though it remains a place with a scolding inner nanny somewhere in its civic brain—crackdowns on nightclubs, strip joints, and street people keep occurring fairly regularly—it is still not very supportive of Republicans of any kind. A few exceptions: former U.S. Attorney John McKay received positive press coverage and local-hero status after he was fired by the Bush administration and took a lead role in criticizing the Justice Department under Alberto Gonzales (who later resigned). And in 2007, after the untimely death of longtime Republican King County Prosecutor Norm Maleng, voters elected as his replacement Dan Satterberg, a fellow moderate Republican. A confessed Republican was also elected to the Seattle Port Commission that year.

Meanwhile, Seattle's suburbs have been turning increasingly Democratic. A number of key Eastside Republican legislators have switched parties and GOP politicians are finding it increasingly difficult to count on the suburbs as safe turf.

Seattle proper still has no effective opposition party on the right or left. A political alliance of environmentalists, developers, and labor has solidified during the Nickels years and neighborhood activism has ceased to be a citywide, independent force, at least for now.

2008

What the Right Does Right

In the Soviet of Seattle, the far right often seems like a distant dog barking in the night. Most of us tune out right-wing radio and Fox TV and live in neighborhoods chock-full of anti-Bush signs. Last weekend, there was a John Kerry bake sale on almost every block.

But in this burg of best liberal intentions, it's time to give some credit to those on the other end of the political spectrum—especially the far end. The conventional wisdom is that the most interesting politics are in the middle, where red- and blue-state Americans agree and where majorities are forged. This turf is where, increasingly, both the Democrats and Republicans find themselves fighting for hearts and minds.

Yet that's not often where the most principled or provocative discussions occur. I'm much more interested in where the far right and far left find common cause. It's out on the farther reaches of the spectrum that the more interesting critiques take place. Where the two ends meet, left and right, there's the possibility of a political spark.

Globalization is one such area. One of the chief critics of globalization is Pat Buchanan—no turtle he—who was in Seattle during the 1999 protests against the World Trade Organization and still writes powerfully and effectively against the imperial pretensions of the Bush administration. Many of the old left support a kind of globalization—a Marxist one. Republicans and Democrats support a vision that seems to boil down to this: one world, one market.

But for many on the far right and pro-union left, globalization poses a threat to peoples and cultures whose value transcends economics. I might disagree with Pat Buchanan about which are the most important American values, but at least we agree that America should be a values-driven country, not a money-driven one.

Earlier this week, I attended a forum at Town Hall on the effects of globalization and outsourcing on our region. It triggered a frustration that I have around these topics. Per usual, the discussion was couched mostly in the economic terms that suit the business and political interests who want us good and worried about job security and the state's "competitive" climate. But these discussions rarely get down to actual values. What kind of city or state do we want to live in? What does the land mean to us? How do we protect those things that are important to us but cannot be commodified? Both major political parties have painted "protectionism" as an evil thing. The suggestion is that anyone who wants to protect a way of life—anyone who isn't willing to fully submit to the free market—is somehow harming America. How? By jeopardizing our right to buy cheap stuff at Wal-Mart?

This also leads to the subject of corporate welfare, which has enthusiastic bipartisan support in this state. Virtually all our most powerful elective leaders—Democrat and Republican alike—supported the recent multibillion-dollar Boeing giveaway. Of the major candidates for governor, only Democrat Phil Talmadge has come out swinging against the Boeing deal. But it's interesting to me that the major player in Olympia demanding accountability was former state legislator Bob Williams and his conservative government watchdog group, the Evergreen Freedom Foundation. It led the way in getting the state to more fully disclose what we taxpayers are on the hook for and how the deal came together. While I may not agree with the free-market philosophy of this group, their insistence on disclosure was a public service. And their doggedness grew out of a long-standing skepticism about public spending, tax policy, and the fundamental honesty of government—skepticism that is not misplaced and ought to be thoroughly bipartisan.

Education is another arena where conservatives are helping push the envelope. My children—both doing well in college—were homeschooled after grade school. That kind of education might not have been possible in this state were it not for the Christian right's activism in getting our homeschooling laws liberalized and helping citizens regain the right to educate their own children. For that, I am grateful. The far right has also been active in fighting the proliferation of drugs like Ritalin in public schools. We've turned our schools into medicine cabinets, a trend symptomatic of an increasingly pharmacologically dependent society where drugs are prescribed by authority figures to regulate behavior in controlled settings (getting us ready for the chronic depression induced by the typical workplace, no doubt). One of the leading crusaders against the drugging of America's youth has been cultural conservative columnist Phyllis Schlafly. More recently, conservatives have helped keep the pressure on for charter schools that, I believe, have the potential to demonstrate important reforms for the rest of public education. Instead of fighting them, the state's teachers ought to be embracing charters and the kinds of freedom, energy, and experimentation they represent. Their resistance is a result, I think, of the fact that they too are victims of a sick system.

Does it sound on some level like I miss the culture wars? Well, I'd much rather debate fundamental values than see the world devalued by economic interests. If that means arguing about God (I don't believe in him!), gays (marry them!), and guns (I own them!) rather than fighting imperial wars and sacrificing American sovereignty for corporate wealth, then yeah.

Seattle Weekly 2004

Yearning for a Strongman

Every time the Puget Sound region's powerful are thwarted, the cry goes out for a strongman. Would that someone could lead us out of the Valley of Confusion and Consensus! Our process is broken, our future grim, the villagers are running amuck and consorting with that damnable Tim Eyman again. The voters just don't know what's good for them!

It reminds me of that old line about the guy who asks a group of marching people how he can get to the head of the parade. "They need me up there," he says, "for I am their leader."

Strongman talk is rampant in the wake of the failure of Proposition 1, which would have funded a farrago of road improvements and transit options. The power players are pumping the creation of a regionwide über-agency that would take charge of the transportation "mess." Why this new über-agency would be any more successful than all the "old" regional entities (Sound Transit, the Regional Transportation Investment District [RTID], Metro, the counties) is unclear, but there is certainly a belief that no one is *in charge* around here.

Flash back to a power luncheon at the Olympic Four Seasons Hotel in the mid-1990s. Somehow, I was seated near the powerful lawyer Judy Runstad. The name of General Norman Schwarzkopf was mentioned and Runstad swooned. "Norman Schwarzkopf for president!" she burbled, apparently giddy at the idea of Stormin' Norman whippin' America into shape just like he chased the Iraqis back to Baghdad. (A Schwarzkopf motto: When in command, take charge!)

She hasn't been the only civic leader attracted to a he-man.

The argument goes that most of our regional transportation players aren't up to taking control: King County

Exec Ron Sims flip-flops, Governor Chris Gregoire wallows in the quagmire of Seattle politics, gubernatorial wannabe Dino Rossi avoids specifics, developer Kemper Freeman is old-school and too self-serving, Mayor Greg Nickels mimics strongmanism but doesn't have the chops—if he did, he wouldn't have failed on the waterfront tunnel and ducked on 520. Speaking of chops, House Speaker Frank Chopp is powerful but he can't be trusted—he's a closet populist, you know.

What we need is someone to come in and knock heads and make the trains run on time. A Rudy Giuliani, a Robert Moses, a Richard Daley, an Arnold Schwarzenegger, a—just what *is* Norman Schwarzkopf up to these days?

Such yearnings defy our history. The development of Seattle and Puget Sound has always occurred on a complex battlefield. Power has always been suspect and authority decentralized at every turn. Political machines have been weak or short-lived; the people have ruled with initiatives, ballot measures, advisory votes. Yes, it's frustrating sometimes, but it's us.

In Seattle, visionaries clashed: R. H. Thomson, the engineer who built roads and sewers, and washed away hillsides, fought tooth and nail with parks designer John Olmsted over parks, boulevards, and the shape of the city to come. The voters backed the engineer and the artist at different times. Both visions made Seattle what it is today. One man made the toilets flush, the other infused the modern city with nature and beauty.

We've voted on freeways only to stop them in their tracks (the R. H. Thomson Expressway, scuttled by popular vote in 1972); we've opposed roadways through parks (Woodland), then built them anyway (not unlike some stadiums). We've elected and recalled mayors. We relish changing our minds. We rejected light rail, then passed it, then rejected extending it again; we passed the monorail, then rejected it too. When Metro was first proposed, it was seen as a regional octopus strangling the suburbs with its tentacles. We voted it down, then voted for it, then merged it with King County, then created Sound Transit and the RTID, and now there's talk of yet another incarnation.

A cascade of decisions and revisions. Fitting for a wet place, we're fluid, not fixed. It may look like chaos—it may even *be* chaotic at times—but it hasn't stopped growth or progress or prosperity. Our process, such as it is, has resulted in one of the most loved, most cherished, most desirable, most habitable metropolitan regions in the country. The questions are: How do we take care of it? How do we continue it? How do we improve it?

Part of the answer lies in our "flawed" processes. We've thrived by giving no one too much power, by never ceding anything we can't take back, by approving and disapproving every step of the way. By resisting the strongman urge.

Our leaders aren't all weak. I think they represent a people whose strength is not being too sure of themselves.

Crosscut 2007

Ballot Initiatives:
Enema of the People?

L ast week at Town Hall, a goodly number of civic-minded types forsook the Seattle Mariners opener, a Sonics game, and Bruce Springsteen at the Tacoma Dome to listen to a panel discuss the topic "Do initiatives derail or serve democracy?"

Snoresville, right?

It would be, except that the issue is incredibly hot here in Washington state, where laws are being dramatically rewritten by the initiative process: affirmative action nixed, "three strikes" for felons, state spending capped. Not to mention the infamous I-695, now in legal and legislative limbo, which, if found constitutional, will require all governments—city, county, and state—to raise taxes and fees only by plebiscite. It has also made Tim Eyman, a watch salesman from Mukilteo, the de facto governor of the state.

The panel essentially set up a debate between Eyman and David Broder, the Pulitzer Prize–winning political columnist from *The Washington Post*, who was in town flacking his new book, *Democracy Derailed: Initiative Campaigns and the Power of Money*.

Broder's book, which grew out of reporting on initiatives he did during the 1998 campaign cycle, takes a very skeptical view of the initiative process as it is practiced today in twenty-four states and various cities around the

United States. What began as an innovation of the Populist and Progressive reform movements in the late nineteenth century has now become a tool, Broder says, of special interests, wealthy individuals, political hatchet men, and angry activists who have no notion of the dangers to democracy some of their ideas—and their often crudely written laws—pose.

The founding fathers, Broder says, were very aware that direct democracy could lead to a tyranny of the majority—an approach to ideas and governance that has all the sophistication of thumbs up or thumbs down at the Roman Colosseum. Such direct democracy might work in small villages or in places with homogenous populations, but in a widely diverse state or country, it is problematic. A good illustration is I-695, which explicitly rewards the majority (car owners) at the expense of the minority (bus riders).

That's why the founding fathers created the checks-and-balances system of representative government: to allow for negotiation between differing constituencies. The legislative process is also a public process, whereas initiative drives are private, not subject to the same kinds of scrutiny. Yes, Broder argues, elective government may be flawed, at times even corrupt, but it is reformable; mob rule is not. Broder's motto might be: Give me James Madison or give me death!

But few people agree with him. In his book, Broder cites a poll taken in Washington state in 1999 that found that 84 percent of voters favored initiatives, while only 8 percent wanted to eliminate them. Even in California, which has been arguably ravaged by the Proposition 13 tax-revolt initiative, nearly three-quarters of the voters still felt such ballot measures were a good thing. Despite the damage they do, or the insanity with which some are conceived, or the hidden agendas many represent, people who have access to the initiative and referendum process don't want to give it up.

Many of them, liberal or conservative, are angry. And Eyman, whatever you may think of his initiatives, is passionate on the subject. His view lacks the sophistication of Broder's, but it is in the tradition of mad-as-hell Populists and Progressives. Eyman says the initiative process is "a laxative to a constipated political process." (Eyman, by the way, who has a beer-hall style of speechifying, seems also to have a fondness for anal and proctologic metaphors, which did not go over well with the Town Hall gray hairs.)

He makes a passionate case for initiatives. They are, he says, a way to get elected officials to deal with issues that they otherwise lack the courage to address or the will to undertake. Term limits is one example, spending lids another. Our own public disclosure commission, which daylights campaign contributions, was established by ballot measure. Initiatives are a way to police the pols.

And to let them know the will of the people. Look at I-695, which at the moment has been overturned by a judge. Even so, its agenda goosed Governor Gary Locke, who has now codified $30 tabs. Even an impending initiative can get action, Eyman says. His Traffic Improvement Initiative I-711, which would shift 90 percent of transport funds to roads and open HOV lanes to single-occupancy vehicles, is already spurring elected officials to look at opening up these lanes.

The compromise position on initiatives is to agree that they're here to stay, but that the initiative system could itself be reformed—by better legal vetting of initiatives so they'll be overturned by the courts less often (because that makes everyone more cynical), eliminating paid signature-gathering, requiring a supermajority vote for passage, and allowing legislatures a chance to act on them before they go to the ballot.

At the end of the evening, it seemed that both Eyman and Broder were flawed messengers for their respective viewpoints. While Broder's faith in the system and belief in the ultimate wisdom of political elites is sincere, it seems sadly out of touch. For as much as he touts the public process of our political system, there is a highly private parallel one: Back rooms do exist, influence is purchased, the people's will is subverted.

On the other side, for all Eyman's fire, desire, and frustration with the system, he seems not to care about the damage some of his laws may do to low-income commuters. He comes from the you've-got-to-break-eggs-to-make-an-omelet school. Plus, his new initiatives are not so much about reform per se but for furthering a specific conservative agenda.

Since initiatives aren't going away—and, Broder fears, they may even go national—we're left to find ways to check-and-balance the initiative process itself without gutting its strength to act as the people's wild card.

A potential solution is for voters to become more hip to the tricks, tactics, cons, and consequences of this brand of lawmaking. Certainly the lessons of I-695 aren't lost on its author. And they shouldn't be on the rest of us.

Seattle Weekly 2000

Tim Eyman's traffic initiative, I-711, was modified and went on the ballot as I-745. It essentially mandated that 90 percent of transportation funding be directed to road- and car-friendly projects, with only 10 percent going for transit. It was defeated at the polls in 2000. Eyman continues to propose antitax and transportation-related initiatives, and despite his being the most hated man in Olympia, many of his measures continue to pass. In addition, the Legislature has put his ideas into law even when initiatives have been struck down by the courts. This happened in the case of I-695 (license fees) and in 2007 when the Legislature codified the property tax limits of his I-747 into law. Lawmakers in Olympia, however, continue to look at ways to modify or limit the initiative process in order to hamstring Eyman.

2008

Free-for-Sprawl

The Legislature has passed a massive $8 *billion* transportation bill to send to the people as a referendum. The business lobby says we have to pass this package because gridlock is choking the economy. Labor unions say we must pass it because it will create jobs. To local governments desperate for dollars it offers a few crumbs for some needed local projects. The establishment consensus seems to be that the measure ought to pass but will likely be defeated by a tax-weary electorate. But let me say that after looking at the bill, there is plenty of reason to be against it without being against a tax increase per se.

Isn't it odd that in a time of economic shortfall, our major priority is roads? We're slashing social and health services, cutting back on fundamental state services, making a good public education harder to come by, but the one bill everyone in Olympia can agree upon is a welfare bill for the road lobby?

The Legislature says this transportation package emphasizes road and highway construction, and they promise a second $8 billion package to deal with other projects later. But do we really need this much more concrete? Yes, traffic is annoying, but why pour all of our resources into a deep, black pothole? If we do, it will only make things worse.

A recent study by Northwest Environment Watch indicated that 60 percent of the growth in the Greater Seattle area during the last decade was in suburban sprawl—

faster than our major metropolitan Northwest neighbors. Sprawl accounted for only 20 percent of Vancouver, B.C.'s growth. Our slow-growth laws are weak, and they began to fail almost immediately upon implementation in the '90s because the greed fueled by a booming economy undermined our will to manage growth sensibly. Do you remember concurrency, the idea that growth would pay for itself as we went along, that growth would be limited to the pace with which we could afford to build roads, schools, and sewers? It collapsed under the political pressure of developers and a business community eager for bigger profits, cheaper labor, and more jobs at any cost.

The legacy is that now, in the lean times, we're being asked to pay huge bills for our folly and shortsightedness. But the form of payment—more pavement—will make things even worse by encouraging yet another decade of free-for-sprawl.

It has been proven again and again in America that you cannot build your way out of growth problems. Trying to ease gridlock with more concrete is like using gasoline as a fire retardant. If you like this transportation bill, you're an arsonist.

KUOW 2002

Boeing 7$7

Boeing's suits may have flown Seattle's coop, but they're not done with us. The aerospace giant is a corporate-welfare pig extraordinaire, which we didn't object to very much when it was *our* corporate-welfare pig. Now, however, the Chicago-based company is exercising some of the new clout it has by virtue of having shed its old identity and cut its local roots. As a roving corporate global giant, it is free to stalk the earth in search of profits and friendly regimes that can help the company outsource jobs and slash costs. Then it can turn around and demand protectionist benefits such as subsidies and political favors from the federal government and the states, many of which will go the extra mile to save jobs and keep the company happy.

If you're one of those people whose blood boils upon hearing that Halliburton is getting fat contracts, or if you rage about welfare cheats stealing your tax dollars, then get ready to stroke out over Boeing.

You may have heard our congressional delegation celebrating over the Pentagon's approval of a $16 billion deal to lease one hundred Boeing KC-767 tankers. "This is the day we have been working for," crowed Democratic Senator Maria Cantwell, who is happy about jobs. The deal will keep Everett's 767 production humming and could lead to the eventual replacement of all military tankers with 767s, a huge potential payoff for the company.

But the deal has been found deeply flawed and much more expensive than realistic alternatives such as modernizing the military's current tankers or buying the new tankers from the get-go. (Any car shopper knows it's cheaper to buy than lease.) And the lease arrangement seems specifically designed to put extra cash in Boeing's pocket. Though Boeing agreed to trim the lease price by $2 billion, the total cost to taxpayers, according to the General Accounting Office, could be in the $20 billion to $30 billion range over six years. If true, taxpayers could pay between $12 billion and $22 billion more than necessary to keep tankers flying. That's a lot of winged pork.

Critics of the deal have included Office of Management and Budget director Mitch Daniels, assorted watchdog groups, government budget analysts, and conservatives like columnist Robert Novak, who wrote that in announcing the deal the Pentagon had "declared victory for Boeing over the U.S. taxpayers." The most vocal opponent in Congress has been the independent-minded Arizona Republican, Senator John McCain: "In all my years in Congress, I have never seen the security and fiduciary responsibilities of the federal government quite so nakedly subordinated to the interests of the defense manufacturer. Indeed, any objective analysis of the deal would conclude that the sole purpose served by this lease is to maximize the profits of Boeing, with consequent underfunding of other defense priorities."

Claiming the most credit for getting Boeing the tanker contract is Illinois Republican Dennis Hastert, Speaker of the House, who just happens to represent the state where

Boeing's corporate bigwigs are now ensconced. And that's important because Boeing is now pitting states against one another for the right to assemble the new 787—a bidding process designed to squeeze the most giveaways from desperate state governments. Illinois is in the running. As, you know, is Washington.

I don't know what the process will be like elsewhere, but here our fearful leaders are engaged in selling us out to please Boeing. It's like *Fear Factor*, with contestants eating worms and rolling in spiders in order to win. Our civic leaders have done this kind of thing for years but rarely so desperately as now. Even usually moderate editorialists have gotten carried away, with *Seattle Times* columnist Lance Dickie begging—in what strikes me as a mixed Freudian metaphor—to "smooch the shiny backside of Boeing's corporate fuselage."

Yet despite decades of smooching, Boeing wants more and is using the June deadline of its site-selection process as the gun to our heads. The company wants the state to build a new $16 million pier in Everett; it wants the third-runway boondoggle at Seattle-Tacoma International Airport speeded up; it's demanding the state's unemployment system be revamped to save Boeing money, even though that could slash benefits and throw thousands of seasonal workers off unemployment compensation. And those are just some of the public demands. Much of what Boeing is really asking will be kept secret, according to a story by *Seattle Times* reporter David Postman. We won't get to see what deals and promises have been proffered to lure the 787 because the documents are supposedly exempt from public disclosure.

The near-panic in Washington is palpable because the sense is that if we lose the 787, eventually we'll lose the rest of Boeing. This was the very kind of desperation Boeing sought to induce by shifting to a global strategy and moving its headquarters. Unfortunately, under deadline pressure, we still haven't fully considered the ultimate costs of being even more beholden to a company that demands so much from the taxpayers—especially in an America where the struggle for public dollars is bound to get more intense. Perhaps it would be better to cut Boeing loose.

Or we could push to nationalize them. Between subsidies and defense contracts, Boeing lives off the public dole anyway. We could either be done with their blackmail—which will only get worse—or take the controls of this flying porker ourselves.

Seattle Weekly 2003

Death, taxes, rain, and Boeing's search for public pork are the four inevitabilities in Seattle life. The Pentagon deal to lease up to one hundred 767 Boeing tankers collapsed in scandal. Besides being a bad deal for the public, the proposal fell apart when conflicts of interest were revealed between Boeing's chief financial officer, Michael Sears, and a top Air Force acquisition official, Darleen Druyun. Both lost their jobs and were sent to jail. Current efforts to cut a new Pentagon tanker deal are ongoing.

As to Boeing's threat to move unless it received a multibillion-dollar package of tax breaks, incentives, and public spending to keep the assembly of the 787 here in Washington, the company got its way. Despite major delays, the 787 assembly is taking place here; however, now Boeing has indicated it may change the way it puts together future planes and may (again) be looking to move operations somewhere else. If Washington wants to keep Boeing's business, it may have to cough up more benefits and incentives. An analysis by The Seattle Times *showed that the 787 project had not yet returned the predicted jobs and benefits to the region, though proponents argue that we're certainly better off than if the project had relocated to Nebraska or Georgia.*

However, Boeing's extortion was so blatant and the cave-in by officials so complete that now all businesses expect the Boeing treatment. The threat of relocation is often used to scare Olympia and local politicians into action. In 2008, for example, Microsoft and Yahoo demanded sales tax breaks for "server farms" in Eastern Washington. In a February 2008 story headlined "High-tech giants seeking massive tax break," the Seattle Post-Intelligencer *quoted Senate Ways and Means Committee chairwoman Margarita Prentice (D-Renton) as saying she would support the requests. "Asked if the legislation was a gift to a huge corporate interest, Prentice said: 'We gave another corporation (Boeing) a tax break,' adding that other states are vying for the server farms." The legacy of the Boeing giveaway is a slippery slope leading into the black hole of endless private sector demands.*

2008

The D Word

The D word. A dirty word. A despicable word. A defamatory word.

You might guess that around here on the Eastside, it's Derdowski. Or Democrat. Nah. It's developer.

I offer as evidence a couple of anecdotes. Not long ago, a downtown Kirkland businessman for whom I have much respect made it clear to me that he did not appreciate being called a developer in our paper. "I am a real estate investor," he informed me. Though he is involved financially in local development projects, the connotations of "developer" seemed to make his skin crawl. Our label certainly was not meant as an epithet, but he felt that like "lawyer" or "used-car salesman," the term weighted him with onerous social baggage.

More recently, Duvall City Council candidate Tom Loutsis called *Eastsideweek*, angry because our paper described him as a developer in our preelection endorsements. He complained we had saddled him with an inaccurate label that could cost him the election.

For the record, Loutsis is not a developer, merely a real estate broker who sells vacant property to people who want to build homes and commercial buildings.

To indicate just how outrageous Loutsis considered the charge, he asked us how we'd feel if he started calling us "communists," seeming to imply we were being Joseph McCarthy-ish by pasting the "developer" label on innocent citizens.

If "developer" and "communist" carry an equal stigma, Loutsis should relax, and so should all commies: He won his race. So did a lot of other developer types this year, despite the discomfort they may have with the label. Our culture at large, and our suburban microculture here, has evolving and sometimes unique standards regarding labels. "Communist" isn't as loaded as it was in the '50s. A lawyer recently told me that to call someone "a sexual harasser," today in the post–Clarence Thomas world, could be considered defamatory. But an unenlightened five or ten years ago, it might hardly have raised an eyebrow.

An attorney for an Eastsider accused of wantonly cutting down trees said that such a charge here could not go unanswered in the courts, because in the Northwest, accusing someone of being cruel to our arboreal buddies is akin to accusing him of infanticide.

So how did "developer" become such an ugly accusation? Certainly we haven't always hated all developers. In fact, throughout history, city builders have largely been admired. Why then do we consider it a season highlight when Ken Behring is knocked ass over teakettle on the sidelines at a Seahawks game?

Rightly or wrongly, developers have taken on a villainous aspect because, as with the oil companies, a few visible, symbolic disasters have colored our view: the hideous shaving of the land along I-90 by Lake Sammamish, or the high-rise towers of Bellevue that forever altered some Seattleites' views of the Cascades and therefore came to symbolize sprawl.

And, of course, no one likes the landlord. In the country of planned communities, developers are large, highly visible targets for picky tenants.

And to many of those tenants, developers no longer seem part of the mainstream. Despite their middle-class values and the upstanding nature of much of their work (providing jobs, housing, amenities), their schemes (such as Issaquah's Grand Ridge) seem too big to sustain quality of life for the landed squires of suburbia; their campaign tactics (as against Derdowski) seem uncommonly low; their unrelenting efforts to resist mitigation, to end regulation, to wave the flag of public good over enterprises that will enrich them yet make the landscape poorer give the impression that they are more bullies than good citizens.

But there may be some good news for developers. As the election demonstrated, people look more sympathetically at growth when it has slowed to a stop. Without a Goliath to fight, David is just another runt. Opposition will return as the pace of big projects picks up with the economy. And many old wounds have begun to heal: the once-bald Newport Hills sport a leafy toupee; trees are growing back around the clear-cut California-style subdivisions overlooking Lake Sammamish; in Kirkland, many neighborhood activists and developers recently backed the same City Council candidates, a welcome trend after the last few fractious years.

After the boom decades, some parts of the Eastside landscape have been given a breather. Will our attitudes toward one another also take this opportunity to heal?

Eastsideweek 1993

ABSURDITIES AND CONTRADICTIONS

Mandatory Lutefisk

Recent statistics show a disturbing trend. Northwest Environment Watch reports that the population of Cascadia—Washington, Oregon, Idaho, and British Columbia—is booming. It's not birth rate but migration from other states and provinces that is driving up the numbers. In the past twelve months, 227,000 folks have moved to the region. That's a 1.5 percent population increase in a year, due almost entirely to what they call "domestic migration." In other words, thanks, California.

Growing the most is Washington. *The Seattle Times* finds that Washington's population has grown by more than 400,000 people from 2000 to 2005. We're America's fourteenth most populous state and the twelfth fastest growing. The *Times* reports that the state's demographer, Theresa Lowe, predicts Washington will continue to draw more than 100,000 people per year for the rest of the decade as our population soars to 6.8 million.

Clearly, we are not doing enough to make ourselves unappealing to the rest of the country. Despite all the dire predictions that we would drive away people with the bad breath and acne blooms of high taxes, overpriced real estate, and onerous laws and regulations, we have not done nearly enough to make ourselves repellent. I mean, when Boeing stormed out of Seattle and relocated its corporate headquarters in Chicago, you would have thought we were some kind of drooling plague monkey. Even the dot-com bust failed to be a deterrent to growth. Our state is adding tons of jobs, and our vaunted "livability" apparently has the appeal of a Paris Hilton sex video.

Mossback doesn't like the way things are going. Too much growth, too much change, too many outsiders trying to grow palm trees—or skyscrapers—in our backyards. I think the only way to turn this thing around is to adopt measures that will turn newcomers off, yet reinforce local values.

Hire consultants—from North Dakota. This is the only state in the union that is losing population. What can we learn from them? Seattle has always been a sucker for guys with briefcases from out of town, so let's tap the wisdom of Bismarck. Maybe we need to develop a really annoying regional accent, like those folks in *Fargo*.

Mandatory lutefisk. Everyone loves to joke about this grotesque, gelatinous fish dish from Scandinavia, but few have ever eaten it. Fewer still have been forced to eat it on a regular basis. Mossback had to choke down a pile every Christmas Eve to get his presents. That's Calvinism on a plate! Served properly, this steaming pile of lye-soaked, boiled cod takes on the consistency of sperm and exudes a fishy odor. The Legislature should pass a law: Once a week, everyone has to eat a plate—or maybe a barrel—of lutefisk. Lutefisk testing stations at the state border can pass out samples, giving immigrants a chance to turn around before it's too late.

Recycling or death. Seattle has passed, and has just begun enforcing, a mandatory recycling law. No one really wants garbage Nazis picking through the trash, but it's good public policy, and the National Security Agency already knows everything else about us, so don't be paranoid. But the law's penalties aren't stiff enough. I mean, a $50 fine? Put some real teeth in it. Make recycling statewide and make noncompliance a death-penalty offense. Not only will this make our state tidy and green, it will cause newcomers to think twice about whether they're ready to live up to our standards. Such a law might be a good occasion to bring back hanging, by the way. Non-recyclers could be strung up curbside (for convenient pickup) by burly sanitation engineers.

Outlaw designer pets. Republican legislator Pam Roach is proposing to recriminalize bestiality in the upcoming legislative session, but this will only make a slight dent in the number of Californians who move here. A tougher, less appealing pet law would be to ban pure- and specialty-breed dogs. Doesn't anyone own a plain, old-fashioned, just-as-God-made-them mongrel pooch anymore? Outside my local Tully's, it seems that every dog is some rare product of canine eugenics. I am convinced that if we ban such pets, their owners will breed them elsewhere. Another suggestion while we're on the topic: In addition to protecting animals from human sex predators, what about protecting humans from animal sex predators? Senator Roach, protect the rights of people who get a leg humped or an unwanted nose in the crotch—now!

Weather restoration act. That asshole George W. Bush is destroying our weather as part of a right-wing plot to turn our blue state into a red-hot, Sun Belt real estate market. Last winter, we had a drought. This winter, an uncommonly dry November. When was the last time

Seattle had a real snowstorm? Green Lake used to freeze over. Our climate's gone screwy. "The bluest skies you've ever seen are in Seattle" goes the song, and it's true—but that used to be an annual event, not the freaking norm. We need new laws that will help put bumbershoots back in Bumbershoot. Without the endless rains that drove Ulysses S. Grant to drink and Lewis and Clark insane, we are defenseless.

I have many other ideas. Year-round hydroplane races; a law requiring the display of Elton Bennett silk-screened art in every home; a diabolical scheme involving Kenny G music. Perhaps you do, too. We need them. Our future is at stake.

Seattle Weekly 2006

Seattle Weekly Needs a New Arena

An open letter to Mayor Greg Nickels, the Seattle City Council, King County, and the delegation in Olympia:

This year, *Seattle Weekly* celebrates its 30th anniversary. Founded in 1976, we have demonstrated staying power as an important civic amenity. This year, we also joined the "big leagues" by becoming part of an even larger national newspaper chain, a major local franchise, if you will.

Over the years, we have followed with interest as the government has showered other major-league franchise owners with largesse. Billionaire Paul Allen and the Seattle Mariners' Nintendo-backed ownership group have received hundreds of millions of dollars in public subsidies for new facilities. They have their own dedicated tax-revenue streams. Even salmon don't have that.

As I write this, Starbucks chairman Howard Schultz is asking the taxpayers to build a new sports arena at Seattle Center to house the Sonics basketball team owned by him and 57 others. He wants the people to pick up the eventual $400 million tab (counting interest). Schultz says he is only asking for the same perks the public has already given the Seahawks and Mariners.

Schultz is no stranger to public perks—why, he once built his private driveway on city park property. He was surprised that people made such a stink about it.

A sorehead would have moved to Bellevue. Fortunately, he didn't, because if he had, we might have missed the opportunity to pay him hundreds of millions of our money to stay right where he is.

Schultz says the issue really is fairness.

We couldn't agree more.

Given that this is a major anniversary year, and that *Seattle Weekly* is operating in an increasingly competitive climate, we think it's time to level the playing field when it comes to public pork.

All we want is what the city's other franchises are getting.

Our offices here on Western Avenue are barely adequate. We aren't major South Lake Union property holders like *The Seattle Times*. We don't have a cool spinning globe over our heads like the *Seattle Post-Intelligencer*. We're not part of a government-sanctioned media monopoly like the two daily papers.

What have we got? We lease space in a brick warehouse close to the death-trap Alaskan Way Viaduct. You used to be able to rent a loft for what monthly parking costs in this neighborhood. The heating and air conditioning work in the wrong seasons, and the elevators frequently take riders to mystery destinations. And have you tried our "coffee"?

A rip in the carpet in my office was recently repaired with blue duct tape. Do you think Schultz has ever used duct tape in his suite?

We think a new arena for *Seattle Weekly* employees and fans is just the ticket. It would add to the economic vitality of this booming part of downtown—the snappily named West Edge—strategically located between the waterfront and First Avenue and between Pike Place Market and Pioneer Square. This place is vibrant, historic, and, when our next lease comes due, likely unaffordable.

We don't relish making threats, but if we don't find a permanent solution, we might have to leave Seattle. Do you really want 100,000 copies of *Tukwila Weekly* circulating downtown? I didn't think so.

And consider the other significant benefits to keeping *Seattle Weekly* in Seattle.

Unlike the Mariners, Seahawks, and Sonics, our product is free—and our salary structure is way cheaper. Our entire editorial department budget is less than a quarter of Raúl Ibáñez's annual salary. Raúl Ibáñez!

In building a new arena for *Seattle Weekly*, taxpayers will be getting value instead of subsidizing rich kids with Nike contracts.

And think of the economic impact of *Seattle Weekly*'s readers. We circulate about 100,000 copies per week and have more than 2.5 readers per copy. That means at least 250,000 people a week read the *Weekly* (not counting the Web). That's five consecutive Safeco Field sellouts, a whole lot of twelfth men. That's more than fifteen weeks of Sonics attendance!

Our readers spend big bucks on food, movies, and clubs. We generate millions of dollars in retail activity and jobs, and I'm not just talking about the sex ads.

And consider the benefits of *Seattle Weekly* spinoffs. The *Best Places* book series, for example. Or how *Seattle Weekly* founder David Brewster went on to start Town Hall. And did I mention the former *Seattle Weekly* staffer who married Conan O'Brien? Conan O'Brien!

City Council President Nick Licata says the cultural impact of the Sonics is "close to zero," but he can't say that about us. We reviewed that children's book he wrote. You're welcome, Nick.

We'll be happy with half of what Schultz is demanding. OK, a third. A tenth? Look, we'll even kick in some of our own money—unlike Schultz. How much is a pallet of duct tape at Costco?

And we promise not to demand more public "invest-ment" every ten years like the Sonics. We can wait another thirty.

Seattle Weekly 2006

The city of Seattle balked at building the Sonics a new arena. Howard Schultz sold the team to a group of Oklahoma City investors who were likewise denied a new publicly funded facil-ity. This makes it slightly more palatable that Seattle Weekly *has been given neither a new office nor a bulk discount on duct tape. To remedy that, however, the newspaper has discovered that by folding its issues into paper airplanes, it qualifies as an aerospace manufacturing company and therefore is eligible for all benefits, subsidies, and tax breaks accorded to Boeing. The* Weekly *promises to continue to "assemble" the paper planes in Seattle as long as that is the case. Otherwise, the* Weekly *may follow the Sonics to Oklahoma City.*

2008

Hobbits Versus Hobbes

A recent story in *The Washington Post* pointed out that Seattle is benefiting from "brain gain" instead of "brain drain." The *Post*'s local correspondent, Blaine

Harden, looked at census data and compared Seattle with that Emerald City of the Midwest, Cleveland. He provided empirical evidence that Seattle is the better—as in smarter—city. How ignominious that such proof warrants front-page treatment. Once a burg of world-class pretensions, the Pacific Rim's Athens, Seattle is now viewed as a bit more respectable than a rust belt has-been.

Except for that extraordinary scoop, the story's main effect will be to feed the city's ever-insecure sense of self. (See the *Seattle Post-Intelligencer*'s recent editorial extolling the virtues of that enviable brainpower.) Let's face it: We've been on a serious ego diet since Jean Godden went into politics and stopped writing her *Seattle Times* column. That dried up our most reliable fount of civic self-flattery: Stop the presses! Seattle's been voted America's sixth-most-livable city again!

While the *Post* story suggested that smart, young, college-educated entrepreneurs were flocking to town, it also contained the tidbit that these demographically desirable hotshots were staying, even if they'd lost their jobs. Which suggests to me that they're less ambitious than the story makes them out to be. It's also nothing new: Except in a few areas, Seattle isn't the best choice for claw-your-way-to-the-Ring-of-Power types. The city tends to attract bright people searching for an ineffable "quality of life" that has less to do with founding a start-up than leaving time for life. Remember that "Old Settler" song Ivar Haglund used to sing that says the real Northwest pioneer came here to escape the world's shams, like ambition? Great-grandpa was the original slacker.

I think the *Post* missed this year's most important Seattle trend, which wasn't the influx of smart kids, but the outflow of screwups.

A year ago, I wondered what it took to get fired in this town. To my surprise and delight, in 2003 the citizens revolted against the more flamboyant mediocrities. They sacked the school superintendent, the head of City Light, the head of our public TV station, three School Board incumbents, three City Council incumbents, an incumbent Port of Seattle commissioner, the president of the University of Washington, and a partridge in a pear tree.

So in addition to brain gain, we're cutting our losses with lamebrain drain. Not that we'll see dramatic improvement, as the bungled school superintendent search reminds us. But we can at least fulfill that first part of Mossback's modified Hippocratic oath: "Do no *more* harm." At least until the new guys get warmed up.

The other thing the *Post* story ignored is the growing trend of the outsourcing of some of our best jobs. During the 1990s, we reassured ourselves that the fading timber, fishing, agriculture, and even aerospace industries we once relied on were easily replaced with smarter, virtual businesses. We could cope with the loss of salmon because people were willing to pay for ideas.

Look at the Microsoft phenomenon: The world's richest man, Bill Gates, created and dominated the software industry by virtue of his homegrown brain. The Washington Apple Commission went out of business, timber workers were retrained as "knowledge" workers at community colleges, and Boeing moved to Chicago (sorry, Cleveland!),

No matter: With Starbucks's marketing savvy and Microsoft's monopoly, we'd be OK. The world itself was now our giant oyster. From our place on the Pacific Rim, we were free to roam the globe, flourishing our imagination and crowing about free trade.

But like that of a straw through a mummy's nose, that giant sucking sound you now hear is a new kind of brain drain. Big corporations—even very profitable ones—are exporting smart-people jobs to India, Russia, China, and Japan, countries, by golly, with a lot of smart people who will work cheap. That seamless, wireless, virtual world has come back to bite our butts. Seattle has no monopoly on intelligence or livability, we now know. And our general populace is no match for the heartless marauders of the Darwinian global market who are dog-eat-dogging out there. For Seattleites, it's a cage match: hobbits versus Hobbes.

If all the smart people are moving to Seattle, I don't see any evidence of it. I see politicians and business leaders still gushing the same rhetoric that keeps us hooked on the boom-and-bust cycle we've been in for years. They want to tie up our tax money in real estate projects for the rich. They want to compete globally, without really understanding the globe or even our little piece of it. They want to "grow" us out of recession by constructing the next bubble, biotech, because it fits the fantasy that we're somehow smart, superior beings who know best how to reshape the species. The Silicon Forest can soon be transformed into Frankenstein's Forest.

How smart is that?

Seattle Weekly 2003

Hallowed Be Thy Newsroom

There's a brouhaha over at *The Seattle Times* over a management pronouncement that top reporters and editors should begin attending Christian fundamentalist churches on Sunday in order to put the staff in touch with the paper's more traditional readers. One can hardly imagine a more ham-handed way of getting writers and reporters to do anything of the kind. Managing a news staff is as easy as herding cats, and just as you cannot order a cat to love you (let alone "go fetch"), you cannot command newspaperfolk to go forth and become sensitive.

Such commandments, however, are the extension of two bankrupt notions often touted by diversity buffs. One is that you must *be* something in order to write about it. Thus, only blacks or Asians or Hispanics can cover their respective racial and ethnic groups. To write about Christians, you ought to become one. Or at least go spend a Sunday or two at God's place.

The second is that failing conversion (or a sex change or a race swap), you can "sensitize" one group to the needs of one constituency by throwing them in the same room together for a political reeducation confab. What harm can it do? Exposure can make you more sympathetic, just as we're all more sympathetic to—let's see, doorbelling Jehovah's Witnesses. Or just as long-term exposure to feminism and professional women made Bill Clinton, Bob Packwood, and Brock Adams more, uh, sympathetic to the opposite sex.

Christian fundamentalists should be outraged by the kind of shallow tokenism implied by the *Times* edict (not to mention the staff's own Christians, Jews, Buddhists, and atheists). The point is, when it comes to someone's deep-rooted ethnic, racial, sexual, and spiritual identity—whatever the complex brew is that makes you who are—exposure to others can have less than predictable results. The *Times* edict is already producing one unanticipated response: fueling staff resentment toward the very people the higher-ups wanted to please.

What the *Times* may need is not more writers and editors exposed to fundamentalism, but simply more empathetic, more curious, and more imaginative ones. People who are not primarily hired to fill affirmative action quotas or whose work is not turned into pulp by layers of editors who seem trained to squeeze the creative juice and power out of stories. People not desensitized by the rough culture of daily journalism that rewards the cynical, the tough, the callous. People who are not asked to break the world down into competing special interest groups or warring factions.

Which is not to say that writers and editors should not get out and nose around, especially in unfamiliar territory. But the best writing comes from within, and spending mental time inside someone else's shoes can pay off better than time in someone else's pews.

Here's a very specific suggestion for the *Times* bosses worried about the short shrift given the Christian righties. Examine the issues involved in the U.S. Senate's passage of a bill imposing harsh federal penalties on anti-abortion protesters.

Just apply a little memory. Remember the 1960s and the antiwar movement. Remember how you worshiped Thoreau's "Civil Disobedience" and the writings of liberal U.S. Supreme Court Justice William O. Douglas. Remember how, when antiwar protesters broke the laws in Chicago, at Kent State, in the streets of Washington, D.C., you resented The Establishment as it cracked down (and cracked skulls).

Sure, you told yourself, the SDS (Students for a Democratic Society) shouldn't bomb campus research facilities, even though they were making weapons used to kill babies; sure, freeways shouldn't be blocked, preventing people from getting to work; sure, peaceful marches that turned to riots were counterproductive. But it was all for a good cause.

And when the government attempted to impose harsh penalties on draft resisters and antiwar activists, or used Cold War–era anticommunist or conspiracy laws to mete out special punishments, it didn't seem right because you knew the law was being used to oppose ideas, not lawbreakers. But you felt better, because civil libertarians such as Douglas reminded everyone in books such as *Points of Rebellion* how Americans must be exceedingly tolerant, even of illegal acts carried out in the name of social justice.

Some reporting on the dangers of cracking down on protesters of conscience, right or left, might be of interest to readers. And it might produce some provocative pieces that the Christian right would appreciate far more than rubbing elbows with reporters on some summer Sunday.

Eastsideweek 1994

Sighting the Great American Peckerwood

Last weekend I watched a bunch of suburban drivers fill up their black SUVs and 4x4s at an Eastside gas station. One of the vehicles sported "W" bumper stickers, and everyone seemed jolly. The source of joy was a gas station giveaway: a free plastic cup filled with soda pop for every driver who filled up with premium gas. That's right, with a $45 tankful of $3-per-gallon gas, you get a few pennies' worth of sugary battery acid.

And people wonder what's wrong with Kansas.

Democrats continue to be baffled as to why so many Middle Americans vote against their interests. Why is it that the great American heartland, which is most shafted by Bush and Republican policies, remains so steadfastly in the GOP's corner?

One answer is that many Americans are ignorant fools.

Let me state for the record that these ignorant Americans who enjoy being ripped off by the oil companies in exchange for a bubbly moment of bliss with a straw are not all Republicans. Many idiots vote for Democrats, too, or at least attempt to. They include the legions of folks who cannot do something as simple as walk into a polling place and fill in a written ballot properly because this involves the incredibly difficult task of coloring inside the lines of a small circle.

This "skill" is the kind of thing we used to learn in nursery school or kindergarten, and the fact that our public educational system is so broken that it cannot teach coloring in circles—let alone reading, writing, and arithmetic—means that while the country's rarest bird is the ivory-billed woodpecker, the *Ignoramus americanus*, otherwise known as the American peckerwood, is quite common.

If I sound like I'm being too hard on my fellow Americans, it's because I have been reading the polls. Last week there was a lot of coverage—including in this column—of "intelligent design," the notion being popularized by Seattle's conservative Discovery Institute that an unspecified creator (who sounds an awful lot like the Christian notion of God) is responsible for the design and development of everything, including human beings. In short, the Darwinian theory of random natural selection is all wrong. Many of our country's most important political leaders, including the president, believe intelligent design should be taught in schools as an alternative to evolution, even though it has no basis in science.

They, too, have apparently been reading the polls.

PollingReport.com cites a Harris poll in June that revealed 54 percent of Americans believe humans did not evolve from an earlier species, 47 percent do not believe we share a common ancestry with apes, 48 percent disagree that fossil evidence offers proof of evolution, and 64 percent believe humans "were created directly by God." Another 10 percent said God guided things through intelligent design. Only a measly 22 percent believe in evolution.

An NBC News poll in March found that 57 percent of Americans believe God created the universe, and 44 percent say he did it in six days, just as described in the Bible.

In a CBS News/*New York Times* poll last year, when asked if Darwinian theory was well supported by evidence, 35 percent said no and 29 percent said they didn't know enough to make a judgment. That means roughly two-thirds of the country is either wrong or totally ignorant about one of the fundamentals of modern science.

Now here's a humorous sidelight. The Bill & Melinda Gates Foundation is a major contributor to the Discovery Institute. And while the money doesn't go toward work on intelligent design per se, it does support the institute's own intelligent designer, Bruce Chapman, who runs the place. Bill Gates has also been a vocal advocate for improving public education in this country and has lamented loudly the low level of science education in particular. His foundation has poured at least $1 billion into the effort of remaking schools, and he is reportedly prepared to spend at least $1 billion more. Gates is making a concerted effort to be education reform's own intelligent designer, a worthy and noble cause.

But the Discovery Institute is a bit like a hole in his pocket: For every dollar Gates spends abetting the intelligent design agenda, he is setting back his own effort to promote good science and learning.

The challenge of education reform that Gates has taken on is big enough without this self-imposed burden. Turning around overcrowded schools that are held back by too many lousy teachers, bloated bureaucracies, and clueless parents who drop their kid off for twelve years of state-run, underfunded day care is no easy task, even for one of the world's richest—and smartest—men. Actively funding the march toward a dumber America by enabling the creationist crowd is ultimately self-destructive.

Gates is famous for announcing to Microsoft employees that one idea or the other they've offered is "the stupidest thing I ever heard." Well, Bill, when it comes to funding Discovery, right back at you.

Seattle Weekly 2006

Score One for Googie

Fans of preserving modern architecture had two victories to celebrate after a recent meeting of the Seattle Landmarks Preservation Board. Two mid-twentieth century modern buildings took big steps toward landmark status. One was officially designated a landmark; the other had its landmark nomination approved and is headed for an official designation hearing where its fate will likely be decided.

Interestingly, the two buildings anchor opposite ends of modern architecture's bell curve: One is a sleek, high-rise box of reflective glass that epitomizes the sophisticated International style, the other a swooping 1960s diner in the Googie style with all the chic of a Stan Boreson polka.

The first is downtown's Norton Building, a marvelous 1959 glass-curtain-walled box that is one of the last remaining examples of its kind in Washington. The building was commissioned by Northwest timber baron, businessman, and patriarch Norton Clapp. It was among the first nominations in a controversial new city initiative to proactively landmark nearly forty important downtown structures. While some downtown building owners have objected to the city's nominations, the owners of the Norton Building did not—they only expressed hope that the board would show some future flexibility if they need to change or upgrade it to continue to offer Class-A office space in the downtown core.

The second was the Denny's in Ballard (formerly Manning's Cafeteria), which locals called "Taj Mahal" because of its exotic, swoopy roofline that brought a certain exotic flavor to the neighborhood. The distinctive building has been described as reflecting both Polynesian and Nordic longhouse traditions, but it also had a flair many associated with the Century 21 Exposition, which ended its run shortly before the diner was built. It resembled one of the pavilions, so much so that it was rumored to have been moved from the fair site. It was, however, an original creation.

The building is currently owned by Benaroya Companies and occupies the site of a planned condo development on a key intersection—Northwest Market Street and 15th Avenue Northwest—that serves as the gateway to the Ballard business district. It was built in the mid-1960s as part of the Manning's restaurant chain, a company founded at the Pike Place Market in 1908 as the city's first premium coffee company (the Starbucks of its era). It was designed by Clarence W. Mayhew, an important modern architect from the San Francisco Bay Area. The building was saved from demolition once before in the mid-1980s when Denny's took it over.

While the vote for the Norton Building was a no-brainer (the board approved it unanimously), the diner posed a more difficult problem. For one thing, the current owner and the prospective condo developer, Rhapsody Partners of Kirkland, want to tear it down and had submitted the nomination to the board in the hope that it would be denied. As Benaroya's attorney Jack

McCullough told the board, they were "not looking for a positive outcome."

The vote blindsided the property owners. For one thing, the Seattle Monorail Project had planned to tear it down for a station. When that project went belly-up, Benaroya picked up the property, confident that the site had been cleared in a review of possible historic sites along the route. However, the monorail project only looked into buildings fifty years old or older, so the Denny's was never researched. Marc Nemirow of Benaroya said the diner looked "like it ought to be torn down and replaced."

To get the landmark hurdle out of the way, Rhapsody first hired an architectural consultant, Mildred Andrews, then reportedly dismissed her for being too sympathetic to the building. They then hired a second consultant, Larry Johnson. At the meeting, he did a PowerPoint presentation that frequently seemed designed to put the building in the worst possible light. He used grim shots of the now-boarded-up diner when other perfectly good pictures were available—some even included in Johnson's own written report. One opponent called the tactic "cynical." The owner insisted that shuttering the diner was not a ploy to make the place look worse, but Johnson certainly took advantage. The pictures were meant to underscore Johnson's argument that the building met none of the six criteria for a landmark and that it was too altered and too junky to be a viable landmark.

The building, however, had its passionate advocates, including Eugenia Woo of Docomomo WEWA, the modern architecture preservation group; Alan Hess, California architect, author, and expert on modern roadside architecture; Andrews, the spurned consultant, who submitted a letter to the board saying that she disagreed with Johnson's conclusion and thought the diner may well be worth saving; Christine Palmer of the preservation group Historic Seattle; and a number of other architects and Ballard residents.

Architectural historian Alan Michelson, head of the Architecture and Urban Planning Library at the University of Washington, led the pro-Denny's case. He wrote a lengthy report that outlined why the building met several of the landmark board's qualifications, notably that it

- "embodies the distinctive characteristics of an architectural style" (Googie)

- "is an easily identifiable visual feature of its neighborhood . . . and contributes to the distinctive quality or identity of such neighborhood or the city" (everyone passing by Ballard knows it)

- "is associated in a significant way with a significant aspect of the cultural, political, or economic heritage of the community, city, state, or nation" (the Manning's coffee/restaurant chain)

- "is an outstanding work of a designer or builder" (Clarence Mayhew)

No one seemed to have a handle on how the landmarks board would vote. During the course of the evening, the board issued death sentences for three charming old brick apartment buildings on Capitol Hill near Cal Anderson Park. They were almost unanimous that the buildings failed to meet the city's landmark standards. In addition, making the case for modern landmarks can be difficult. Older buildings are more easily regarded as historic while younger ones (less than fifty years old) often fall into arguments about taste rather than significance.

But the landmarks board agreed with most of Michelson's points. Some members were downright enthusiastic about the diner's qualifications. At least one lamented that they hadn't had the chance to save the old Twin Teepees diner on Aurora. Some members didn't seem to want to let another unique piece of roadside architecture slip through their fingers. They approved it, 8-1. The vote stunned both proponents and opponents, who immediately left the hearing room and formed two caucuses in the hall outside. Everyone seemed shocked that the preservationists, fighting above their weight class, had won a round against the big boys.

One group, mostly in suits and ties, could be called the "What the Hell?" caucus. These were the shocked representatives of the owners and developers who couldn't believe anyone was taking the building seriously. Benaroya's Nemirow said he was "surprised and disappointed." The developer's spokesman, PR man Louis Richmond, said they would continue to fight the landmark designation and predicted that no developer would want to develop the property as long as the building was standing. It'll just become "another blighted block," he said, and he criticized the process for not taking into consideration the financial implications of the decision.

The other stunned group, dressed mostly in designer black, were the pro-diner architects and preservationists. Call it the "What Now?" crowd. They powwowed to figure out how to bolster their case and counter the next moves of Benaroya and company.

It seemed like a vindication of modern architecture—even the kitschy, commercial kind. It was also a victory for old Ballard, a community once defined by its quirky character, not just its proliferating condos.

Crosscut 2008

In February 2008, the Ballard Manning's/Denny's was officially designated a Seattle landmark by the city. In response, the owners appealed the decision and sued the city to overturn the designation. They won their appeal when the city Landmarks Board voted to put no restrictions on what could be done with the landmark building. The board decided that preserving it was not financially viable for the owner. Proponents of preservation attempted to prove otherwise. The resulting decision was a Seattle absurdity: a city landmark that could not be protected from demolition. As a consequence, the diner was demolished in June 2008, a year after the landmark battle began.

2008

Index

INDEX

Population, 257–60
Populism, 188–89, 242
Port Angeles, 19
Port Townsend, 9
Portland, 58–59
Ports, 10
Postman, David, 249
Potter, Harry, 136–37
Price, Mike, 185
Pringle, Heather, 206
Pritchard, Joel, 231
Privatization of roads, 142–43
Proposition I, 237
Protests, 33–34
Public art, 53–56
Public schools, 112–17
Puget Sound Community School, 115–16
Puget Sound Indians, 75, 159
Puget Sound Regional Council, 11, 16–17
Pugetopolis, 3–4, 7

R

Race, 74–83, 204–7
Racial profiling, 76
Rain, 157–61
Raines, Howell, 185
Rainier Valley, 36
Ravenna, 37
Reams, Bill, 194
Reclaiming Cluster, 34
Recycling, 258–59
Regional governance, 11
Reichart, Dave, 230
Religion, 124–28
Renton, 13, 166
Rhapsody Partners, 276–77
Rice, Norm, 76
Richardson, Dana, 184
Richmond, Louis, 279
Ritalin, 235
Roads, 130–32, 140–44, 245
Rolfe, Stuart, 226
Rossi, Dino, 238
Runstad, Judy, 237

S

Safeco Field, 53
Salmon, 6, 14–15, 19, 196
Sammamish, 12
San Juan Islands, 172–76
Saulter, Carla, 44
Schell, Paul, 52, 191, 230
Schlafly, Phyllis, 235
Schools, 112–17, 184
Schultz, Howard, 261, 263–64
Sculptures, 51–53, 55

Seattle, 8–9, 11–16, 59, 192
Seattle Area Industrial Council, 18
Seattle Art Museum, 54
Seattle Center, 50
Seattle City Council, 218–19
Seattle First United Methodist Church, 70, 73
Seattle Intelligencer, 17–18
Seattle Landmarks Preservation Project, 275
Seattle Monorail Project, 217–27, 277
Seattle Police Department, 76
Seattle Post-Intelligencer, 44, 57, 95, 103, 161, 262, 265
Seattle Times, The, 45, 72, 103, 188–89, 218, 225, 249, 262, 268–69
Seattle Weekly, 260–64
Secularism, 127–28
Seeger, Pete, 105, 132
Selig, Martin, 70
September 11, 2001, 139, 168–69
767 Boeing tanker, 247–51
Sewage spills, 94–95
Seward Park, 147, 165
Shaw Island, 172–76
Sidran, Mark, 35, 88, 228–29
Sightline Institute, 42–43, 56–57
Simmons, Bob, 196
Sims, Ron, 23, 76, 143, 238
Singapore, 35–36, 89, 230
Skagit County, 19
Smallman, Andy, 115–16
Smith, Edward, 81
Somali immigrants, 76
Sound Transit, 229
South Lake Union, 66, 68, 227
Space Needle, 227
Spellman, John, 229
Sprawl, 245–46
Starbucks, 12–13, 140, 261, 267
Stegner, Wallace, 16
Steinbrueck, Peter, 210–14
Stern, David, 30
Stevens, James, 101
"Stickers," 16
Stockill, Lewis, 39
Strongmanship, 236–39
Students for a Democratic Society, 270
Stump homes, 129–30
Suburbs, 12–13, 37, 138–40, 232, 245
Sullivan, John J. "Jack," 208–9
Sustainability, 40, 43

T

Tacoma, 9
Tacoma Ledger, The, 102
Tacoma Narrows Bridge, 144
Talbot, C. B., 162
Talmadge, Phil, 234–35
Taxes, 62–65
Taylor, Joyce, 66
Taylor, Quintard, 75
Technology, 96–99, 133, 143–44
Terry, Bill, 210
Thomson, R. H., 238
Toll roads, 141–42
Traffic congestion, 130–32, 242–43
Traffic Improvement Initiative I-711, 242–43
Transportation, 42–44, 240–42, 245–46
Trees, 6–7, 129–30, 164–67
Truman, Harry, 209–10

U–V

U Village, 37–38
Uhlmann, Wes, 191
University of British Columbia, 55
Urban Forest Management Plan, 167
Utopian communities, 19–23
Van Geldern Cove, 20
Vance, Chris, 228, 231
Vancouver, 58
Vancouver, George, 9
Vatican, 125
Victor Steinbrueck Park, 33–34
Vidal, Gore, 59
Vietnam War, 200–3
Volcanoes, 26–27
Vulcan, 66

W

Wailers, 49–50
Waiting for the Interurban, 52–54, 217
Wallis, Jim, 127
War Against Terrorism, 139
Washington Standard, 105
Watson, Emmett, 103
Weather, 157–63
Whidbey Island, 19
Wildlife, 6, 14, 18, 170–72
Williams, Bob, 235
Wilson, John Arthur, 230
Woo, Eugenia, 277
World Trade Organization, 33, 87, 197, 233

Z

Zumdieck, Georgia, 195

283

About the Author

Photo by Kari Berger

Knute Berger is a Seattle native. He writes the Mossback column for Crosscut.com, a Pacific Northwest online daily. He also writes a monthly back-page column for *Seattle* magazine, where he is editor-at-large, and is a political columnist for *Washington Law & Politics*. In addition, he is a regular news commentator on Seattle's public radio station, KUOW. Between 1990 and 2006, Berger did three stints as editor of *Seattle Weekly* and was founding editor and publisher of *Eastsideweek*, a suburban alternative newspaper. He lives in Seattle, and can be reached at knute.berger@crosscut.com.

_____

_____

_____

_____

2. What Scripture is being referred to in these verses?

_____

_____

_____

_____

3. What are some of the doctrines you have learned since becoming a Christian?

_____

_____

_____

> "Christianity explains the facts of reality better than any other worldview **because it relies upon divine inspiration**. If the Bible is truly God's special revelation to man, as we believe it is, then the only completely accurate view of the world must be founded on Scripture."
>
> —*The Battle for Truth* by Dr. David Noebel, p. 18

ADDITIONAL THOUGHTS

_____

_____

_____

_____

_____

DEMOLISHING STRONGHOLDS

FIND THE FOCUS

Whenever God gives us new information or repeats something we've heard in the past, He wants us to pay attention. Think for a moment … look back over the notes you have for this lesson, and write down a couple of things that were an encouragement or a challenge, or that stood out to you. (Ideas: Maybe you were made more aware of <u>why</u> you believe or should believe that the Bible is the **only** holy, inspired Word of God; or maybe it became apparent to you through Ken's talk that science—true science—and the Bible are on the same page.)

Whatever you write, be specific and be prepared to share it with the group.

1. _____
   _____
   _____
   _____
   _____

2. _____
   _____
   _____
   _____
   _____

HOMEWORK

1. Memorize 2 Timothy 4:1.

2. Read over the article "Biblical Authority Unleashed" several times and be prepared to share three items you could use to defend the authenticity and accuracy of the Bible.

WAR OF THE WORLDVIEWS
PART 2
CAN WE REALLY TRUST THE BIBLE?

LAYING THE GROUNDWORK

In 2 Timothy 4:2b, we are commanded to "Be ready in season and out of season. Convince, rebuke, exhort, with all longsuffering and teaching."

Let's read how the Amplified Bible explains this verse and think about it a little more personally:

"Keep your sense of urgency [stand by, be at hand and ready]..."

- Do you live each day as if it could be your last?

- Do your choices show that you are ready, willing, and able to speak up for the Lord without advance notice?

- Are you ready in the sense of knowing what you believe and why you believe it?

- Are you ready to defend your faith in relation to salvation, creation, daily life, etc.?

"...whether the opportunity seems to be favorable or unfavorable. [Whether it is convenient or inconvenient, whether it is welcome or unwelcome, you as preacher of the Word are to show people in what way their lives are wrong.]"

- Do you avoid being in conversations/situations in which your beliefs might be questioned or attacked?

- Do you know how to present your beliefs using God's Word so that He can use His Word to convict others of the truth?

"And convince them, rebuking and correcting, warning and urging and encouraging them, being unflagging and inexhaustible in patience and teaching."

- Do you have a concern and compassion for others and understand the urgency of reaching them for Christ?

- Do you pray for your unsaved friends regularly?

- Do you live your life so that others see Jesus Christ in your thoughts, words, and actions?

Are you prepared for spiritual battle? The commands presented in this verse are a sobering reminder that we need to ready ourselves by understanding our enemy and his tactics. In this lesson, you will be made aware of how evolutionists and evolutionary textbooks try to lead you to unbiblical conclusions about origins. You will also see clear evidence presented that supports biblical creation and be reminded of the fact that the Bible confirms what true science shows.

Before watching the DVD, however, let's define some terms.

Presupposition: A starting point accepted as true; an established principle or law of science, art, etc.

Straw Man: As a rhetorical term, "straw man" describes a point of view that was created *in order to be easily defeated in argument*; the creator of a "straw man" argument does not accurately reflect the best arguments of his or her opponents, but instead sidesteps or mischaracterizes them so as *to make the opposing view appear weak or ridiculous.*

> An example of this is when person A says "I don't think children should run into the busy streets." Person B responds "I think that it would be foolish to lock up children all day with no fresh air." This insinuates that person A's argument is ridiculous and far more severe or extreme than it is.

VIEW THE DVD

(Watch for the key thoughts that complete the statements below and fill them in as you watch and listen.)

How do you find out who's __right__ [about origins]?

We can use __observational__ science and apply it to those interpretations of facts.

When we apply observational science to changes in dogs, it really confirms biblical _____ because dogs _____ dogs, elephants remain _____, etc. There's ___ evidence of a mechanism to change one ____ into another when you study genetics. When you study _____ and you study the rock layers, actually what you find over the earth is more consistent with __Biblical__ processes, NOT __millions__ of years of processes.

Definition #1 for Evolution—Dictionary definition: a process of _____ in a certain direction; an unfolding; i.e., _____.

True or False

"Before Charles Darwin, most people believed that God created all living things in exactly the form we see them today. This is the basis of the doctrine of creation." (Quotation from a display in the *Natural History Museum* in London, England)

BEWARE OF THE STRAW MAN!

The evolution they are referring to is _____-to-____ evolution, but all they define it as is _____. People get indoctrinated here!

What Darwin observed was not a process of _____ that would change one kind into _____; he observed the hand of _____ in the phenomenal _____ that God placed there.

_____science and _____ confirm the Bible's account of kinds; it _____ confirm molecules-to-man evolution! The Bible's history is _____!

YOUR STARTING POINT DETERMINES YOUR WHOLE
_____

DEMOLISHING STRONGHOLDS

Bible's history confirmed!

Use observational science

Look at the evidence

Start from the Bible

Quotation from Dr. Richard Dawkins: "My personal feeling is that understanding _____ has led me to atheism."

When you have no _____ authority, who determines right and wrong?

The worldview battle is really a battle between the _____ and the anti-gospel.

Gospel	Anti-gospel
"the _____ news"	Man is just an _____
Jesus died on the cross & was raised from the dead for _____	When you die, that's it.
_____ is truth.	_____ determines truth.

GET INTO THE WORD

Read **Romans 1:19–20** and **Psalm 19:1**, then be ready to respond to the following items:

1. Discuss and write down two or three things that God has shown you in His creation to indicate He is the eternal Creator.

   _____

   _____

   _____

   _____

   _____

2. How do the "heavens declare the glory of God"? Give an example.

   _____

   _____

   _____

   _____

3. The phrase "without excuse" is literally, "without an apologetic" or "without a defense" (Greek *apologia*—the same word used for "answer" in 1 Peter 3:15). As Ken pointed out in this session, there

is absolutely no evidence to support molecules-to-man evolution. In contrast, the evidence for creation is all around us. Discuss with the group and write down several examples that provide additional evidence of the divine creation.

_____

_____

_____

_____

Note: Even though people instinctively know there is a God (Psalm 19; Romans 1) by looking at creation, they still must be told what His name is. It is not enough to simply know and believe there is a Creator—we must know Him by name—thus, the Gospel.

ADDITIONAL THOUGHTS

_____

_____

_____

_____

_____

FIND THE FOCUS

Whenever God gives us new information or repeats something we've heard in the past, He wants us to pay attention. Think for a moment … look back over the notes you have for this lesson, and write down a couple of things that were an encouragement or a challenge, or that stood out to you. (Ideas: Maybe you were made more aware of how you have been indoctrinated by humanistic thought, or maybe it became apparent to you through Ken's talk that evolution is <u>not</u> supported by science but is a "blind faith" religion.)

Whatever you write, be specific and be prepared to share it with the group.

1. _____
   _____
   _____

2. _____
   _____
   _____

HOMEWORK

1. Memorize 2 Timothy 4:2. Practice saying verses 1 and 2 together.

2. Complete any part of the lesson that you were not able to finish in class. Be prepared to discuss your answers.

3. Read Ephesians 4:14–15 and 2 Thessalonians 2:1–12 to prepare your heart for next week's Bible focus.

EVOLUTION IN POP CULTURE

PART 1

WHAT'S WRONG WITH IT?

LAYING THE GROUNDWORK

In 2 Timothy 4:3, we are warned, "For the time will come when they will not endure sound doctrine, but according to their own desires, because they have itching ears, they will heap up for themselves teachers."

Once again, the Amplified Bible can provide a detailed commentary on the content presented in this verse:

> For the time is coming when [people] will not tolerate (endure) sound and wholesome instruction, but, having ears itching [for something pleasing and gratifying], they will gather to themselves one teacher after another to a considerable number, chosen to satisfy their own liking and to foster the errors they hold...

Discuss and answer the following questions with the group and ask God to prepare your heart for the message He has for you in today's lesson.

What "time" does this verse remind you of?

_____

Where can you go for sound doctrine? How do you know this?

_____

_____

_____

In this lesson, you will come face to face with some of the false teachings presented to you in TV shows and movies you may watch or may

have watched. The intent of this session is to get you excited about really getting to know God and His Word. We need to be equipped to stand against the obstacles that humanists and non-Christians use to try to trip us up. Knowing what you believe and why you believe it will enable you to develop the mind of Christ and overpower the influence of the media in your life.

VIEW THE DVD

(Watch for the key thoughts that complete the statements below and fill them in as you watch and listen.)

We as the body of Christ have to start getting _____ about our _____. We need to get out into the _____ and start _____ people.

Evangelism is a _____ not a presentation. Are you _____? To do that we need to understand the way that the world is seeing us and how we can break down those _____ that keep us from being able to have _____conversations with people (2 Corinthians 10:4–5).

The very first step in being able to be real with people and to talk with people and to have conversations with people is to _____ there's a _____ going on.

Without recognition there can be no _____.

"It is time to recognize that the true tutors of our children are not school teachers or university professors but _____, _____ _____ executives, and _____ purveyors. _____ does more than Duke, _____ outweighs Stanford, _____ trumps MIT."—University of Maryland Professor

Lot's Fall into Worldliness (Genesis 13:8–9)

1. "He lifted up his eyes." – Lot looked around with his _____ eyes. He used his physical eyes to make a very important _____ (Proverbs 3:7; 16:25).

DEMOLISHING STRONGHOLDS

Application: When you and I use our physical eyes, we use *our* wisdom; we can be _____ because the world can make things look really _____.

2. "He pitched his tent towards Sodom." – Lot didn't live __ the city because he wanted the best of both worlds.

3. In chapter 19 Lot's living _____ the city walls! –Years had passed between chapters 13 and 19; He didn't get sucked in all at once; it was a slow, gradual _____.

Application: What happens to us is many times we get sucked into the world:

Slowly and gradually we start _____ the ways of the world.

We start _____ the world.

We start _____ the world's standards instead of the Word's standards.

KEY THOUGHT

"The vast majority of Christians do not behave differently because they do not _____ differently, and they do not think differently because we've never _____ them, _____ them, or held them accountable to do so."

> If Satan can get you to _____ [God's Word] in the first chapter, the second chapter, the third chapter,
>
> where do you quit doubting?

DEMOLISHING STRONGHOLDS

The Bible is like a _____ system and if you don't use it properly, you're not going to like the _____ that you get.

Satan's tool that's being used on our culture today to get us to doubt is _____ and evolution.

**Watch as Carl shares several clips from TV shows/movies that support evolutionary thought.

CARL'S OBSERVATION ABOUT SCIENCE FICTION

Science fiction is a _____. You do not get from "There is a God" to "There is no God" just like that most of the time. There has to be a bridge—you can believe in God, He just used evolution; He just directed the Big Bang.

Opportunities (or obstacles?) for biblical conversations

Messages from the Media through:

Advertising   Movies

TV   Music

Internet

Recognize that when you open up your mind [when] watching a movie, you open up your mind to the messages inside of those movies. Be discerning and confront these messages with the Truth!

GET INTO THE WORD

Read Ephesians 4:14–15; 2 Thessalonians 2:1–12.

Discuss and answer the following items:

1. What does the word "deceive" mean in these passages?

   _____

2. Who is constantly trying to deceive us? What tactics does he use?

   _____

_____

_____

3. According to Jeremiah 17:9 and James 1:14, what else can we be deceived by?

_____

4. Name one or two things you can do to avoid being deceived by evolution's lies.

_____

_____

_____

Throughout the next week, take the challenge of digging even deeper into the message and power of this passage.

ADDITIONAL THOUGHTS

_____

_____

_____

_____

FIND THE FOCUS

Whenever God gives us new information or repeats something we've heard in the past, He wants us to pay attention. Think for a moment ... look back over the notes you have for this lesson, and write down a couple of things that were an encouragement or a challenge, or that stood out to you.

1. _____

_____

_____

2. _____
   _____
   _____

HOMEWORK

1. Memorize 2 Timothy 4:3. Practice saying verses 1–3 together.

2. Complete any part of the lesson that you were not able to finish in class. Be prepared to discuss your answers.

3. Read through the entire article on Inductive Bible Study before next week's lesson. Ask God to prepare your heart for deeper study of His Word.

4. Pre-read 2 Corinthians 10 and 2 Timothy 2 to prepare your heart for next week's Bible focus.

EVOLUTION IN POP CULTURE

PART 2

WHAT ARE YOU TALKING ABOUT?

LAYING THE GROUNDWORK

1 Peter 3:15 says "But sanctify the Lord God in your hearts, and always be ready to give a defense to everyone who asks you a reason for the hope that is in you, with meekness and fear."

By this time in the study of *Demolishing Strongholds*, you should be beginning to identify worldly influences in your day-to-day life. More importantly, you are becoming more aware of the false teachings perpetrated in the media and the humanistic worldview from which they stem.

Your challenge in this lesson will be to do something about the worldly influences in your life. This may include "raising the bar" in your viewing standards (TV/movies), pointing out the humanistic/evolutionary influences to fellow believers, and/or confronting the culture head-on to make an impact for Christ. Whatever role God may have you play, it will necessitate the need for really knowing His Word and knowing how to answer some of the tough questions non-Christians might come up with.

Before watching the DVD, however, let's define some terms.

New Age: a broad movement of late twentieth-century and contemporary Western culture, characterized by an individual eclectic approach to spiritual exploration.

Syncretism: the attempt to reconcile opposing beliefs and to meld practices of various schools of thought; i.e., in the realm of religion to say that there are many ways to get to Heaven so that no one is offended.

Wicca: the polytheistic nature religion of modern witchcraft whose central deity is a mother goddess. Wicca incorporate a specific form of witchcraft, with particular ritual forms, involving the casting of spells, herbalism, divination, and other magic.

VIEW THE DVD

Much of Carl's video presentation for this lesson is focused on movie clips. Though there will not be many notes to fill in, the ones chosen are to the point and powerful.

Be careful with Intelligent Design . . ., because unless you name the Name [of Jesus], the designer's not going to get you into Heaven. Jesus Christ—at the name of Jesus every knee shall bow and tongue confess. . ."

There's something that's even better than spider sense. It's called _____ sense.

- God has given us a _____.

- He's the only one who's _____ been there.

- He's given us a _____ _____ book to be able to deal with the world that we're living in.

You can have Bible sense when you _____ from the Word of God to _____ the world that we live in, to have _____ to real issues.

We've been trained to put on those glasses to think like the _____. Think about it.

- Average time a child in America spends in school = _____ _____

- Average time a child in America spends in front of the television set = _____

- Average time we spend in church = _____ (about 100–150 hrs. per year)

DEMOLISHING STRONGHOLDS

IN ORDER TO CONFRONT THE CULTURE

_____ the Word of God _____ from the _____ verse. Use it as a real solid _____.

You need to have a _____, rational explanation of _____ you believe what you believe.

> "_____, not science, is the ultimate test of all _____ and the further evangelicalism gets from that conviction, the less evangelical and the more humanistic it becomes."
> —Dr. John MacArthur

> **Christian, are you ready, _____, and able to answer the _____ that the world has?**

> **God's Word is ____ from the beginning.**

We need to get _____ and start thinking from the _____ of God—with no apologies, and have _____ from the Word of God—*using* the culture, not being abused by the culture.

GET INTO THE WORD

2 Corinthians 10:3–5; 2 Timothy 2:15

Beginning with this lesson, our Scripture passage will be covered in much more detail as we work through the Inductive Bible Study process. Your assignment from last week was to read the context passages of our Scripture verses for this lesson, so we'll begin by discussing the overview of the passage.

2 Corinthians 10: _____

_____

2 Timothy 2: _____

_____

_____

Now let's take a closer look at the key verses. We'll answer as many of the six questions as we can, and we'll look for key words.

2 Corinthians 10:3–5

"For though we walk in the flesh, we do not war according to the flesh. For the weapons of our warfare are not carnal but mighty in God for pulling down strongholds, casting down arguments and every high thing that exalts itself against the knowledge of God, bringing every thought into captivity to the obedience of Christ."

Who? _____

_____

_____

What? _____

_____

When? _____

_____

Where? _____

Why? _____

_____

How? _____

_____

DEMOLISHING STRONGHOLDS

Key Words: _____

_____

CROSS-REFERENCES

Summarize each of the verses and relate them back to 2 Corinthians 10:3–5.

2 Timothy 2:3–4; Ephesians 6:13–18; Colossians 2:8; 2 Corinthians 4:4

What do these verses mean to me?

_____

_____

How am I going to apply these Scriptures to my life?

_____

_____

This reference will be assigned for homework for the next lesson. Take the time to get as much as possible from the study of this verse, keeping in mind the context in which it is found.

2 Timothy 2:15

"Be diligent to present yourself approved to God, a worker who does not need to be ashamed, rightly dividing the word of truth."

Who?_____

What?_____

When?_____

Where?_____

Why?_____

Key words

Diligent	Approved	Worker	Not ashamed
Dividing	Truth		

CROSS REFERENCES

John 17:17; Psalm 119:160; John 14:6

What is this verse saying to me?

_____

_____

_____

_____

How am I going to apply this verse to my life?

_____

_____

_____

_____

ADDITIONAL THOUGHTS

_____

_____

_____

_____

FIND THE FOCUS

Whenever God gives us new information or repeats something we've heard in the past, He wants us to pay attention. Think for a moment … look back over the notes you have for this lesson, and write down

DEMOLISHING STRONGHOLDS

a couple of things that were an encouragement or a challenge, or that stood out to you.

1. _____

   _____

2. _____

   _____

HOMEWORK

1. Memorize 2 Timothy 4:4. Practice saying verses 1–4 together.

2. Complete the Inductive Bible Study for 2 Timothy 2:15 from this lesson. Be prepared to discuss your answers.

3. Read through the article on death and suffering before next week's lesson.

4. Pre-read Colossians 2 to prepare your heart for next week's Bible focus.

COUNTERFEIT REALITY

PART 1

IS THIS FOR REAL?

LAYING THE GROUNDWORK

2 Timothy 4:4 says, "and they will turn their ears away from the truth, and be turned aside to fables."

The more a person exposes himself to something that does not reflect God's truth or the light of Christ, i.e., things that are honest, just, pure, lovely, of good report (Philippians 4:8), the easier it is to turn away from the truth and lose interest in knowing it and standing up for it.

This lesson is all about understanding that it's more than just evolution we have to be aware of and watch out for in our society. Thoughts that emerge from evolution that cause us to rationalize sinful behavior and practices can lead us down a destructive path and keep us from making an impact on our culture.

VIEW THE DVD

(Watch for the key thoughts that complete the statements below and fill them in as you watch and listen.)

Your _____ is your view of the world. . . It is your _____ for understanding existence.

We (Christians) are to be _____ in season and out of season. The bad news is it's out of season to preach the _____. The worse news is it's __ season on Christians.

When you go out and you _____ the truth of the Gospel, you

proclaim that the _____ is true; people are going to come after you. Why?

Because they are immersed in a _____ reality. We have a _____ that is filled with "myth" information.

Secularism (indifference to or rejection of religion or religious considerations) is a belief that there may or may not be a _____, but even if there is a God, He's _____ in history, art, science, literature, music, philosophy, etc. Secularism is not _____, [it] is a _____ system that is _____ and at the core of [it] is the question of _____.

> **Ideas have _____.**

Our assumptions determine our _____.

(As Bill gives the fact or assumption statements below, circle the correct response beside each statement.)

Dimensions of velociraptor	fact	assumption
Half-moon shaped wrist	fact	assumption
"No wonder these things learned how to fly."	fact	assumption
"Perhaps dinosaurs had more in common with modern-day birds than they did with reptiles."	fact	assumption
". . . you spot velociraptor, and you stand still because you think his visual acuity is based on movement just like T-Rex."	fact	assumption

That's _____ on top of assumption on top of _____!

"bobbing his head like a bird"   fact   assumption

"Velociraptor is a pack hunter."   fact   assumption

"The attack doesn't come from the front, but from the side."

                                        fact   assumption

Just because you have _____ teeth, does that necessarily mean you were designed to eat _____?

Six-inch retractable claw   fact   assumption

"slashes at you"   fact   assumption

We are immersed in a counterfeit _____, and we must realize that people like Dr. Grant are neither stupid, crazy, unintelligent, nor insane. They're _____.

FYI:

*Science—knowledge; something observable, testable, and repeatable

*Science Fiction—elements of science with a lot of fiction (make believe)

GET INTO THE WORD

Colossians 2:8

"Beware lest anyone cheat you through philosophy and empty deceit, according to the tradition of men, according to the basic principles of the world, and not according to Christ."

Colossians 2 key idea: Don't be led into false teaching or legalism, but follow Christ completely.

Who? _____

What? _____

When? _____

DEMOLISHING STRONGHOLDS

Where? _____

Why? _____

How? _____

KEY WORDS

Underline or highlight these words in the verse above.

cheat   philosophy   deceit
tradition   principles   world

CROSS REFERENCES

**Acts 17:18; 1 Corinthians 1:30; Colossians 1:16–17;
Galatians 4:3, 9–10; 1 John 2:15–17**

What is this verse saying to me?

_____
_____
_____
_____

How am I going to apply this verse?

_____
_____
_____
_____

ADDITIONAL THOUGHTS

_____
_____
_____
_____

FIND THE FOCUS

Whenever God gives us new information or repeats something we've heard in the past, He wants us to pay attention. Think for a moment … look back over the notes you have for this lesson, and write down a couple of things that were an encouragement or a challenge, or that stood out to you.

1. _____

_____

_____

_____

_____

2. _____

_____

_____

_____

_____

HOMEWORK

1. Memorize 2 Timothy 4:5. Practice saying verses 1–5 together.

2. Finish any parts of the lesson that were not completed during the lesson time.

3. Complete the Research Project before the next lesson (see below). Be sure to study the "Attributes of God" chart as well.

4. Pre-read 1 Corinthians 8 to prepare your heart for next week's Bible focus.

RESEARCH PROJECT

Choose a movie to watch with "biblical glasses" that your parents approve ahead of time. Try to think in advance of movies you know that might have evolution or humanistic thinking in it.

Name of Movie _____

Please write at least three ideas or statements from the movie that are factual and at least three that are assumptions. Also, note situation ethics (justifying wrong behavior because it might have a favorable result). Watch critically—you may be surprised at the amount of counterfeit reality the movie contains.

Facts	Assumptions	Situation Ethics
_____	_____	_____
_____	_____	_____
_____	_____	_____
_____	_____	_____
_____	_____	_____

Oftentimes we can be drawn into "Christianizing" a movie because some of the characters/themes resemble biblical ideas. When we educate ourselves about who God is and what He is like, we will be much less likely to fall for this type of counterfeit reality.

Take time to review the "Attributes of God" chart. Search the Scriptures (Acts 17:11), do deeper study, and really get to know God. Keep in mind that God's character will never contradict itself. For example, if a movie character you think represents God lies, then that character is not a picture of our Lord.

Many movies lend themselves to spiritual discussions. For example, you could use a movie like "Star Wars" to initiate a conversation on the topic of "the Force" and explain how "the Force" cannot be representative of God. (Feel free to use the solid reasons Bill gave in his presentation.)

NOTE: For deeper study, you can find the full version of this chart with commentaries at www.preceptaustin.org/attributes_of_god.htm

COUNTERFEIT REALITY

PART 2

TIME FOR A REALITY CHECK

LAYING THE GROUNDWORK

Read Romans 1:21–22. The Amplified Bible elaborates upon the concept presented in these verses.

> Because when they knew and recognized Him as God, they did not honor and glorify Him as God or give Him thanks. But instead they became futile and godless in their thinking [with vain imaginings, foolish reasoning, and stupid speculations] and their senseless minds were darkened.

In the last lesson, Bill Jack zeroed in on tactics used by humanists to support their theories, i.e., using assumptions and stating them as fact. At the end of the video presentation, Bill made a statement that provided a reasonable explanation for why they (evolutionists) would use counterfeit reality to deceive—they are blind, spiritually blind. They are not saved, and therefore will behave as someone who is influenced by sin and the characteristics of it.

This lesson will continue in the same vein of thought but will also challenge us to use our biblical glasses to be discerning and to be aware of our testimony to those who are not believers or who are new Christians. We have a responsibility to the Lord and to others.

You have been given a lot of information over the past few weeks. Your sense of awareness to the world's influence has been sharpened. Use the tools you've been given to chip away at this counterfeit reality.

DEMOLISHING STRONGHOLDS

VIEW THE DVD

(Watch for the key thoughts that complete the statements below and fill them in as you watch and listen.)

What is the difference between science and science fiction? Science fiction is _____ with elements of science. . .science is constrained by _____.

We who are steeped in a counterfeit reality must tell the world that your best time is after you _____ because you can then get to be with your _____ forever.

Matthew 11:25

We need to be people of the _____. We need to be wise in whom we _____. Are we going to trust God's _____ or man's wisdom?

_____ your way through [a] film so you are not taken captive by counterfeit reality, but you can use it to start _____ with those around you.

> Movies are not just entertainment—movies are the most _____ teaching tool in the culture.

Romans 1:25b

This counterfeit reality affects our quest for _____ and significance.

Turn [conversations about movies] into a pulpit from which you can _____ the truth of the Gospel of Jesus Christ.

"See to it that no one takes you _____ through philosophy or empty _____ according to the tradition of men ... rather than according to Christ." Don't get _____!

The best prison to build is a prison in which the prisoner doesn't even realize he's in prison, because he'll never try to _____.

We are all prisoners of our _____.

If your assumptions are false, it could be _____ . . . _____ kills people!

BILL'S CONCLUSION

We are steeped in a counterfeit reality, and we have to take what is common to the _____ just like Paul did in Acts 17, and we have to turn it into a _____ from which we proclaim the _____ of the Word of God.

GET INTO THE WORD

1 Corinthians 8:1–2

"Now concerning things offered to idols: We know that we all have knowledge. Knowledge puffs up, but love edifies. And if anyone thinks that he knows anything, he knows nothing yet as he ought to know."

1 Corinthians 8 key idea: Though we have freedom in Christ to live as we would like, we need to make sure our behavior does not become a stumbling block to other Christians or to non-Christians.

Who?_____

DEMOLISHING STRONGHOLDS

What?_____

When?_____

Where?_____

Why?_____

How?_____

KEY WORDS

Underline or highlight these words in the verse above.

idols   knowledge   puffs up   edifies   knows

What do these verses mean/say?

_____

_____

_____

_____

How can I apply these verses?

_____

_____

_____

_____

ADDITIONAL THOUGHTS

_____

_____

_____

_____

_____

FIND THE FOCUS

Think for a moment … look back over the notes you have for this lesson, and write down a couple of things that were an encouragement or a challenge, or that stood out to you.

1. _____

_____

2. _____

_____

HOMEWORK

1. Memorize 2 Timothy 4:6. Practice saying verses 1–6 together.

2. Finish any parts of the lesson that were not completed during the lesson time.

3. Read the handout about extraterrestrials before next week. If you have internet access, go to the Answers In Genesis website for further information on this subject (www.answersingenesis.org/go/aliens).

4. Pre-read John 3 and Acts 17 to prepare your heart for next week's Bible focus.

ANSWERS TO DIFFICULT ISSUES
PART 1
FOSSILS: FACT OR FICTION?

LAYING THE GROUNDWORK

2 Timothy 4:5a says, "But you be watchful in all things, endure afflictions." The Greek word for "watchful" in this verse means "to be calm and collected in spirit; to be temperate, dispassionate, and circumspect."

- Temperate: steady, restrained

- Dispassionate: fair, objective

- Circumspect: careful, alert

In other words, Paul's charge to Timothy (and in turn, God's charge to all believers) is to "keep your head" in times of hardship or trouble.

This series of lessons is providing you with many tools to discern truth from myth, increasing your knowledge of the enemy's world system, and equipping you with the Word of God upon which your faith should be founded and solidified. Often, an arsenal such as this can generate a righteous indignation against the evolutionistic/humanistic worldview. When you realize how evolutionists have indoctrinated our schools and culture with false claims, it can stir up your anger. We must guard our hearts to exhibit the self control of a Spirit-filled Christian. The Scriptural command, "Be angry and sin not" means to be angry at the sin, not the sinner. Satan would like nothing better than to discredit our message of truth through a lack of self-restraint when dealing with the opposition. Claim Scripture with confidence: "For God has not given us the spirit of fear; but of power, and of love, and of a *sound mind*" (2 Timothy 1:7).

In lessons 7 and 8, Carl Kerby makes an incredible presentation of the evidence for the biblical account of creation and the Flood through the

DEMOLISHING STRONGHOLDS

fossil record. He first reminds us of our great commission to share the good news of the Gospel message. To do this effectively, he challenges us to affirm our faith by always making the Word of God our starting point. When we do this, we have an unshakable foundation upon which to stand and will be able to discern between the scientific facts and evidence we encounter and the fiction of speculations and misleading artwork.

VIEW THE DVD

(Watch for the key thoughts that complete the statements below and fill them in as you watch and listen.)

As a Christian, do you realize that you are a _____ of the Gospel of Jesus Christ?

Fossils are one of those areas that many, many difficult _____ come from.

2 Timothy 4:1–4

What does the world accuse Christians of believing? _____

But the Word of God says that when we start from His Word, we should end up with _____.

When you start learning to look at things through the lens of God's _____ and start learning how to figure out what's _____ and what's not real, you get excited!

John 3:12

Your starting point is going to _____ the way that you _____ the world that you live in.

The Word is true—_____ is the only one who's always been there. He told me what happened, and when I _____ with His word, and then I go to the world that I live in, I will understand the world _____ than somebody who says there is no God. . .

My bias, my axiom, my _____ absolutely _____ the way that I understand fossils, stratagraphic layers, light from the furthest star—all of those things!

43

DEMOLISHING STRONGHOLDS

Carl discusses the concept of going through a museum and looking for the evidence that's presented for the evolution side . . .

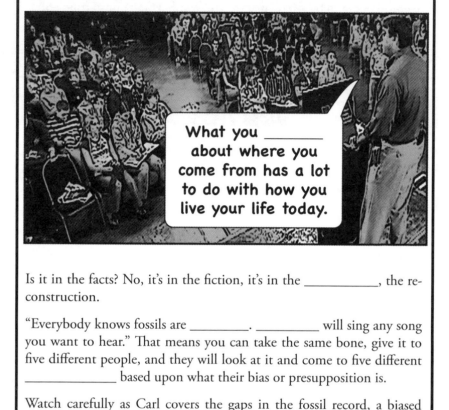

Is it in the facts? No, it's in the fiction, it's in the _____, the reconstruction.

"Everybody knows fossils are _____. _____ will sing any song you want to hear." That means you can take the same bone, give it to five different people, and they will look at it and come to five different _____ based upon what their bias or presupposition is.

Watch carefully as Carl covers the gaps in the fossil record, a biased scientific observation from *Earth* Magazine, and how fossils are formed.

If God _____ sin the way that He said that He did in the past ... we should find a _____ of it—and we do.

GET INTO THE WORD

John 3:12

"If I have told you earthly things and you do not believe, how will you believe if I tell you heavenly things?"

CONTEXTUAL KEY IDEAS

John 3—Nicodemus, a ruler of the Pharisees, visits Jesus by night to discuss spiritual things. He recognizes that Jesus has been sent from God. Jesus gives Nicodemus a very clear Gospel message and answers his deep questions. In verse twelve, Jesus makes a very relevant connection between believing the earthly things He speaks of, and believing the spiritual truths of the Bible. You can't believe one without the other.

Who?_____

What?_____

When?_____

Where?_____

Why?_____

How?_____

KEY WORDS

tell   earthly   believe   heavenly

What do these verses mean/say?

_____

_____

_____

How can I apply these verses?

_____

_____

_____

Acts 17:11

"These were more fair-minded than those in Thessalonica, in that they received the word with all readiness, and searched the Scriptures daily to find out whether these things were so."

DEMOLISHING STRONGHOLDS

CONTEXTUAL KEY IDEAS

Acts 17—This chapter encompasses Paul and Silas' visits to Thessalonica and Berea, and then Paul's experiences in Athens, including the speech he gave on Mars Hill. The first half of this chapter clearly emphasizes the importance of deep personal Bible study for believers.

Who?_____

What?_____

When?_____

Where?_____

Why?_____

How?_____

KEY WORDS

Fair-minded   received   readiness   searched
Scriptures   so

What do these verses mean/say?

_____

_____

_____

How can I apply these verses?

_____

_____

_____

ADDITIONAL THOUGHTS

_____

_____

_____

FIND THE FOCUS

Think for a moment … look back over the notes you have for this lesson, and write down a couple of things that were an encouragement or a challenge, or that stood out to you.

1. _____
   _____
   _____

2. _____
   _____
   _____

HOMEWORK

1. Memorize 2 Timothy 4:7. Practice saying verses 1–7 together.

2. Complete the Inductive Bible Study for Acts 17:11.

3. Read the article about radiometric dating before next week's lesson. Write down any questions or comments you may have in the margins as you are reading.

4. Pre-read Revelation 4 to prepare your heart for next week's Bible focus.

ANSWERS TO DIFFICULT ISSUES
PART 2
WHERE'S THE BEEF?

LAYING THE GROUNDWORK

2 Timothy 4:5b boldly states, "Do the work of an evangelist." *Webster's New World Dictionary* defines "evangelist" as "a bringer of good news." Evangelism is defined as a "zealous effort to spread the gospel."

In light of the context of this verse, it is even more vital to share the saving work of Christ at a time such as this when people are not "enduring sound doctrine and are turned unto fables." Are you living your faith? Are you finding opportunities to turn conversations into a pulpit for sharing the evidence of an all-knowing, merciful Creator? Now more than ever Christians need to be proactive in communicating the truth of God's Word.

In this lesson, Carl Kerby continues his focus on fossils and how they provide yet another area of science that confirms the biblical account of Creation. Carl will also show the evidence that refutes the idea that fossilization requires long periods of time.

VIEW THE DVD

(Watch for the key thoughts that complete the statements below and fill them in as you watch and listen.)

If evolution is true, this is what it should show from the secular quotes:

"_____ provide the only historical documentary evidence that life has evolved." (** see contradictory statement below.)

(Note: As Carl shows the charts displaying the fossil evidence, it will become painstakingly apparent that the fossil record does not provide enough evidence to support evolutionary claims.)

THINK ABOUT IT!

Christian, why are we so willing to sell out the Word of God, the _____ that changeth _____, for something that every time they find a new _____ somewhere, it _____ everything we've known for a hundred and fifty years?

What does the _____ really show? People have always been _____; monkeys have always been monkeys …

When you look at the charts, it's almost always the same—_____ evidence where _____ is supposed to have happened.

When you start from the _____ of God, what we see in the world around us …

absolutely _____ what we read in the Word of God.

**"The gradual change of _____ species has never been a part of the _____ for evolution." No real evolutionist uses the fossil record as evidence in _____ of the theory of evolution.

They even disagree about what evidence to consider for their side!

The only place you will find evidence for evolution is in the _____.

Carl revisits the question of "Why would a loving God allow death, pain, and suffering? and explains that they (evolutionists) have been blinded to the Gospel because of the "millions-of-years" bias presented by evolution.

When you teach _____ of years of death and suffering, and that's how we got man, that absolutely _____ what the Word of God

DEMOLISHING STRONGHOLDS

teaches. The Word of God teaches that _____ action—sin—led to death and _____.

Fossils—friend or foe? Fossils are our _____ when we use the Bible as real history to explain them because ... we see that bats have always been bats, cats have always been cats, and that is that. God's _____ is _____ from the beginning.

GET INTO THE WORD

During this lesson's Bible study, we will be applying an inductive method of study based on the "golden rule of interpretation" (refer to lesson 12 for further explanation on biblical hermeneutics—the principles for accurate interpretation of the Scriptures).

The golden rule of interpretation is: "When the plain sense of Scripture makes common sense, seek no other sense." Therefore, take every word at its primary, usual meaning, unless the facts of the immediate context, studied in the light of related passages and fundamental truths, clearly indicate otherwise.

We take the Bible at face value, or plainly, in the same way that we read other literature. This is a common sense approach. We understand that history is history, poetry is poetry, metaphors are metaphors, etc. The Bible is written in many different literary styles and should be read accordingly.

After reading these verses and their cross references and discussing their plain meaning, write down the message you believe God has for you in them.

Revelation 4:11

"You are worthy, O Lord, to receive glory and honor and power; For You created all things, and by Your will they exist and were created."

Cross-reference: Acts 14:15

What do these verses mean/say?

_____

_____

How can I apply these verses?

_____

_____

Revelation 10:6

"And swore by Him who lives forever and ever, who created heaven and the things that are in it, the earth and the things that are in it, and the sea and the things that are in it, that there should be delay no longer."

Cross-reference: Jeremiah 10:10

What do these verses mean/say?

_____

_____

How can I apply these verses?

_____

_____

Ephesians 6:17

"And take the helmet of salvation, and the sword of the Spirit, which is the word of God:"

Cross-references: Hebrews 4:12: Isaiah 49:2; 1 Peter 1:23

What do these verses mean/say?

_____

_____

How can I apply these verses?

_____

_____

DEMOLISHING STRONGHOLDS

ADDITIONAL THOUGHTS

_____

_____

_____

FIND THE FOCUS

Think for a moment ... look back over the notes you have for this lesson, and write down a couple of things that were an encouragement or a challenge, or that stood out to you.

1. _____

_____

_____

2. _____

_____

_____

HOMEWORK

1. Memorize 2 Timothy 4:8. Practice saying verses 1–8 together.

2. Finish any parts of Lesson 8 that did not get completed during the lesson time.

3. Read the article "Only Three Ways to Make an Apeman." Write down any questions or comments you may have in the margins as you are reading.

4. Pre-read Colossians 2, Hebrews 9, and 2 Corinthians 10 to prepare your heart for next week's Bible focus.

SIMPLE TOOLS FOR BRAIN SURGERY

PART 1

MAY I ASK YOU A QUESTION?

LAYING THE GROUNDWORK

In 2 Timothy 4:5c, Paul exhorts Timothy to "fulfill your ministry." The Greek word for "fulfill" is *plerophoreo* (*play-rof-or-eh'-o*) meaning "to carry out fully (in evidence), i.e., completely assure (or convince), entirely accomplish: most surely believe, fully know (persuade)." Since apologetics is the branch of theology having to do with the defense and proofs of Christianity, it sounds as if this charge encompasses the idea of fully communicating one's faith so that the ministry of reaching the lost for Christ can be realized.

You've been given many ideas in prior lessons as to how you can defend and share your faith. In this lesson, Bill Jack presents another platform that can be used to impact your culture for Christ. In addition, Bill will give you four specific questions that you can learn to use effectively to cause your opponent to think seriously about his/her own beliefs.

VIEW THE DVD

(Watch for the key thoughts that complete the statements below and fill them in as you watch and listen.)

Christians ought not to be ignorant of anything around them.

Four questions that will stand you in good stead no matter what the topic

DEMOLISHING STRONGHOLDS

WARNINGS:

1. Christians are to speak the _____ . . . in _____ . . . by the power of the Holy Spirit.

2. Do _____ use these questions as a _____ _____, but as one would use a crowbar.

Aristotle said that those who wish to _____ must ask the right preliminary—the right beginning—questions.

Sometimes the best you can do is simply get people to _____ about their own position.

The Four Questions

1. What do you mean by what you're saying?

2. How do you know that what you're saying is true?

3. What difference does what you're saying make in your life? (or So what?)

4. What if you are wrong? (or What if you're wrong and you die?)

PASCAL'S WAGER

"If I as a Christian am _____ about there being a God, then all I've done is live my life by a set of rules out of a book that has provided nothing but good and _____ for mankind, and when I die, that's all there is. But, if you as a non-Christian are wrong about there not being a God and you die, are you willing to _____ the consequences?"

What is a humanist?

Humanists

• believe _____ is supreme

• do not believe in God—atheistic

• deny anything _____

- believe man is inherently _____

- believe we can build a civilization by each person deciding for himself what is _____ and what is _____

Consider the only three answers that could be used to answer, "What happens when you die?"

1. _____—you die, you rot, you stink, and become extinct

2. _____ or Hell

3. Reincarnation

GET INTO THE WORD

As you embark on this lesson's study of key verses brought out in Bill's talk, your focus will be once again to interpret these verses at face value. Work in small groups, discuss the context of these verses, and come to a consensus on the meaning. Your leader will guide you through a final discussion to ensure that your interpretation is in line with the intended interpretation for these verses.

Colossians 2:8

"Beware lest anyone cheat you through philosophy and empty deceit, according to the tradition of men, according to the basic principles of the world, and not according to Christ."

Cross References: Jeremiah 29:8; Matthew 15:2–3; Hebrews 13:9

What do these verses mean/say?

_____

_____

_____

DEMOLISHING STRONGHOLDS

How can I apply these verses?

_____

_____

Hebrews 9:27

"And as it is appointed for men to die once, but after this the judgment."

Cross References: Genesis 3:19; Ecclesiastes 3:20

What do these verses mean/say?

_____

_____

How can I apply these verses?

_____

_____

2 Corinthians 10:5

"Casting down arguments and every high thing that exalts itself against the knowledge of God, bringing every thought into captivity to the obedience of Christ;"

Cross References: Isaiah 2:11

What do these verses mean/say?

_____

_____

How can I apply these verses?

_____

_____

ADDITIONAL THOUGHTS

_____

_____

_____

FIND THE FOCUS

Think for a moment … look back over the notes you have for this lesson, and write down a couple of things that were an encouragement or a challenge, or that stood out to you.

1. _____

   _____

   _____

2. _____

   _____

   _____

HOMEWORK

1. Review 2 Timothy 4:1–8.

2. Finish any parts of the lesson that did not get completed during the lesson time.

3. Read the article "General Humanist Beliefs" in preparation for next week's DVD presentation.

4. Pre-read Romans 1 to prepare your heart for next week's Bible focus.

SIMPLE TOOLS FOR BRAIN SURGERY
PART 2
THE UNCUT VERSION

LAYING THE GROUNDWORK

In 2 Timothy 4:6–7a, the Apostle Paul writes,

> "For I am already being poured out as a drink offering, and the time of my departure is at hand. I have fought the good fight . . ."

Wow! What an incredible testimony! Paul knows that he has done God's will and served Him faithfully. He knows he is close to death, and he is ready to meet his Lord. This is a peace that passes all understanding. Though he still refers to his Christian walk as a "fight," he is completely at peace because he is confident that he has fulfilled God's purpose for his life and is now ready to "be present with the Lord" (2 Corinthians 5:8). When a Christian walks according to God's will and actively lives and shares his faith, he too can have the confidence conveyed here by Paul.

In this session, Bill Jack will be interviewing a humanist and an atheist. As you observe, you will hear some philosophies that have no basis in truth, or evidence to support them. Try to view these individuals through the eyes of Jesus, i.e., see them as lost and in need of Christ, and notice how blinded they are by their false religion.

At the end of this lesson, you will find some very sound advice from Ken Ham, President of Answers in Genesis, on how to effectively talk to an evolutionist using the Bible as your starting point.

VIEW THE DVD

(Watch for the key thoughts that complete the statements below and fill them in as you watch and listen.)

During this video, write down some of the words/phrases used by the humanist and the evolutionists at the "Freedom from Religion" booth at the People's Fair in downtown Denver.

Humanist Ideas:

_____

_____

_____

_____

_____

_____

_____

_____

_____

_____

_____

_____

> Too often not only are we soft-headed, but we are hard-hearted ... We ought to be thinking God's thoughts after Him. We ought to be the most tender-hearted towards people.

Evolutionist Ideas:

_____

_____

_____

_____

_____

DEMOLISHING STRONGHOLDS

_____

_____

_____

_____

_____

GET INTO THE WORD

Write down and reference key phrases from **Romans 1** that refer to creation, evolution, and consequences. God is very clear in these verses, and it's important that you understand the cause and effect present in this key passage of Scripture.

Creation_____

_____

_____

Evolution_____

_____

_____

Consequences _____

_____

_____

Isaiah 55:11

"So shall My word be that goes forth from My mouth; it shall not return to Me void, but it shall accomplish what I please, and it shall prosper in the thing for which I sent it."

Cross reference: Isaiah 46:10

What do these verses mean/say?

_____

_____

How can I apply these verses?

_____

_____

_____

FIND THE FOCUS

Think for a moment … look back over the notes you have for this lesson, and write down a couple of things that were an encouragement or a challenge, or that stood out to you.

1. _____

   _____

2. _____

   _____

HOMEWORK

1. Review 2 Timothy 4:1–8.

2. Complete the Inductive Bible Study for Isaiah 55:11.

3. Read the article "Debate Terms."

4. Pre-read Revelation 5 and Colossians 3 to prepare your heart for next week's Bible focus.

SPECIAL FORCES FOR THE SAVIOR

PART 1

A MINORITY REPORT

LAYING THE GROUNDWORK

"I have finished the race, I have kept the faith" (2 Timothy 4:7b).

In spite of opposition, persecution, prison, beatings, shipwreck, weariness, hunger and thirst, cold, and numerous other perils (2 Corinthians 11:23–27), Paul endured as a servant and soldier of the Lord. His faith never wavered. Why is that?

If you have never read all of Paul's epistles, let this be a challenge to you to do so. Not only will you discover why he was so committed to Christ, you'll also learn foundational Christian doctrine that is vital for all believers. Paul was consistent in his witness because his starting point was *always* God's Word. He knew a joy and peace only God can give because he had a heart of gratitude for what the Lord had done for him. Paul's example to us is to know the Bible and know the God of the Bible.

You are about to see and hear Dr. Charles Ware who uses this inspiring session to get us to acknowledge what an awesome God we have. He also calls us to stand firm in our faith as a Christian minority. We are called out to stand up for Jesus, and we are to be prepared for the opposition we face. We must be ready to answer their questions and accusations.

TERM TO DEFINE:

Jim Crow laws—*Jim Crow laws* were state and local laws enacted in the Southern and border states of the United States and in force between 1876 and 1964 that restricted access of African-Americans to public facilities. *Jim Crow*, or the *Jim Crow period* or the *Jim Crow era* refers to the time during which this practice occurred. The most important laws required that public schools be segregated

by race, and that most public places (including trains and buses) have separate facilities for whites and blacks. School segregation was declared unconstitutional by the Supreme Court in 1954 in Brown v. Board of Education. All the other Jim Crow laws were repealed by the Civil Rights Act of 1964.

VIEW THE DVD

(Watch for the key thoughts that complete the statements below and fill them in as you watch and listen.)

Revelation 5

You need to understand that you're partnering with a God who ulti-mately _____ this battle, and you'll go on to be amongst those thousands of thousands, ten thousand times ten thousand as we worship Him who alone is _____!

_____ Forces are not majorities, they are _____.

Dr. Ware wants to "challenge you to dream a bit, to _____ about what a sovereign all-powerful God can do through a minority, what he can do through one person like you."

Listen carefully as Dr. Ware gives deep insight into understanding the cultural differences we may encounter in America.

In the Scriptures, the _____ of God were a called-out group. Those who come to faith in Christ _____ of their sins and come to faith in Christ. They are brought together as one in Christ. We are the _____ of God. We stand against a society . . . that has a culture and a worldview that _____

The problem is not skin, it's __.

Jesus Christ wants us to ____ _____ across racial and economic lines for the glory of God!

our God and denies the _____ of His Word. We're not to be
_____, but we're to be unified on biblical _____.

Do you know that one of the strongholds of your society is that they're
continually attacking Christianity based upon bigotry and _____?

Expect _____. . . 2 Timothy 2: "Endure hardness as a good
soldier."

DISCUSSION/THOUGHT QUESTIONS:

1. Maybe the only cultural difference of which you could be a victim
   has to do with your Christian worldview versus the anti-Christian
   worldviews. Are you prepared to stand alone or be a leader in this
   minority? If not, what's holding you back?

2. Less than 6% of Protestant churches are what we can call multieth-
   nic or multicultural. Why do you think that is? Examine yourself.
   Are you biased or prejudiced?

GET INTO THE WORD

Each of the passages for today's lesson has a different thrust. The first
one is focusing on the person and work of Jesus Christ. Answer the following questions after reading the passage to gain a deeper understanding of the context of this passage as you apply the contextual principle
of hermeneutics.

Revelation 5:6–14

The apostle John describes Jesus as what animal? _____

Why? _____

_____

What is the purpose of the book of Revelation? _____

_____

_____

Jesus is called "worthy" to receive what seven blessings from His people?

_____

The events of the book of Revelation will usher in the restoration of all things to God's created perfection and the consummation of all His purposes in creation. What an all-wise God we have, and what a wonderful future we have to look forward to!

How can I apply these verses?

_____

_____

_____

_____

The second passage reminds us of who we are in Christ and how we are to exemplify the "new man" within us.

Colossians 3:10–15

v. 10 Whose image are all believers created in? _____

v. 11 What point is Paul trying to get across here? Who is to be the center of our thoughts?

_____

_____

_____

_____

vv. 12–14 List and explain in your own words the godly character traits we are commanded to attain. After your leader gives deeper insight into these traits and their biblical significance, be sure to add to your notes. What you see, hear, say, and do will remain in your memory much longer than if you are only listening.

_____

_____

_____

DEMOLISHING STRONGHOLDS

How can I apply these verses?

ADDITIONAL THOUGHTS

FIND THE FOCUS

Think for a moment ... look back over the notes you have for this lesson, and write down a couple of things that were an encouragement or a challenge, or that stood out to you.

1. _____

_____

_____

2. _____

_____

_____

HOMEWORK

1. Review 2 Timothy 4:1–8.

2. Finish any parts of the lesson that did not get completed during the lesson time.

3. Read the article "Is There Really Just One Race?"

4. Read Romans 1 again to prepare your heart for next week's Bible focus.

SPECIAL FORCES FOR THE SAVIOR
PART 2
THE "DREAM" TEAM

LAYING THE GROUNDWORK

Today, we will first take a closer look at 2 Timothy 4:8, the final verse in our memory passage. By itself, it could lead one to believe that all believers might be entitled to a "crown of righteousness" when we stand before the Lord; however, within the context of the passage and the Apostle Paul's life, it is apparent that this special reward is presented to those who have stayed faithful and committed to serving the Lord, and as a result, "love his appearing."

What an encouragement it is to read 2 Timothy 4:8, the final verse in our memory passage:

> Finally, there is laid up for me the crown of righteousness, which the Lord, the righteous Judge, will give to me on that Day, and not to me only but also to all who have loved His appearing.

Dr. Joe Temple, Bible teacher for over 50 years, in his sermon series on "The Five Crowns" makes the following observation: "Every man who loves the appearing of the Lord will receive the crown, because you cannot love His appearing without fighting a good fight. You cannot love His appearing without running a good race. You cannot love His appearing without guarding the faith."

Because as Christians we believe that this life is simply preparation for eternity, we have a goal and a hope. Our work is not in vain (1 Corinthians 15:58) and it *shall* be rewarded (2 Chronicles 15:7; 1 Corinthians 3:10–15) by the King of Kings and Lord of Lords. Even when we fall, and we *will* fall, we can come to God's throne of grace, confess, receive restored fellowship with our Lord (1 John 1:9), and carry on His work with renewed wisdom and experience (James 1:2–5).

In this second session of "Special Forces for the Savior," Dr. Ware reiterates the concept that Christian people make mistakes and fail because we live in a sinful, fallen world. He states that, "God has revealed in His Word that some of the people He has used in His mercy and His grace to accomplish His will have been people of clay feet. They have fallen. God has (through their experiences) shown me . . . the pattern that I need to follow." Dr. Ware then uses the acronym DREAM to show us the pattern God has established for those whom He has called to demolish the strongholds of the world's belief system.

VIEW THE DVD

(There are no notes to fill in for this session, but students may want to jot down some thoughts during the DVD.)

Understand (that) just because one (or more) of God's people fell, it doesn't mean that _____ is unfaithful. God has been working His _____, in His _____ and His grace, through ordinary fallen sinners for years, and still is!

_____

_____

_____

_____

_____

_____

_____

_____

_____

_____

DEMOLISHING STRONGHOLDS

Will you have a biblical worldview that you can both "lip" and live in such a way that others will be convinced you're for real—you're genuine?

GROUP DISCUSSION

1. Part of the application is studying for yourself, getting to know the subject that you will be defending. Become a Berean and search the Scriptures for yourself (Acts 17:11). Discuss what areas would be good for an in-depth personal study.

2. Discuss the difference between the original definition of tolerance (to respect others as people while not agreeing with their beliefs/practices) and the current cultural definition (to condone or agree with others' beliefs/practices without sharing them).

3. Dr. Ware states that the greatest marketing tool for Christianity is the love we have for one another. Discuss with the group what you believe this conveys.

4. Are you prepared to defend your faith from God's Word? Are you ready to commit to the authority of God's Word?

5. What did Dr. Ware mean by: "God doesn't have fans. We are all players"?

GET INTO THE WORD

In this lesson, we are going to apply some of the hermeneutic principles to Romans 1, the chapter we looked at in Lesson 10. Our focus will be Principle #3: The Scripture interprets Scripture Principle. Listed below are cross-references to most of the verses in this chapter. You will work in small groups to share the responsibility of looking up the verses and comparing them with the corresponding verse from Romans 1. Do as many as you have time for and try to get to the rest of them throughout the next week.

1:2 (cf. Luke 1:70; Titus 1:2) _____

_____

1:4 (cf. Hebrews 9:13–15) _____

_____

1:5 (cf. Ephesians 3:8–9)_____

_____

1:9 (cf. Ephesians 1:16; Philippians 1:3; 1 Thessalonians 1:2)

_____

_____

1:13 (cf. Romans 15:22; 1 Thessalonians 2:18)

_____

_____

1:16 (cf. Acts 3:26; 1 Corinthians 1:18)

_____

_____

1:17 (cf. Habakkuk 2:4; Galatians 3:11)

_____

_____

1:19 (cf. John 1:9; Acts 14:17)_____

_____

1:20 (cf. Psalm 19:1)_____

_____

DEMOLISHING STRONGHOLDS

1:21 (cf. 2 Kings 17:15; Ephesians 4:17)

_____

_____

1:22 (cf. Jeremiah 10:14; 1 Corinthians 1:20)

_____

_____

1:23 (cf. Psalm 106:20; Jeremiah 2:11)

_____

_____

1:24 (cf. Psalm 81:12; 1 Peter 4:3)

_____

_____

1:26 (cf. 1 Thessalonians 4:5) _____

_____

1:27 (cf. Leviticus 18:22; Leviticus 20:13; 1 Corinthians 6:9)

_____

_____

1:28 (cf. Ephesians 5:4) _____

_____

1:30 (cf. 2 Timothy 3:2) _____

_____

1:31 (cf. 2 Timothy 3:3) _____

_____

1:32 (cf. Romans 6:21, 23) _____

_____

What is the overall message of Romans 1 in light of the comparable Scripture?_____

_____

How can I apply these verses?

_____

_____

FIND THE FOCUS

Think for a moment … look back over the notes you have for this lesson, and write down a couple of things that were an encouragement or a challenge, or that stood out to you.

1. _____

   _____

   _____

2. _____

   _____

   _____

HOMEWORK

1. Review 2 Timothy 4:1–8.
2. Finish any parts of the lesson that did not get completed during the lesson time.
3. Read the article about biblical hermeneutics—the principles of accurate interpretation of the Bible.
4. Write down one or two things you've learned from God's Word and be prepared to share when you come to the final class for Lesson 13.

LESSON

13 Q&A SESSION

LAYING THE GROUNDWORK

The Christian life can be a real battleground! Throughout his epistles, Paul uses military terminology to emphasize the Christian's role and goes as far as to relate our spiritual "equipment" to that of earthly armor and weapons (Ephesians 6:10–18).

Paul's first letter to Timothy is filled with encouragement for a young Christian man who was facing many difficult problems in his place of service for the Lord.

> "One of the key words in 1 Timothy is 'charge,' sometimes translated 'commandment' (1:3, 5, 18; 4:11; 5:7; 6:13, 17). It was a military term, referring to an order to be passed down the line. God had entrusted the Gospel to Paul (1:11), who had passed it along to Timothy (1:18–19; 6:20). Timothy was 'charged' to guard this treasure (2 Timothy 1:13–14) and pass it along to faithful people who would, in turn, entrust it to others (2 Timothy 2:2)."
> —*Weirsbe's Expository Outlines*, p. 619.

1 Timothy 4:16 is one of those charges given to Timothy:

> "Take heed to yourself and to the doctrine. Continue in them, for in doing this you will save both yourself and those who hear you."

Just like you, Timothy lived in a day and age where false teaching, worldly philosophies, and heresies permeated his culture.

74

In this verse, Paul emphasizes the necessity of first *examining yourself* to find out where you are spiritually and where you are going.

Next, he focuses in on *examining your doctrines* to make sure they are in line with God's Word.

Finally, the challenge shifts from examination to *application—continue, remain faithful, persevere in your faith and the teachings of God's Word.*

Why? It's about salvation—yours and others'. In Christ alone is eternal security, love, joy, and peace.

VIEW THE DVD

To culminate our study of what it takes to demolish strongholds, we will watch Bill Jack as he does some man-on-the-street interviews and demonstrates how one might use the "The Four Questions." Below are lines for you to take notes. Be sure to jot down any questions or comments that you find helpful or interesting. Remember, it is through the work of God's Word that He can break down the barriers and demolish the strongholds of opposing worldviews.

_____

_____

_____

_____

_____

_____

_____

_____

_____

_____

_____

_____

_____

_____

_____

_____

_____

_____

GET INTO THE WORD

Look back over the previous lessons and pick two or three verses that have really challenged your faith through this study. Discuss them with the group and use your discussion as a springboard to share how this series of lessons has made a difference in your walk with and service for God.

What verses have really spoken to you throughout the *Demolishing Strongholds* course?

_____

_____

_____

_____

_____

_____

How will you apply or how have you already applied what you've learned?

_____

_____

_____

_____

_____

_____

FIND THE FOCUS

Think for a moment ... look back over the notes you have for this lesson, and write down a couple of things that were an encouragement or a challenge, or that stood out to you.

1. _____

_____

2. _____

_____

A FINAL WORD

Now you can say with Paul, "I have finished my course," though this "course" was quite insignificant compared to Paul's journey through life. The challenge to you now is to stay faithful and to use what you have learned. You now have several important tools with which to arm yourself.

1. Your sword, God's Word, is your offensive weapon against the opposition you will face in life. Read it, learn from it, and apply it.

2. The information you have gleaned from this course has better equipped you to defend your faith, counter the skeptics, and challenge nonbiblical worldviews.

3. Use the Answers in Genesis website where you will find over 5,000 free articles with faith-building content to engage and equip you.

Matthew 25:21

His lord said to him,
"Well done, good and faithful servant;
you were faithful over a few things,
I will make you ruler over many things.
Enter into the joy of your lord."